ANDREW WELSH-HUGGINS

No Winners Here Tonight

RACE, POLITICS, AND GEOGRAPHY IN ONE OF
THE COUNTRY'S BUSIEST DEATH PENALTY STATES

Ohio University Press Athens

Ohio University Press, Athens, Ohio 45701
www.ohioswallow.com
© 2009 by Ohio University Press

Printed in the United States of America
Ohio University Press books are printed on acid-free paper ⊗ ™

16 15 14 13 12 11 10 09   5 4 3 2 1

Library of Congress Cataloging-in-Publication Data
Welsh-Huggins, Andrew.
  No winners here tonight : race, politics, and geography in one of the country's busiest
death penalty states / Andrew Welsh-Huggins.
    p. cm. — (Ohio University Press series on law, society, and politics in the Midwest)
  Includes bibliographical references and index.
  ISBN 978-0-8214-1833-8 (cloth : alk. paper) — ISBN 978-0-8214-1834-5 (pbk. : alk. paper)
  1. Capital punishment—Ohio—History. I. Title.
  HV8699.U6O394 2008
  364.6609771—dc22

                                                                    2008043918

No Winners Here Tonight

Ohio University Press Series on Law, Society, and Politics in the Midwest

SERIES EDITORS: PAUL FINKELMAN AND L. DIANE BARNES

For my parents,

Richard and Mary Anne Huggins,

who let me walk to the library

when I was six

CONTENTS

ACKNOWLEDGMENTS

To the outside observer, the man running a marathon appears to do so alone, an island unto himself as he plods endlessly along city streets. What the observer doesn't see are the people who got this solitary athlete to that point: those who coached the runner, offered him advice, gave him the time to train and provided encouragement and sustenance along the way, and above all forgave him the crazy idea in the first place. Similarly, with this book, I, the one, am indebted to you, the many, who got me to the starting line and stayed with me all the way to the finish. Eva Parziale, Ohio bureau chief for the Associated Press, agreed to my initial idea to study the state's death penalty system and continuously supported the endeavor even when a quarterly project stretched into years. Nancy Nussbaum and Deb Martin, my AP editors, oversaw the initial reporting and stories that led to this book. I am grateful for their suggestions, advice, keen eyes, and patience, especially their patience. Liz Sidoti, my former AP Statehouse colleague, labored long and hard to help develop our database before her skills covering presidential politics were recognized and rewarded. John Seewer of the AP's Toledo bureau and Kate Roberts, formerly of the Columbus office, contributed powerful stories to the initial AP series on the discrepancy of outcomes in death penalty cases and the cost of capital punishment, respectively. Gillian Berchowitz at Ohio University Press encouraged my proposal and proved instrumental in helping shepherd the project from hopeful outline to finished product. Likewise, the press's Rick Huard expertly guided me through the laborious editing process while fielding the questions of a book-writing rookie with unending politeness. Lisa Lynch, of the Ohio Supreme Court's library, was generous with her time helping me track down death penalty court rulings from over the years. Lee Leonard and Tom Suddes, retired Statehouse correspondents for the *Columbus Dispatch* and the *Plain Dealer*, respectively, read early drafts of the book and offered invaluable suggestions, caught egregious mistakes, and made sure I held politicians' feet to the historical fire they deserved. Larry Herman, Ohio State University law professor emeritus, read a rough draft of the history he helped make and kindly pointed out what I got right and what I got not so right. Victor Streib, the Ella and Ernest Fisher Professor of Law at Ohio Northern University, was good enough to check my legal history for accuracy and context. Sadly, three giants in the field of capital defense, David Bodiker, Max Kravitz, and Benson Wolman, died before the book was completed. They were among my earliest interviews and provided me with a strong starting point; I hope I have honored their memory adequately. As a fellow journalist, Carrie Ghose used her brilliance as a writer and editor to pinpoint places for improvement and raised the appropriately skeptical eyebrow whenever needed. As my friend, she did it with a thoroughness and selflessness for which I am forever indebted. My children, Sarah, Emma, and Thomas, gave me the space, both physical and temporal, to conduct my research and carry out my writing. They were especially kind enough to win several acting roles at the community theater around the corner from the main branch of the Columbus Metropolitan Library, providing me plenty of opportunities to dig through history while glowing with parental pride. I also owe considerable thanks to the many reference librarians who steered me toward the books and documents I needed but was sure could not be found.

To the man mad enough to run that marathon, lucky is he who finds a team of supporters along the way; blessed is he fortunate enough to have a spouse devoted to his undertaking. My wife, Pam, is such a partner. She accepted days of vacation lost to early research, complained not a whit as the home office table disappeared under boxes of file folders, and didn't blink at sunny Saturday afternoons spent in the Ohio Historical Society archives. She read early drafts closely and made countless suggestions that improved the book. One bit of advice, a simple reminder not to give too much away too soon, was typical of her help: genius, gently offered. I appreciate her efforts, I value her contributions, I treasure our partnership. "Just do it," many marathoners are fond of saying today. Fair enough, except let's be honest: I couldn't have done it without her.

Introduction

Killing people is wrong. Please end the death penalty in Ohio.

—*January 8, 2007, letter to newly elected Governor Ted Strickland*

Please don't mess with the death penalty. It is the only tool that we have left to deal with killers.

—*January 20, 2007, e-mail to Strickland*

LEWIS "LITTLE Lew" Williams, an inmate at the Southern Ohio Correctional Institution for one day in the winter of 2004, did not seem the type of person destined to make headlines around the world. Diminutive at five feet three inches, rough-spoken and defiant, he had been quietly incarcerated for nearly two decades. His only claim to fame until that January was his barely remembered reputation as a Cleveland street punk— a punk whose career was cut short by his arrest and conviction for the robbery and murder of Leoma Chmielewski, a seventy-six-year-old woman on the city's east side for whom he'd occasionally done odd jobs. Sentenced to die, he had been on Ohio's death row for twenty years before finally exhausting his appeals and receiving an execution date of January 14, 2004.

The only thing remarkable about his scheduled execution was that it would be the first in which the entire procedure would be public. During the state's previous eight executions by lethal injection, the first sight of the condemned inmate that reporters, lawyers, and witnesses for both the accused and the victim's family had was when a curtain opened in the death chamber and the inmate was revealed lying on a gurney, strapped down with an intravenous shunt in his arm and prepared to give a final statement. It was a tidy presentation—a tableau of calm inevitability that in a morbid way recalled the beginning of life, the stereotypical viewing of the newborn through a nursery window, the viewers spared the messy struggle that had preceded this peaceful moment.

Mindful of this contradiction, the Ohio chapter of the American Civil Liberties Union had sued in 2003, arguing that the state was preventing full public access to executions by beginning, as it were, at the end. In response, the Department of Rehabilitation and Correction agreed, beginning with Williams's execution, to broadcast on closed-circuit TV the process under which guards in an adjoining room inserted the shunts into an inmate's arm before leading the inmate to the death chamber. The procedure was not taped, and, under already existing rules, no recording of the event was allowed. To this day reporters are barred from bringing their own notebooks into the death chamber and must use state-issued paper and pencils.[1]

In Williams's case, it was clear from the instant the first images appeared on the TV screen in the witnesses's viewing room that something unusual was happening. A struggle was underway. Williams was kneeling on the floor, gripping the edge of the table he was supposed to be lying on and refusing to be lifted up. Disembodied hands from all sides of the screen were grabbing him and trying to pull him onto the table. It was a surreal and confusing image, made even more disturbing by the lack of sound—the closed-circuit process didn't include audio—and trying to figure out exactly what was happening.

After two minutes, the execution team finally hoisted Williams up from his knees, pried his hands free, and placed him on the table. Several guards held him down as the shunts were inserted; it then took four guards to carry him into the death chamber. As soon as the door to the room opened, Williams's voice became audible for the first time, a combination of groaning and cries for help: "I'm not guilty. I'm not guilty. God, please help me." His pleading continued for the next few minutes while he struggled with the guards strapping him down. Those of us reporting the execution—it was my second as a witness for the Associated Press—strained to catch every nuance of what was happening, aware we were watching grotesque history being made. A few feet away in the viewing room, Williams's mother, sixty-six-year-old Bonnie Williams, of Columbus, sobbed as she watched. Standing next to her, prisons spokeswoman Andrea Dean, a veteran of the execution process, gently rubbed her shoulder.[2]

Williams made no final statement as such; he just pleaded and groaned until the drugs kicked in and silenced him. Officially, the words he said at 10:07 AM were recorded as his last statement: "God, please help me. God, please hear my cry." But in fact, after Warden James Haviland pulled the microphone away, Williams continued yelling until 10:08 AM, when he abruptly stopped speaking. As the muscle relaxant Pavulon took effect, Williams's chest rose and fell a couple of times, as is common in executions. He was declared dead a few minutes later, at 10:15 AM. "I'm just glad that it's over," said Dorothy Beverly, Chmielewski's stepdaughter, informed of the outcome. "It still shouldn't take that long for the justice system to work."[3]

In hindsight, it's difficult to figure out exactly what was going on that day at the prison in Lucasville. Williams's outburst surprised everyone, including public defender Stephen Farrell, who had spoken to him as recently as that morning and described him as calm. A prison log of Williams's minute-by-minute activities his last day also gives no hint of a struggle in the offing. ("Inmate Williams laughing and talking with his attorney and his spiritual advisor," reads the entry at 8:21 AM, ninety minutes before the execution was scheduled to begin.) There was an element of exhibitionism about the behavior, as though Williams were not actually begging to be spared but consciously giving a demonstration of an inmate pleading for his life. On the other hand, it's possible his cries for help were genuine. Williams had changed his story several times but generally had professed his innocence of the crime, though his explanations—he wasn't there, or he was there but he fired after the victim's dog attacked—tended to fall flat. Maybe something in him snapped. Maybe he figured, what have I got to lose?

While Williams will be best remembered for the way he went to his death, in the long run he played a more significant role in the modern history of the death penalty. He and his criminal justice experience are emblematic of the ways in which capital punishment is carried out unevenly, not only in Ohio but across the country. This unevenness manifests itself in three general areas: race, both of the perpetrators of crimes and of the victims; the discretion of prosecutors from county to county; and public sentiment, or more precisely, the way juries specifically and the entire justice system generally react to death penalty cases depending on the demographics of the counties where judgment is served.

Williams's home of Ohio is also a useful place to study these trends, since the state—sometimes to the surprise of both death penalty supporters and opponents—had one of the most active death chambers in the country during the first decade of the new century. In 2006, Ohio executed five people, second-highest in the nation after Texas, which executed twenty-four. From 2002 through 2006, Ohio executed twenty-two people, a tie for third with North Carolina and behind only Texas and Oklahoma. It is a state where support for the death penalty remains strong, though not overwhelmingly so. In early 2007, after newly elected Governor Ted Strickland temporarily delayed three executions to give himself time to study their cases, a poll taken by Quinnipiac University found Ohioans supported his decision by a two-to-one ratio. The same poll found that voters still supported the death penalty over life without parole, but only by 48 percent to 38 percent. This may reflect Ohio's reputation as a politically moderate bellwether state, another factor that makes it useful as a laboratory for examining the history of capital punishment. While voters in the state returned President George W. Bush to the White House in 2004 and at the same time enacted one of the country's most restrictive gay-marriage bans, for example, they also chose two years later to dump almost the entire statewide Republican power structure in favor of a new slate of Democrats.

In Williams's case, to begin with, he was black, like almost half the men on death row in Ohio and across the country, a rate far out of proportion to the actual population of African Americans, about 11 percent of Ohioans and about 13 percent across the country. Although statistics show that African American men commit violent crime at a higher rate than whites, the overrepresentation of blacks on death row has been a hallmark of the capital punishment system in this and most other states. Far more important than Williams's own skin color, however, was that of his victim, Leoma Chmielewski, who was white. Researchers have known for years that the chances of facing a death sentence in the United States vary considerably based on the race of the victim. A groundbreaking study of murders in Georgia in the 1970s by David Baldus of Iowa State University found that killers of white victims were far more likely to end up on death row than killers of blacks. More recently, University of Maryland researcher Ray Paternoster found a nearly identical pattern in Maryland. Similarly, a 2005 study of a decade of capital cases in California by researcher Glenn Pierce found that offenders who killed whites were more than four times more likely to be sentenced to death than those who killed Latinos and more than three times more likely than those who killed blacks. And in Ohio, a three-year analysis that I conducted for the Associated Press of capital indictments between 1981 and 2002—including the case of Williams—found that people who had killed one or more white people and been charged with a capital crime were twice as likely to be sentenced to death than those whose victims were black. As Paternoster puts it, killers of whites are always "more likely to have death sought. More likely to have their case advance to the penalty phase. More likely to have death imposed."[4]

Secondly, Williams's case intersected with another death penalty inequity: prosecutors' use of plea bargains. Ohio lawmakers rewriting the state's capital punishment law in 1981 wanted the death penalty for the worst of the worst, killers whose crimes were so heinous that nothing short of execution was appropriate. Over the years, however, prosecutors charged with administering the law had treated the statute less as a cudgel than as a bargaining chip. A capital indictment, after all, was a powerful negotiating tool, especially in a case with multiple offenders. In Ohio, as my analysis found, half of all capital indictments were resolved with plea bargains over the first twenty years of the new death penalty law, including dozens of crimes with multiple victims and some twenty-five cases in which at least three people had been killed.

Excessive plea bargains create disparities in the system because of both who accepts them and who doesn't. In 1983, the year Williams was indicted, fifty-three other offenders in Cuyahoga County were also charged with death penalty crimes. Thirty of those individuals accepted plea bargains to escape the death sentence. But Williams refused to discuss a plea, insisted on a trial, and ended up on death row, even as more than half the county's capital offenders that year, accused of crimes just as bad or worse, went to prison and served sentences that in some cases were up by the time Williams was executed. As Timothy Miller, criminal division chief for the county prosecutor's office, would put it, death sentences can be avoided at many stages of a capital case based on decisions made by a judge, the jury, or the accused, as well as prosecutors. Had Williams made a different decision, he might have been free in January 2004 instead of facing death.[5]

Prosecutors may offer plea bargains when the strength of the evidence changes between the time of indictment and the time of trial. They may be reluctant to risk a jury trial and possible acquittal against the certainty of a long prison term that could in itself be a death sentence. They may be willing to listen to the victim's family, which, more often than is realized, asks for a plea agreement to avoid the pain of a drawn-out trial and the equally painful possibility of years or decades of further litigation if a death sentence is achieved.

Another reason prosecutors allow plea bargains, though they generally won't talk about it because of its explosive political ramifications, is the cost of a death penalty trial, especially for a small county. Sending a person to death row can mean hundreds of thousands of dollars in legal expenses as well as untold hours of preparation. David Yost, prosecutor in suburban Delaware County in the middle of the state, said that half his office's resources were tied up for three months for the 2003 trial of Gerald Hand, a serial killer who had arranged the deaths of three of his four wives. David Landefeld, prosecutor in southeastern Fairfield County, described the price tag on a capital case as "a fiscal horror-fantasy."[6]

The financial burden that capital punishment places on local government was brought home in 2002 when a judge threw out the death penalty charges against a man accused of killing two people in rural Vinton County, an Appalachian area among the state's poorest. The judge said the county's financial problems could hurt defendant Gregory McKnight's hopes for a fair trial. In the uproar that followed—including the appearance of the prosecutor and one of the victim's parents on the *Today* show—the judge overturned his decision, and, tellingly, the state agreed to help with the prosecution. McKnight was sentenced to death later that year, though questions about his case lingered, including a discrepancy in the way he was charged with killing a white college student—a murder that carried the death penalty charge—and a black acquaintance, which did not merit a capital indictment.

The variables of race and prosecutorial discretion underscore perhaps the most subtle way in which the death penalty is applied unevenly in Ohio and beyond, and that is the role of simple geography. Hamilton County, home to Cincinnati in the southwest corner of the state, is not more than a three-and-a-half-hour drive from Cuyahoga County, home to Cleveland, along the shores of Lake Erie. Ohioans cheer on both the Cincinnati Reds and the Cleveland Indians, the Cincinnati Bengals and the Cleveland Browns. Cincinnati's chili is as much a part of the state's culinary claim to fame as pierogies in Cleveland. Yet during the first twenty years of the state's new death penalty law, 43 percent of all capital indictments in Hamilton County resulted in death sentences, the highest rate of any county in the state. During the same period, just 8 percent of people indicted in Cuyahoga County for crimes punishable by death ended up on death row. That, despite the fact that prosecutors in Cuyahoga County, a Democratic stronghold, indicted more than 700 individuals with capital crimes during that time span, contrasted with just 130 in conservative Hamilton County. In the middle of the state, in Franklin County, whose largest city, Columbus, is a moderate Democratic seat of state government, only 5 percent of 330 capital indictments resulted in a death sentence. While these three counties and their big cities— Cincinnati, Columbus, and Cleveland—have their differences, and while their murder rates are not identical, there is no evidence that the number of death sentences bore any relationship to the actual number of homicides committed in a given year.

Proponents of the death penalty in Ohio look at these disparities and say the system works fine because it relies on the judgment and standards of local communities, the violent crime equivalent of the community standards that rule obscenity laws. Jim Canepa, the former capital crimes division chief for the state attorney general, put it this way: "So based on where you are in the state of Ohio you're going to get fair on crime, tough on crime, consistent on crime."[7] Yet it's difficult to avoid the conclusion that a hardened criminal who knew what he was doing was better off committing his crime near the winding Cuyahoga River in northeast Ohio than along the wide expanse of the Ohio River in the southwest corner of the state.

Where the crime was committed mattered deeply, as did who prosecuted and defended the criminal and then who passed final judgment. By

1986, just five years after Ohio enacted its new capital punishment law, the state supreme court expressed its concern over the quality of lawyers representing death penalty defendants and the way judges appointed those lawyers. Indeed, incompetence by defense attorneys became the chief reason for death sentence reversals as cases slowly worked their way through the federal courts. In 1988, the state supreme court raised similar concerns about misconduct by prosecutors. Moreover, some county judges questioned the appropriateness of certain death sentences, rejecting juries' capital sentences on eight different occasions. Meanwhile, one of the chief architects of the new law, Republican state senator turned supreme court justice Paul Pfeifer, began to raise doubts about the law's fairness. And on the Sixth Circuit Court of Appeals, the chief review panel for Ohio death sentences, one judge, Boyce Martin, appointed by President Jimmy Carter, suggested the death penalty was so flawed as to be beyond repair, while another, Danny Boggs, appointed by President Ronald Reagan, famously complained that a majority of his colleagues would delay an inmate's execution based "on a hot dog menu."

A system meant to be fair turned out, contrary to lawmakers' expectations, to be subject to the same frailties as the rest of the criminal justice system—capricious, uneven, and dependent on that most nonjudicial of factors, human sentiment. State officials echoed this notion in the wake of Lewis Williams's execution, pointing out that a disagreement between Sixth Circuit judges over the constitution of the panel hearing Williams's case was nothing new. "Jurists often disagree on points of law and procedure," said Bob Beasley, a spokesman for then–Attorney General Jim Petro. "That's the way our system is set up."[8]

In the case of the death penalty, of course, there is no way to resolve those disagreements once the sentence has been carried out. Right or wrong, all decisions are final.

ONE

Early Justice

All day yesterday the Central Station was thronged with visitors, anxious to catch either a glance of the prisoner or at least of the scaffold from which he is to make his plunge into the other world.

—Cleveland Leader, *June 22, 1876, on the crowds gathering to watch the execution of triple-murderer William Adin*

THE BIGGEST event of the year 1844 in Columbus, Ohio, was not scheduled until two o'clock in the afternoon on February 9, but that didn't stop crowds from gathering around the hill near the Scioto River for days ahead of time. Roads into the city, then a small municipality of about eight thousand, were filled for more than a week with men on horseback and families in wagons on their way to the entertainment. For hours on February 8, people poured into the ravine around Penitentiary Hill, black and white, young and old, continuing to arrive into the night and well into the next day. This was a special occasion, after all, a double hanging, two individuals convicted of separate crimes to be put to death together, in a day when the public execution of even one person was a defining moment for a community. Despite the bitter cold, thousands of people flocked to witness the hangings; the fact that at least a quarter of the spectators were women was disturbing to those chronicling the occasion, especially when reporters were nearly pushed underfoot by some of these women as they surged to get a better view.

The condemned inmates had little in common except the nature of their crimes and the location of both murders: the Ohio State Penitentiary. Three years earlier, James Clark, a white man from southern Ohio serving time for highway robbery, had murdered a prison guard, Cyrus Sells, by attacking him from behind with an axe. Sells had whipped Clark's entire prison work crew for breaking a rule a few months earlier, and Clark had made it clear he would get back at the guard. A few months later, Esther Foster (some accounts call her Hester), a black woman serving time in the penitentiary's female wing for assault, was in the prison kitchen when she attacked Louisa White, a white female convict, and bludgeoned her to death with an iron fire shovel. Clark and Foster ended up together on the gallows about two miles from where the prison stood.

Many in the crowd had been drinking on the day of the execution, and the situation was unruly at best. As the pair left the penitentiary for the gallows in a procession common in those days of public hangings, bystander Sullivan Sweet was jostled by the crowd, fell into the street, and was fatally trampled by a horse. As the hour drew near at the gallows, several ministers prayed publicly with the convicts as the crowd looked on. Foster was emotional, kneeling and praying fervently along with the pastors. Clark was unrepentant, twice refusing a request to go to his knees as the ministers conducted the service. His defiance was all the more remarkable given that his execution was overseen by members of the Columbus Guard, a local militia whose ranks had included his victim at the penitentiary. As was typical of public executions, a last sermon, "short, fervent and solemn," was delivered. Then the sheriff adjusted the nooses, and the two were hanged. Though no contemporary account exists of the precise nature of their death, numerous histories of death by hanging make it clear the two would have been lucky if they were killed immediately. More likely they hung for several minutes as their hearts slowed and finally stopped. Foster arranged for a Columbus doctor to get her corpse after her execution in exchange for as much candy as she could eat while alive.[1]

With the exception of a thirty-six-year gap from 1963 to 1999, Ohio executed convicted murderers throughout the state's entire history. The creation of laws to punish killers was a natural part of Ohio's development, as much an element of the state's evolution as the building of roads, the planting of farms, and the construction of towns and cities. Even with the temporary halt in executions late in the twentieth century, it's safe to say that from statehood in 1803 until the present, hardly a year has passed in Ohio without one or more individuals sitting in a jail or prison and waiting to die.

That the death penalty should take root so quickly and strongly in the United States should come as no surprise. After all, humans have passed fatal judgment on themselves for all of recorded history. The Babylonian Code of Hammurabi prescribed capital punishment for a number of offenses, from theft to sloppy building construction that led to someone's accidental death. Ancient Jewish tribes mandated death for many crimes, and the Old Testament is filled with references to the death penalty, as in the twenty-first chapter of Exodus: "Whoever strikes a man so that he dies shall be put to death." Greece's Draconian Code in the seventh century BC stipulated death for even the smallest of crimes, putting idleness on the same level as murder. (The code's harshness ultimately limited its actual enforcement.) The Roman Law of the Twelve Tables spelled out several capital offenses while making social distinctions in their application, such as executing slaves for killing their masters but not vice versa.[2]

Following this tradition, the history of the death penalty in Ohio begins not in North America but in Europe—in England, in particular— where the laws and practices that would govern capital punishment in the United States were first established and carried out. Europeans settling the eastern seaboard in the early seventeenth century began almost upon arrival to execute convicted criminals. As the American colonies grew, many of them followed English criminal law, dubbed the "bloody code" after Parliament authorized capital punishment for dozens of crimes by the mid-eighteenth century, many of them narrow property offenses.[3]

Colonists in Jamestown, Virginia, put Captain George Kendall to death in 1608 on a charge of spying for Spain, the eastern colonies' first recorded execution. Early laws mandated death for a variety of crimes, sometimes the least of which was murder. Virginia governor Sir Thomas Dale enacted laws in 1612 that made stealing grapes, killing chickens, and trading with Indians capital crimes. In 1636, the Massachusetts Bay Colony passed laws making murder, witchcraft, sodomy, and rape punishable by death. On June 1, 1660, Boston Puritans hanged Quaker Mary Dyer for violating a law that banished Quakers from the colony under pain of death.

After independence, states slowly began to reduce the number of capital crimes, and in many cases, especially in the North, to eliminate the death penalty for all offenses but murder. In 1794, spurred by Benjamin Rush, an early capital punishment opponent, Pennsylvania limited executions to those convicted of first-degree murder. Michigan abolished the death penalty in 1847, followed by Rhode Island in 1852 and Wisconsin in 1853. Nine other states abolished the death penalty by 1917, although several, including Arizona, Iowa, and Missouri, restored it within a few years.[4] The movement to restrict the range of capital crimes did not generally include southern states, however. There, executions had a dual role that affected their practice for centuries: they were a tool of the state to punish those guilty of the worst of crimes, but also a means to control and manipulate an enormous slave population. Even as southern states reduced the number of capital crimes for whites, they kept the death penalty as an option for slaves and even free blacks for a far greater number of offenses. In the antebellum South, attempted rape of a white woman was a capital crime in Florida, Louisiana, Mississippi, South Carolina, Tennessee, Texas, and Virginia.[5]

The Marietta Code of 1788, the first criminal statutes of the Northwest Territory, an expanse including the area that would become Ohio, spelled out five crimes punishable by death: treason, murder, arson, burglary, and robbery resulting in death. Between 1799 and 1805, arson that did not result in a death was also a capital crime, the only such property crime eligible for the death penalty in the state. However, in 1805, two years after Ohio achieved statehood, lawmakers removed nonfatal arson from the death penalty law and mandated capital punishment for murder, rape, arson with prejudice to life, murder, and "maiming with malice aforethought." Lawmakers dropped maiming from the statute four years later, making it punishable by whipping instead. In 1815, the state followed the lead of Pennsylvania and distinguished murders by degree, making offenders eligible for the death penalty only for first-degree murder and treason. In 1824, lawmakers eliminated treason as a capital crime under state law, recognizing that it overlapped with similar federal death penalty statutes: no one could commit treason against a state who wasn't also committing treason against the country.[6]

The earliest executions in what would become the state of Ohio—at least the earliest that involved some sort of judicial process, however flimsy—

were those of soldiers who deserted their command. In the fall of 1792, troops under the command of Major Michael Rudolph arrived at Fort Hamilton for frontier duty in what is now Butler County in the southwest corner of the state. Fort life was arduous, and desertions were common. The following spring, seven soldiers left the fort, fleeing Rudolph's tyrannical leadership, and made it to the Ohio River, where they started toward New Orleans by canoe. They were apprehended a few miles down the river and returned to Fort Hamilton. After a court-martial, two were sentenced to run the gauntlet, two to lie in irons in the guardhouse, and three— John Brown, Seth Blinn, and a soldier named Gallagher—to die by hanging the next day. Five hundred armed soldiers surrounded the gallows to watch the execution. As Brown prepared to die, a sergeant acting as executioner asked him if there were any reason the execution shouldn't proceed. Brown pointed to Rudolph and said he would "rather die nine hundred deaths than be subject to the command of such a man." Unfortunately for the three, a pardon obtained by a friend immediately following their death sentence arrived fifteen minutes too late. (Rudolph was later forced from command and died en route to Europe when pirates captured his ship and hanged him from the yardarm.[7]) In civilian life, James Mays was executed that same year in Hamilton County for fatally stabbing a man who had beaten him. County commissioners provided the sheriff fifteen pounds, eight shillings, and ninepence for the cost of the gallows, coffin, and grave digging.[8]

After statehood, public executions in Ohio—almost exclusively hangings—took place under conditions familiar to most nineteenth-century Americans and almost unimaginable today. Counties conducted their own executions, often shortly after a conviction and sometimes not far from the scene of the crime itself. Today, months or years can pass between an indictment and a trial and decades between a death sentence and an actual execution. Not so in 1846, when David Work murdered Christopher Hocker in April, was sentenced to death in September, and was hanged in October.[9] Prisoners, often dressed in a robe and accompanied by ministers, doctors, and sheriff's deputies, walked from the jailhouse to the gibbet through the gathered crowds in a solemn parade. The condemned commonly addressed the waiting crowds, which could number in the thousands, sometimes for more than an hour, and the spectators, friendly or abusive, weren't afraid to speak up. "Where is your wife?" a bystander asked Jesse Ransbottom, sentenced to die for cutting his wife's throat, as the convicted man awaited hanging on January 25, 1850, in Xenia in Greene County. In Cleveland on June 1, 1855, James Park mounted the scaffold, took a drink of wine, then said to those gathered, "I shall detain you but a short time. If I wished to say more, I have hardly strength to do so," before proceeding to speak for almost an hour.[10]

As at the executions of James Clark and Esther Foster, thousands of people typically gathered on the day of a hanging to try to catch a glimpse of the condemned and, if they were lucky, the springing of the gallows trap. These crowds could be enormous: an estimated fifty thousand people saw Andrew Hellman hanged near the courthouse in Bellefontaine, Ohio, on January 12, 1843, for poisoning his children.[11] The size of the crowds was not unusual given the enormity of the spectacle and the relative lack of other public entertainment. Yet there is no modern equivalent to these gatherings, which continued even after lawmakers banned public hangings in the 1840s and tried to limit them to jail yards. The closest we have today, massive crowds jammed into semioutdoor spaces for concerts or sporting events, may produce a similar level of energy (not to mention mayhem) but have nothing of the peculiar combination of voyeurism and civic duty that accompanied hanging-day crowds.

In 1812, almost the entire population of the village of Cleveland came out to watch the hanging of an American Indian named John Omic, convicted of killing two white trappers near Sandusky, Ohio. Taken to the gallows, Omic twice seized the gallows post and refused to let go, relenting only when offered two large cups of whiskey. Omic was one of six Indians executed in Ohio's early years, the other five at the hands of fellow Indians after being convicted by tribal councils. Those executions included the October 1830 death by firing squad in Wyandot County of Wyandot Indian Soo-de-nooks for killing Too-ra-hah-tah, another Indian, in a fit of drunkenness.[12]

In 1837, thousands gathered in Cincinnati to watch the hanging of John Washburn, convicted of beating a shopkeeper to death and sentenced to die near where he had committed the crime. In his last words, Washburn denied involvement in the crime but boasted of involvement in several other murders. After the execution, doctors examining the body found a watch that Washburn had stolen earlier that day from a minister who had come to his cell to pray for him. In January 1852, in Ashland, thousands of people, many of whom had been drinking, massed to watch the execution of Charles Steingraver for murdering a blind ten-year-old girl the previous July 4. Steingraver, wearing a long white robe and accompanied by the sheriff and five ministers, declared, "I'm innocent," and dropped to his death.[13]

In 1878 in Mansfield, a crowd estimated at ten to fifteen thousand people poured into the city for the hanging of Edward Webb, an ex-slave convicted of beating farmer William Finney to death during a robbery. Special execution-excursion tickets were available for residents of Ashland for sixty cents round trip. Getting inside the jail yard enclosure that day required a second, black-bordered ticket. Despite deputies' attempts to control the throng, the boisterous crowd tore down the wooden fence to see better, causing the panicked sheriff to telegraph the governor for advice. The terse response of Governor Richard Bishop: "Execute the law by carrying out the sentence of the court upon the criminal, without reference the inclosure."[14]

As the size of the crowds that poured into towns demonstrated, a hanging was big news whenever it happened. Yet despite their novelty, hangings were also part of the backdrop of life in nineteenth-century America, events common enough as to be, if not trivial, not all that remarkable, either. "Today's Hangings," went the headline in the *Dayton Daily Herald* on one occasion in June 1885. On a particularly bloody day in 1880, the twenty-eighth of May, authorities carried out executions in Hartford, Connecticut; Memphis, Tennessee; Little Rock, Arkansas; Hanover Court House, Virginia; and Woodsfield, Ohio, where twenty-one-year-old Peter King was hanged for killing David Trembly in a robbery the year before. The fall didn't break King's neck, and he slowly strangled to death over the next seventeen minutes, drawing up his legs and kicking at the gallows trap in his convulsions.[15]

Hanging was the most effective and publicly palatable of execution methods in Ohio and elsewhere in the 1800s. Yet, as King's death demonstrated, it often failed to get the job done immediately or humanely. Those who put offenders to death in Ohio, sheriffs or their designees, were by their very nature amateurs at the job and in smaller counties might carry out only one execution in their lifetimes. The luckiest inmates were those whose necks were broken instantly. But even for those, death took its time. Doctors checking the condition of Albert Myers, hanged in Columbus in 1858 for killing a fellow inmate at the Ohio State Penitentiary, were able to detect a pulse for ten minutes and forty-five seconds after the drop.[16] James Greiner, hanged in the Franklin County Jail in October 1885, took eleven minutes to die of strangulation. Greiner had begged doctors to make sure he was dead before he was buried, citing a fear held by condemned inmates at the time based on accounts of people revived after hanging. Making matters worse, Greiner had read of the execution in Cincinnati three months earlier of Joseph Palmer, who had hung for half an hour, slowly strangling to death, before being declared dead. Greiner's execution overlapped with the new state law moving executions to the penitentiary, about two miles from the county jail, where authorities had already executed the first inmate two months earlier. As a result, Greiner, twenty-seven, a German immigrant, appears to have been the last person executed in Ohio outside the control of state authorities.[17]

Authorities often didn't bother building their own gallows but instead borrowed from another county, an ad hoc approach that may have contributed to some of the gruesome mistakes littering the accounts of nineteenth-century executions. In September 1876, the Coshocton County sheriff obtained Cleveland's rope and scaffolding, fresh from the June execution of William Adin (and used several times previously as well), for the hanging of Frank Ept, sentenced to die for killing the son of his employer during a failed robbery. Ept mounted the gallows stoically and showed no emotion while the sheriff placed the noose around his neck. Ept raised his chin to help the sheriff guide the noose to his neck, leading a spectator to cry, "Ain't he game," using a common expression of the day to refer to condemned killers who refused to show fear in the final moments before death. But in the next minute disaster struck, as the fall not only failed to break Ept's neck but left him hanging with the knot of the noose under his chin as he begged in German to be cut down. The minister attending Ept encouraged him to die like a man. The sheriff hauled Ept back up onto the trap of the gallows and hanged him a second time, more efficacious than the first.[18]

The following year, in Mount Vernon, hundreds watching the hanging of William Bergin looked on as the knot of the noose slipped when the trap opened and Bergin fell to the ground. Unperturbed, the sheriff and his assistants hauled Bergin back up and refitted the noose. "It is all right Johnny," Bergin assured the sheriff. "Go ahead; you are choking me a little now." Bergin fell again, this time with the noose tight enough to slowly strangle him over twenty-five minutes. Eight years later, in the second execution in the Ohio State Penitentiary, Patrick Hartnett was almost decapitated after dropping through the trap; guards rushed forward to support his lifeless body for fear his head would be severed altogether.[19] Perhaps in fear of these mistakes, some inmates tried to kill themselves beforehand. Historical records show at least eight condemned prisoners who attempted suicide in jail and at least two who succeeded, including Allen Ingalls, a black Cincinnati man who hanged himself with bedclothes; he had been sentenced to die for beating a couple and their adopted daughter to death and then selling their bodies to a medical college. His accomplice, Benjamin Johnson, was executed.[20]

Nineteenth-century sensibilities also allowed the executions of a number of juveniles, some scarcely more than boys. On April 30, 1867, in Cincinnati, the sheriff put to death three convicted murderers, including Samuel Case, just fifteen years old. "I am not very old, and cannot talk much before men," he said, standing on the gallows. "If there was a crowd of boys here I might tell them how to behave."[21] On June 25, 1880, three boys, Gustave A. Ohr, sixteen, George Mann, seventeen, and John Sammitt, also seventeen, were hanged for a pair of unrelated murders, including the slaying of an elderly traveling companion of Mann and Ohr for five dollars and a silver watch. The day before their death, the boys sat in their cell chatting and eating ice cream. Later, Ohr gave a concert on the cithera, a lyre-like instrument, accompanied by Sammitt on the violin. "Goodbye, grandma," Mann said just before the trap dropped.[22]

In all, at least eighty-four men and one woman were put to death in Ohio by individual counties between statehood in 1803 and 1885, when the legislature voted to move executions to the state penitentiary. The first man put to death in the pen under the new law was Valentine Wagner, Prisoner No. 17,409, convicted of killing his brother-in-law in Morrow County three years earlier. Wagner came close to collapsing when entering the execution annex, cried, "Oh, don't hang me," and had to be lifted to his feet by guards once he reached the trap doors. A black cap over his face, he was dropped at 2:40 AM on July 31, 1885, and hung for twenty minutes before a doctor pronounced him dead.[23]

Even as Ohio tried, convicted, and executed murderers throughout its early history, debate raged over the practice, and lawmakers considered several times whether to abolish capital punishment altogether. This abolitionist spirit had its roots in a 1764 essay, "On Crimes and Punishment," by the Italian lawyer Cesare Beccaria, who argued that the purpose of a state was to protect its citizens, not to harm them. In the late eighteenth century, the aforementioned Benjamin Rush, a signer of the Declaration of Independence, published pamphlets opposing capital punishment and predicting its demise. Many, including Benjamin Franklin, supported Rush's proposal to rehabilitate rather than execute criminals. These arguments, suffused with religious sentiments and debates over the role of society, colored Ohio's discussion throughout the nineteenth century and beyond.

In 1835, the state legislature established a select committee of three lawmakers to study the issue of the death penalty and report the following year. Their recommendation, to abolish capital punishment, was proposed as a bill and debated at length before the House of Representatives voted to postpone the legislation indefinitely. Two years later, Governor Joseph Vance, a death penalty opponent, tried unsuccessfully to push through a bill abolishing the practice, which he called "a relic of barbarism, that ought to be struck from the code of civilized nations."[24] In 1844, lawmakers in Columbus were so appalled by the spectacle surrounding the double hanging of Foster and Clark in February that they approved a bill in March banning public executions, instead requiring sheriffs to hold executions in or around the jail and inside enclosures tall enough to hide the gallows. Given the circus-like atmosphere of many subsequent executions, where thousands were in attendance, the practical effect of the legislation was limited. That same March, lawmakers declined to approve a second bill banning capital punishment altogether, instead agreeing to postpone the legislation indefinitely. In the 1845–47 session of the General Assembly, Representative Clement L. Vallandigham pushed an abolition bill that led to hours of debate, including one session that ran to three o'clock in the morning. But ultimately the bill failed on December 4, 1847, "amended to death," after supporters allowed it to be tabled rather than put up to a vote of certain defeat. (Vallandigham later became best known for his opposition to the Civil War and his banishment to the Confederacy by President Abraham Lincoln.[25])

Delegates to Ohio's 1850–51 constitutional convention debated the issue vigorously. On the opponents' side, some abolitionists contended the death penalty defeated its own purpose because juries would acquit people rather than risk imposing a death sentence. Others, echoing Vance, said the practice was a relic of an earlier, barbaric age that had no place in modern society. Still others said it eliminated any possibility of reforming a criminal. "Certainly it were better that a man should be reformed, than that he be exterminated," argued Trumbull County Democratic delegate Rufus Ranney (later a state supreme court justice) during the long final debate on December 6, 1850. So long "as it remains possible to extend the power of reformation, it were certainly better to do so, than to consign a man, at once, to hopeless perdition," he said.

But proponents were no less fervent in their arguments in favor of keeping the death penalty. They took a position as familiar then as it is today, that the death sentence was a deterrent to potential criminals. They argued that government had a duty to protect its citizens, including in some cases duty to impose the most absolute form of punishment. They cited biblical arguments on behalf of capital punishment, arguments common for much of the 1800s, in particular God's command to Noah in the ninth chapter of Genesis, "Whoever sheds the blood of man, by man shall his blood be shed." As Samuel Quigley, a convention delegate from Columbiana County and a death penalty supporter, wryly noted, "No intimation of its repeal is found in the sacred volume that ever I could see." The measure to abolish the death penalty finally fell short in December 1850 by a vote of 50 to 34.[26]

In 1853, a select committee of the Ohio House of Representatives on capital punishment took the position that society had never granted the government the power over human life. Representative Durbin Ward, writing in the committee's final report, argued that the taking of life was not guaranteed by any constitution or embedded in any fundamental law: "It is at best but a doubtful implication—an excrescence which has grown like a foul tumor upon the body politic."[27]

Durbin's arguments reflect a sentiment first cited almost a century earlier by Beccaria. "What manner of right can men attribute to themselves to slaughter their fellow beings?" Beccaria queried. "Certainly not that from which the sovereignty and laws are founded." Beccaria also argued that a long prison term was a greater deterrent than a quick execution. The death penalty, he added, was useless as a criminal justice tool because of its barbarity. "It seems to be absurd that the laws, which are an expression of the public will, which detest and punish homicide, should themselves commit it, and that to deter citizens from murder, they order a public one." (This two-hundred-year-old argument survives today in the adage often cited by opponents, "Why do we kill people to show people that killing is wrong?"[28])

As Durbin posed the issue in 1853, a man had a right by natural law to protect his son, neighbor, or wife from immediate danger. But society, facing no immediate danger from a criminal in custody, had no injury to prevent by executing that offender. The following year, writing in the Senate minority report on capital punishment, lawmaker Isaac Wright took that argument and turned it on its head. "A man has, by nature, the right, if his wife, children or himself be set upon by a murderer, to defend them or himself to the extreme even of taking life. As a party to the compact of society, everyone yields to some extent this right. Government, composed of individual members, having respectively this right, will certainly be acceded to possess as much power, and the same abstract rights to protect itself against the traitor or its members from the assassin."[29]

Discussion of capital punishment waned with the coming of the Civil War. Yet in 1859, Governor Salmon P. Chase, in his annual address to the General Assembly, noted the rarity of death penalty convictions in comparison to the number of indictments and questioned whether judges should have the discretion to sentence first-degree murderers to life in prison as well. (It took until 1996, more than a century later, for Ohio to establish a sentence of life in prison with no chance of parole as a death penalty alternative.[30]) In 1873, Representative Isaiah Pillars presented a report to the House of Representatives advocating the abolition of capital punishment, arguing that it was more just to sentence killers to a lifetime of solitary confinement. "*He is dead to the law* and all rights under the law, and he is dead to the world and *every human being* of the world—he is in a living tomb," Pillars wrote.[31] He based his argument on first-hand knowledge; in December 1871, he had represented Andrew Brentlinger, of

Allen County, charged with stabbing his wife to death in a fit of jealousy. Brentlinger was convicted, sentenced to die, and hanged April 7, 1872.

The debate over capital punishment flared up again in 1912 when a constitutional amendment to abolish the death penalty in Ohio was one of several proposals brought before voters, including suffrage for women. Edward Turner, prosecutor of Franklin County, expressed his strong opposition to the measure, arguing it would further embolden criminals. "I want to raise my voice in behalf of the almost forgotten children and dependents of murdered men and women," he wrote in the September 1, 1912, edition of the *Ohio State Journal;* "in behalf of those law-abiding citizens who, when awakened from peaceful slumbers by society's outlaw, the burglar, will be murdered to insure his escape and subsequent acquittal if capital punishment be abolished." Others supported the measure just as strongly, citing Christian charity and the responsibility of society to reform rather than solely punish. Letter writer E. P. Lovett of Jolly, Ohio, in the same edition of the *Ohio State Journal,* asked advocates of capital punishment to rise above the spirit of revenge. People "should remember that capital punishment was born of that spirit and will never rise much higher than its source. Capital punishment is not elevating or refining, but, on the other hand, it is repulsive and degrading." In the end, the issue failed overwhelmingly on September 3, 1912, by a vote of 303,246 to 258,706.

World War I interrupted debate again, but Governor Harry Davis, a capital punishment opponent, revived the issue after the war with an article published in the national magazine the *Outlook* in 1922. Davis examined the more than sixteen hundred murders committed in Ohio between 1900 and his day and pointed out numerous disparities in indictments, convictions, and sentencing. Only four of every one hundred of those murders resulted in an execution, and, Davis argued, many offenders convicted of equally heinous murders went to prison instead. He also pointed out that there was no correlation between the imposition of the death penalty and the overall crime rate and argued that there were some offenders guilty of terrible crimes who had shown themselves capable of being reformed. He predicted that a movement to abolish capital punishment would soon sweep across many states. Yet Davis, a politician, was also a practical man. He reminded his readers that twenty-six murderers had been condemned to death since he became governor the year before, that sixteen had already been executed, and that another ten awaited the electric chair. He promised to enforce the death penalty as "long as capital punishment is the law of the state."[32] The intensity of the country's death penalty debate emerged five years later in the pages of the *Congressional Digest,* which devoted its issue of August–September 1927 to the range of opinion on the subject. Famous proponents like Ambrose Bierce weighed in alongside equally famous opponents like Clarence Darrow and Henry Ford. One of the most impassioned defenses of capital punishment came from Cuyahoga County, Ohio, prosecutor Edward Stanton, who argued that the death penalty was not only a deterrent but also the fitting punishment for those found guilty of premeditated murder. Wrote Stanton: "The frightful toll of murder in this country will be decreased only when mawkish sympathy yields to common sense and all murderers are promptly executed."[33]

Between 1923 and 1961, Ohio lawmakers took up eighteen proposals to either abolish capital punishment or prohibit the execution of juveniles. In 1949, the House voted 69 to 35 to abolish capital punishment, almost exactly one hundred years after the Senate had passed a similar bill in 1850. The 1949 bill, however, died in committee in the Senate without action.[34]

In the midst of the debate over whether to execute, Ohio and many states, mindful of problems with hanging, were busy considering a better way to put people to death. In 1886, a New York legislative commission became the first to explore the possibility of using electrocution, and the commission's 1888 report urged its adoption: "It is the duty of society to utilize for its benefit the advantages and facilities which science has uncovered to its use." Death by electrocution represented a perfect intersection of American industrial development and criminal justice advancement. Just as proponents of capital punishment were searching for a more humane method of execution, electricity, hailed as a miracle of modern technology, was emerging as a common and widespread power source. On August 6, 1890, William Kemmler, a New York produce peddler convicted of killing his mistress, became the nation's first man put to death in an electric chair. The execution could not have gone worse. After the first seventeen-second dose of electricity failed to kill Kemmler, the operator of the generator powering the chair produced a second charge lasting for more than a minute. The capillaries in Kemmler's face burst, beads of blood appeared on his skin, and the smell of burning flesh filled the room. Despite the shock and revulsion Kemmler's death created, however, New York continued to use the chair, and its second application the following year, for a quadruple execution, went smoothly. Ohio became the next state to adopt the chair, passing a law allowing the practice in 1896 and carrying out its first electrocution in 1897, using a chair built by a penitentiary inmate. Six other states quickly followed suit, and seven more chose the chair by 1913. A new method of capital punishment had arrived.[35]

Ohio's first use of the chair came on April 21, 1897, for two condemned inmates convicted of unrelated crimes: William Haas, seventeen, sentenced to die for raping and murdering the wife of a couple he had been living with in Cincinnati, where he did odd jobs in the garden and around the house; and William Wiley, who murdered his wife, also in Cincinnati, in 1896. The state had not planned to execute both at once, but a fire in the dynamo powering the chair had damaged an electrical coil two weeks earlier, the day before Haas's original execution date of April 8; there was some speculation that inmates assigned to clean the death annex had sabotaged the instrument. Governor Asa Bushnell commuted Haas's sentence for two weeks.

The damage repaired, an electrician tested the chair at 5:30 AM on April 20, once again later the same morning, and again late that night just before the crowd of witnesses entered the prison annex where the chair sat. Haas walked in at 12:27 AM, an unconcerned look on his face, dutifully sat down when instructed, and, when asked if he had any last words, said, "No, sir, let 'er go." An electrician applied a dampened conducting sponge to Haas's right ankle while an assistant warden put a similar sponge on his head. The warden and an assisting electrician then activated the 1,750 volts of current in three bursts, ending at 12:32 AM. A doctor, after making sure the current was turned off, pronounced Haas dead. According to newspaper accounts, "When the covering was removed from the face of the dead boy his eyes were half closed, the mouth was open and his face had about the same appearance as if he had died a natural death." Wiley was led into the annex a few minutes later, electrocuted, and pronounced dead at 12:47 AM.[36]

For the next six decades in Ohio, executions by electrocution continued at a regular pace, including at least nine separate years when the state put at least ten people to death each year. The zenith came in 1949, when Ohio executed fifteen men, a total not out of line with the mores of the day but startling today and equaled only among current death penalty states by Texas, which still puts twenty or more to death annually. On December 7, 1938, Anna Marie Hahn, of Hamilton County, became the first woman executed in Ohio in the twentieth century, and one of only four—along with Esther Foster in 1844 and two women in 1954—put to death in the state's history. Through the 1930s and 1940s, the country regularly put more than one hundred people to death a year, including a high of 199 in 1935, thanks in part to anxiety over crime during Prohibition and later the Depression. After 1949, with the coming of the post–World War II economic boom, the number of executions began to decrease dramatically. In Ohio, the number dropped to three or four a year, including 1955, when, for the first and only time since 1897, no one went to the electric chair. Even as the numbers declined, however, Ohio remained one of the country's most active death penalty states. In 1958, of the forty-eight executions carried out nationwide, just four states accounted for half, each with six: Ohio, Georgia, California, and Texas.[37]

On August 26, 1961, grocer Edgar Weaver was in his market on the west side of Columbus with his back to the door when he turned and saw a man pointing a gun at him. As Weaver turned back around, twenty-eight-year-old Donald Reinbolt shot him once in the back. Reinbolt, a garage mechanic, handyman, and convicted car thief, then walked over to Weaver and shot him three more times. Reinbolt took the dying man's wallet and drove off. He tossed the wallet after taking sixty dollars in cash and then headed to a nearby shopping center, where he bought permanent license plates for his car.

Arrested a few days later, Reinbolt was tried the following February and convicted of first-degree murder. He sat with head cocked and hands clasped on February 16, 1962, as the jury sentenced him to death, then he was returned to the county jail, where he immediately went to sleep. He received two reprieves from then-Governor Michael DiSalle, a death penalty opponent, and another delay from the Ohio Supreme Court, but ultimately his execution was set for March 15, 1963. His last day appeared no different from that of the hundreds who went before him. A new governor, James Rhodes, denied Reinbolt's last-minute request for clemency. Reinbolt's final meal included orange juice, steak, french fries, cole slaw, cottage cheese, strawberry shortcake, peanut butter, hot rolls, and a soft drink. He smoked cigarettes provided by the prison. He said prayers with a Roman Catholic chaplain and held a crucifix as he went to the chair. Warden Ernest Maxwell ordered two jolts of electricity; Reinbolt lurched forward after the first, straining against his straps, then slumped back, limp. After the second jolt, a smell of singed hair filled the room, and a reporter witnessing the execution fainted. Afterward, Maxwell noted that before dying, Reinbolt "had a good day."[38] He would be the last person executed in Ohio for more than three decades.

Over the years, Reinbolt's death grew in significance as executions ceased throughout Ohio in the face of reviews and rulings by federal courts around the country that culminated with the U.S. Supreme Court's 1972 decision finding capital punishment unconstitutional. But at the time, executions at the state pen were so commonplace that coverage of the event was almost nonexistent. The now-defunct *Citizen-Journal,* the morning paper in Columbus, marked Reinbolt's death with a three-paragraph story deep inside the paper the following day. The *Columbus Dispatch,* then the afternoon paper, had run its own three paragraphs inside the paper the day before and an even shorter story at the bottom of the front page the day of the execution. An article about county commissioners seeking more state money for the county home overshadowed the five-paragraph story the next day, inside the paper. An important historical footnote in the decades to come, Reinbolt at the time was merely the 315th person executed in the electric chair and the 343rd to die at the penitentiary since the state took over responsibility for executions.

TWO

A New Law

A medicine that has to be taken . . . a spinach that this state has to eat.

—*Republican senator Richard Finan, of suburban Cincinnati,
a death penalty supporter who helped draft
Ohio's current death penalty law*

THE FIRST word came over the radio, shattering the relative calm in the old Ohio State Penitentiary late on the morning of June 29, 1972. By a 5-to-4 vote, the U.S. Supreme Court had ruled against the constitutionality of Georgia's death penalty, a decision that threw out capital punishment laws across the country and spared the lives of hundreds of condemned inmates. Ohio's death row erupted in cheers, the fifty-four men awaiting execution yelling and shouting at the news. The jubilant prisoners included William Jackson, a triple murderer from the Toledo area imprisoned for killing his wife and her parents; Thomas Anderson, of Columbus, just seventeen when he was sentenced to death for the 1969 killing of a convenience store clerk; James Findley, twenty-nine, of Cincinnati, convicted in the mutilation murder of a sixteen-year-old girl; and William Bradley, of Cleveland, condemned to die for killing a man over one dollar in a card game and at the time the longest-serving death row inmate, having arrived nine years before. The day of the decision, Warden Harold Cardwell speculated that problems might have occurred if the ruling had gone the other way. But he said he wasn't concerned about moving the inmates into the prison mainstream. First-degree murderers, he explained, tended to be better behaved than the rest of the prison population.[1]

The Supreme Court's decision that day in late June, *Furman v. Georgia,* capped a decade-long process that ultimately froze the nation's capital punishment system while the federal courts reviewed numerous death penalty cases. The road to *Furman* began in large part in 1963, when the high court declined by a 6-to-3 vote in *Alabama v. Rudolph* to take the case of an Alabama man sentenced to death for rape. Justice Arthur Goldberg, however, in a dissent joined by two other justices, urged the court to hear the case to decide whether the death penalty was constitutional for crimes that did not result in death. For years, death penalty opponents had waged their attacks on capital punishment in state legislatures and in Congress. Goldberg's dissent added to a growing consensus that the assault should take place in the courts instead, and it provided opponents the first real ammunition they needed to launch that assault. Responding to lawsuits by the NAACP's Legal Defense Fund in Florida and California, federal judges imposed moratoriums on executions in those states in 1967. The following year, for the first time since the government began keeping statistics in 1930, no one was executed in the United States.[2]

Legal efforts to end capital punishment then suffered a pair of defeats that would make the *Furman* decision all the more remarkable. In 1970, in *Maxwell v. Bishop,* the court refused to consider the claim of an Arkansas man that black defendants in that state were far more likely to be sentenced to death for raping a white woman than defendants convicted of raping someone of the same race. In May 1971, in a decision involving cases from California and Ohio, the U.S. Supreme Court upheld the right of a jury to sentence someone to death without concrete instructions from a judge. The Ohio case dealt with the death sentence of James Crampton, an amphetamine addict from Toledo convicted of killing his wife, Wilma Jean, on January 18, 1967, by shooting her in the face. A Lucas County jury sentenced Crampton to death, and the Ohio Supreme Court upheld the conviction and sentence in June 1969. Before the U.S. Supreme Court, Crampton's attorneys argued that the lack of standards to guide the jury's discretion on the issue of punishment violated the Constitution. But the court found no evidence that this was true. "In light of history, experience, and the present limitations of human knowledge, we find it quite impossible to say that committing to the untrammeled discretion of the jury the power to pronounce life or death in capital cases is offensive to anything in the Constitution," Justice John Harlan wrote for the majority. Nevertheless, Ohio governor John Gilligan, a Democrat, said following the ruling that no inmates would be executed in the state until the court ruled specifically on the constitutionality of capital punishment. The next month, the U.S. Supreme Court indicated that in the following term it would consider that very issue in a number of appeals.[3]

Furman v. Georgia hit Ohio as lawmakers neared the completion of a historic seven-year rewrite of the state's criminal code, including the capital punishment provisions, the first substantial overhaul of the code since 1815. By 1972, no one had been executed in Ohio for nearly ten years. Governor James Rhodes, a Republican, had allowed the execution of two inmates, including Donald Reinbolt, almost immediately upon taking office in 1963, but had then quietly put the issue on the back burner. He commuted the sentences of eight killers, including two teenagers, and took the neutral public position with other cases that death row inmates should receive the full advantage of appeals available to them under the law.[4]

As the legislature rewrote the criminal code, it debated the implications of the *Crampton* ruling, questioning whether it was wise to proceed with plans to split the death penalty process into two distinct stages, a trial for guilt and a trial for death. The main sponsor of the legislation, suburban Columbus Republican representative Alan Norris, decided to go ahead with the two-part process, known as a bifurcated trial. Immediately after *Crampton* was announced, he pointed out that while the Supreme Court had upheld the current system, "they didn't say they liked it." He also noted that three justices did believe the system was unconstitutional.[5] This reasoning would color legislative debates on capital punishment bills over the next decade, as lawmakers in favor of the death penalty kept a constant eye on the constitutional issue, at times removing provisions they supported solely out of fear that they would ultimately lead to judicial rejection of their overall efforts.

Three months before *Furman* was decided, on March 22, 1972, Ohio's Republican-controlled House of Representatives ended an unprecedented two days of floor debate by voting in favor of a new death penalty law as part of the 266-page criminal statute bill. The legislation, approved by a vote of 72 to 14, took away limitless sentencing discretion from a jury and instructed the sentencer to consider a list of aggravating and mitigating circumstances. Capital punishment opponents tried all the way to the end to eliminate the death penalty from the law, Representative Phale Hale, of Columbus, a black Baptist minister, noting that "there is no record of any wealthy person ever going to the electric chair." Nevertheless, an amendment to remove the death penalty was tabled, a time-honored legislative tactic that killed the proposal without requiring an up or down vote on its merits.[6]

With the update of its criminal code near the end, Ohio had to decide how or whether to proceed now that *Furman* had altered the landscape so profoundly. But from the beginning *Furman* was a problematic guidepost. The 5-to-4 ruling included nine separate opinions and no overarching consensus. While the court found that the death penalty as administered constituted cruel and unusual punishment—a violation of the Eighth Amendment—it stopped short of saying the practice by itself, regardless of how it was carried out, violated offenders' constitutional rights. Justice Potter Stewart, voting to declare the death penalty unconstitutional, said capital punishment had been "wantonly and so freakishly imposed." The death sentences before the court, he wrote, were cruel and unusual "in the same way that being struck by lightning is cruel and unusual." This argument went to the heart of the capriciousness of the capital punishment system as it existed. But it also left the door open to state statutes that could devise a less arbitrary system. The concurring opinion of Justice Byron White determined a violation of the Eighth Amendment "with respect to capital punishment as it is presently administered under the statutes involved in these cases." Justice William Douglas found the lack of standards in determining who received a death sentence troubling, but he also contemplated further consideration, saying the Eighth Amendment required legislatures "to write penal laws that are evenhanded, nonselective, and nonarbitrary." Only Justices Thurgood Marshall and William Brennan argued that the death penalty was on its face a violation of the constitution's prohibition against cruel and unusual punishment. The death penalty, Brennan wrote, violated four chief principles of criminal law: "Death is an unusually severe and degrading punishment; there is a strong probability that it is inflicted arbitrarily; its rejection by contemporary society is virtually total; and there is no reason to believe that it serves any penal purpose more effectively than the less severe punishment of imprisonment."[7]

Following *Furman,* the Ohio Supreme Court had no choice but to declare the state's capital punishment law unconstitutional, ruling 6 votes to none in July of 1972 to overturn the sentence of John Leigh, sent to death row for his role in the September 24, 1969, robbery of the Cabinet Supreme Savings & Loan Association in Delhi Hills Township in Hamilton County, a brutal crime in which a woman teller and three female customers were killed, each shot repeatedly until they stopped moving. Two other defendants in the Delhi Hills robbery were also spared execution, disappointing Joseph Huebner, who had discovered the victims, including his wife, Helen, who had just entered the bank to cash a check. Once an opponent of capital punishment because of his years in the military, Huebner changed his mind after his wife's death. "I still wanted to see them die," he said after *Furman* was announced.[8]

In the end, lawmakers proceeded with their legislative plans through the fall of 1972. "We won't gain anything at this point by putting it off until next year," Norris, who later became a federal judge on the Sixth U.S. Circuit Court of Appeals, told reporters covering the debate. "You'll just retrace all of the ground we have already covered."[9] Trying to respond to the Supreme Court's position that death sentences had been handed down arbitrarily, lawmakers created seven aggravating factors that could send someone to death row—including murders committed during a rape, robbery, or arson—and for the first time added a list of mitigating factors that could spare a defendant. The list was narrow: the victim had to have induced the killer or in some way facilitated his own murder; the offender had to have been unlikely to commit the murder had he not been under "duress, coercion or strong provocation"; and the offense had to have been chiefly the product of a psychosis or mental deficiency.

The bill-writing process was full of emotion, last-minute wrangling, and lawmaking on the fly. Legislators were clearly torn over the issue. On March 2, 1972, the House Judiciary Committee, by a vote of 8 to 7, defeated an amendment by Representative Harry Lehman, a suburban Cleveland Democrat, to eliminate capital punishment altogether. The two-day debate in the full House three weeks later included two additional attempts to strip the death penalty from the bill. In mid-December, as the final days of the

General Assembly wound down, a joint committee of the House and Senate was on the verge of approving a final version of the bill that would permit the death penalty for the killing of a state lawmaker. At the same time, lawmakers had stripped provisions allowing capital punishment for the killing of the very old and very young. David Lore, then a reporter for the *Columbus Dispatch*, asked Senator Howard Cook, a Toledo Republican, early on the morning of Thursday, December 15, why the committee found the killing of a lawmaker more heinous than the killing of a child. Panic ensued, legislators reconvened, and the lawmaker provision was removed.[10] The committee approved the bill later the same day, and after House and Senate passage it was sent to Gilligan, who signed it three days before Christmas. The legislation went into effect just over a year later, on January 2, 1974.

The following month, on February 26, 1974, Carl Bayless, a seventeen-year-old juvenile delinquent with a long history of crime—including a conviction as a fourteen-year-old of killing an Akron rubber worker—kidnapped funeral director Paul Anthony and his wife, Patricia, a fifth-grade teacher, from a Kmart parking lot in Akron and forced them into the trunk of their black-and-white Cadillac. He drove to Perkins Park, home of the city's Children's Zoo, where he shot both in the head, killing Paul Anthony and leaving Mrs. Anthony to die over the next few minutes. A tip led police to the bodies early the next morning. Mr. Anthony was found holding a rosary, Mrs. Anthony clutching a crucifix. Bayless was arrested later that day, February 27, after police detectives discovered him hiding in the attic of his grandmother's house, wearing Mrs. Anthony's wedding ring. Upon conviction, Bayless became the first man sentenced to death under the new law.[11]

As Bayless's appeals were working their way through the state courts, the U.S. Supreme Court handed down a pair of decisions on July 2, 1976, that opened a new era of capital punishment. The rulings reacted to the two different approaches that states had taken following *Furman* as they set out to rewrite their death penalty laws. Some states, like Ohio, had chosen the discretionary route, dividing the process into trials for guilt and trials for punishment and creating lists of aggravating and mitigating factors for juries to weigh. Others, like North Carolina, had chosen the mandatory route, making a death sentence automatic for certain types of crimes, such as first-degree murder. The latter approach, the high court decided, was not good enough. In *Woodson v. North Carolina,* the court ruled 5 to 4 to reject North Carolina's legislative scheme of mandatory death for first-degree murder. As the majority opinion announced by Justice Stevens found, "The two crucial indicators of evolving standards of decency respecting the imposition of punishment in our society—jury determinations and legislative enactment—both point conclusively to the repudiation of automatic death sentences."[12]

But in *Gregg v. Georgia,* decided the same day, the court upheld new death penalty laws in Florida, Georgia, and Texas, making good on the implied premise in *Furman* that it was the imposition of the nation's death penalty laws that was unconstitutional, not the punishment itself. Lending the decision a note of historic finality, a three-justice majority, in an opinion announced by Justice Stewart, also declared that the framers of the Constitution had accepted capital punishment, and for almost two hundred years the high court had recognized that death sentences are not in themselves unconstitutional. Yet the court was also careful to acknowledge that it was dealing with an area of law distinct from other parts of the criminal justice system. The *Furman* decision four years earlier, the *Gregg* majority noted, "did recognize that the penalty of death is different in kind from any other punishment imposed under our system of criminal justice." This understanding that "death is different" would color the court's deliberations time and again.

Not unexpectedly, *Gregg* left Ohio's condemned inmates much quieter than four years earlier. "Most of them kind of look at it as the reality," the officer in charge of death row at the state penitentiary said on the day the ruling was handed down.[13]

Five months later, on the day before Thanksgiving, November 1976, the state supreme court upheld Bayless's conviction and sentence—and hence the new statute—relying largely on the precedent set forth in *Gregg.* "It cannot be claimed that punishment by death in Ohio is excessive because it is grossly disproportional to the severity of the crime," wrote Ohio supreme court justice Leonard Stern. He continued:

> For death is imposed only in cases of purposeful murder and only when one or more aggravating factors are present. Nor can

it be fairly charged that Ohio's statutes are likely to result in capricious, arbitrary and discriminatory death sentences. More clearly than any of the states whose statutes were reviewed by the high court, Ohio has attempted to insulate the determination of guilt and of sentence from any likelihood of jury arbitrariness.

Although Bayless appealed to the federal courts, his case was soon superseded by another challenge to the law, involving yet another Akron slaying. In mid-January of 1975, New Jersey residents Al Parker and Nathan Earl Dew found themselves stranded in Akron on a snowy, cold Tuesday with no money for the drive home. The weekend before, in Jersey City, the two had met Sandra Lockett and her friend Joanne Baxter, both from Akron but in the area to visit some of Lockett's relatives. The couples got along well, partying late both Friday and Saturday evenings. They ran into a little trouble late in the weekend when New Jersey police stopped their car as they returned from New York and arrested them on a concealed weapon charge after finding a gun in their car. The morning of Monday, January 13, the couples went to the Jersey City jail to pay the sixty-dollar bond for Lockett's brother, James, who had also been along for the trip. Later the same day the couples caravanned back to Akron, staying together because of the bad weather and because Sandra Lockett was having trouble with her car. Both cars were stopped for speeding on the way, and the couples had to pay fifty dollars each, depleting what little cash they had left.[14]

Back in Akron, James Lockett did not pay Parker the bond money back as planned. Trying to figure out a way to raise money, Parker debated pawning a ring. But Sandra Lockett nixed the idea, saying the jewelry was too beautiful. Instead, on the way to her methadone clinic appointment on January 14, Lockett told Parker and Dew she knew of places they could "knock off." Ultimately, they settled on Syd's Market Loan in downtown Akron. Lockett's plan called upon Dew and Parker to enter the pawnshop and ask to see a gun, at which point Parker would insert a .38 cartridge he already had and turn the false sale into a robbery. Lockett said she would have to wait outside since the owner, Sydney Cohen, knew her.[15]

Around noon the next day, Dew, Lockett and her brother, James, picked up Parker at a nearby apartment, where he was staying with Joanne

Baxter. After pulling up at the pawnshop, Parker, Dew, and James Lockett went inside while Sandra Lockett went to Larry's, a well-known downtown restaurant, and ordered two cheeseburgers. Inside the pawnshop, everything went according to plan at first. Parker asked Cohen, who was alone, to see a .38-caliber handgun. Cohen handed the gun over, Parker loaded the weapon and announced the robbery. Then things immediately went wrong. As Parker testified at trial, Cohen "snatched the gun" and the weapon went off, shooting him in the chest and killing him. The men fled the pawnshop. Parker ran to the restaurant and dragged Sandra Lockett out, telling her they didn't have time for her to wait for her order. When he told her what had happened, she stashed the gun in her purse and they drove off. Arriving at Lockett's aunt's house, the pair called a cab and headed to the home of Lockett's mother. Police stopped the cab on the way, but Lockett placed the gun under the seat. They were released after being questioned, but later the same day police caught up with them at Lockett's mother's house and arrested them. Outside the pawnshop, Cohen's customers, friends, and relatives struggled to cope. As a businessman trying to help people down on their luck, Cohen had "dealt in humanity," his mourning brother said. The slain storeowner had run his pawnshop for thirty-four years without ever being robbed.[16]

Prosecutors were in a bind looking at the case, since any prosecution of Sandra Lockett, whom they considered the robbery's mastermind and hence the true villain, required the help of Parker and the others. In a painful deal, Summit County assistant prosecutor Stephan Gabalac persuaded Cohen's family that he needed to drop the death penalty against Parker in exchange for his testimony against Lockett. Without her, Gabalac argued, the robbery would never have happened and Cohen wouldn't have been killed. Even so, prosecutors three times offered Lockett a chance to plead to lower charges that didn't carry the death penalty, and each time Lockett refused. She was found guilty on April 3, 1975, and Judge James Barbuto sentenced her to death.[17]

After taking up her case on appeal, Lockett's attorneys were convinced they had a strong case for challenging Ohio's death penalty law. Their client, just twenty-one years old at the time, had been convicted and sentenced to death after a relatively short trial of two and a half days and eight hours of jury deliberation, and, more importantly, she had not been the triggerman.[18] Moreover, prosecutors had never actively sought the death penalty for Lockett. On December 30, 1976, however, a divided Ohio Supreme Court ruled against Lockett, finding no evidence that the state's capital punishment law was a violation of her constitutional rights. Justice J. J. P. Corrigan, writing for the 4-to-3 majority, said the burden was clearly on Lockett and not the state to prove why she should receive a lesser punishment. He also had no patience for the argument that because she wasn't the triggerman in the shooting, death was too harsh a punishment. Lockett, he wrote, "participated in the planning and commission of the robbery and acquiesced in the use of a deadly weapon to accomplish the robbery. Under these circumstances, it might be reasonably expected by all the participants that the victim's life would be endangered by the manner and means of performing the act required."

Lockett's attorneys took some comfort in the split decision and the strong dissent by Justice Leonard Stern, who had written the earlier opinion in *Bayless* upholding the 1974 law. Aggravated robbery is a serious crime, Stern wrote, and there could be some circumstances where an accomplice to that robbery might be punished as if he had participated directly. But he argued that the death penalty may only be applied constitutionally for the most serious of crimes and possibly only for murder itself. Otherwise, he wrote, for defendants like Lockett a death sentence "is both arbitrary and grossly disproportionate to the crime."

Emboldened, Lockett's attorney, Max Kravitz, contacted the NAACP Legal Defense Fund, which agreed to take the case to the U.S. Supreme Court after reviewing the facts. Petitioning on Lockett's behalf would be Tony Amsterdam, the same lawyer who had helped argue *Furman*. In a rare move, the high court agreed to hear both Lockett's case as well as a related case out of Cincinnati, which also involved a death sentence for a non-triggerman. In that crime, Willie Lee Bell had been sentenced to death for his role in the shotgun slaying of sixty-four-year-old Julius Graber, a nursing home operator. Bell, sixteen when the murder was committed, had kidnapped Graber from the parking garage of his apartment complex with an accomplice, eighteen-year-old Samuel Hall, and taken him to a secluded cemetery. There, Hall robbed Graber, marched him into nearby woods, and shot him.[19]

At the hearing in a packed U.S. Supreme Court on January 17, 1978, Bell's attorney, H. Fred Hoefle, argued that the three mitigating factors allowed under Ohio law were so narrow as to give the jury virtually no discretion in deciding whether to sentence someone to death. As he put it, "only a psychotic, or moron or imbecile or idiot had a reasonable chance of surviving the sentencing process." Meanwhile, he and Amsterdam pushed hard on the point that their clients had not been involved in an actual killing. As Amsterdam said, "We are dealing with a case where the defendant has been sentenced to die for doing nothing more than participating in an armed robbery." But Carl Layman, an assistant Summit County prosecutor, would have nothing to do with that argument. Echoing Corrigan's state supreme court opinion, he told the justices that it was reasonably foreseeable that a robbery involves violence. Lockett "dreamed up the idea of the robbery," he told the justices. "It's in her mind that force will be used."[20]

On July 3, 1978, Ohio's death row once again erupted with yells, applause, and foot stomping as the U.S. Supreme Court overturned the state's law, a bloc of four justices arguing that the statute did not provide the individual consideration of mitigating factors required by the Eighth and Fourteenth amendments. As Chief Justice Warren Burger wrote:

> A state that prevents the sentencer in capital cases from giving independent mitigating weight to aspects of the defendant's character and record and to the circumstances of the offense proffered in mitigation creates the risk that the death penalty will be imposed in spite of factors that may call for a less severe penalty, and when the choice is between life and death, such risk is unacceptable and incompatible with the commands of the Eighth and Fourteenth Amendments.

Other justices found different problems with the law. Justice Harry Blackmun said the law was deficient because it allowed a death sentence for Lockett, who did not participate in the actual killing, without allowing the jury any process for considering the extent of her involvement. He also said it was unconstitutional to allow a jury to prevent a death sentence in a case where an offender pleaded guilty but not to have a similar provision if a defendant went to trial. Byron White argued that the death penalty was unconstitutional in cases where it could not be proven the offender meant to kill. Thurgood Marshall again voted to overturn the sentence based on his assertion that the death penalty itself was a violation of the constitutional prohibition against cruel and unusual punishment. William Brennan did not participate, and Justice William Rehnquist dissented, saying the law was not constitutionally deficient. He wrote, "Sandra Lockett was fairly tried, and was found guilty of aggravated murder. I do not think Ohio was required to receive any sort of mitigating evidence which an accused or his lawyer wishes to offer, and therefore I disagree with Part III of the plurality's opinion."[21]

A prison official that day likened the mood on death row to New Year's Eve in Times Square. Elsewhere, there was little reason for celebration. Loretta Prochazka, widow of police Sergeant William Prochazka, of Bedford Heights in suburban Cleveland, killed by a teenager three years earlier when he interrupted a robbery, reflected bitterly that day on the decision that took her husband's killer off death row. "The way I feel, no mercy was given to Bill. When they talk about mercy, they're asking the wrong person." Among those who escaped a death sentence as a result of *Lockett* were Michael Swihart, a suburban Cleveland college student who had clubbed his parents and two brothers to death the year before; Taylor Hancock Jr., of Columbus, a double murderer who killed a roller rink security guard and a taxicab driver; and Carl Bayless, whose own appeal the state supreme court had turned down two years earlier. Prosecutors and lawmakers who had pushed for the 1974 law immediately promised another attempt, and the House Judiciary Committee drafted a new bill over the summer. A constitutional law could be crafted and enacted, Alan Norris promised, "if we can determine what kind of law five of the justices want."[22]

The difficulties of enacting major legislation in an election year temporarily halted the process for the rest of 1978. But lawmakers made good on their post-*Lockett* pledge at the beginning of the new General Assembly. A proposal by Representative Terry Tranter, a Cincinnati Democrat, passed the Democrat-controlled House Judiciary Committee 13 to 8 on February 15, 1979, after the committee, by just one vote, defeated an amendment two days earlier to strip capital punishment from the bill and replace it with life without parole. During the three-hour debate in the full House on February 21, supporters again fended off an attempt to replace capital punishment with life in prison without the possibility of parole, and added an important provision allowing the death penalty for felony murders, such as crimes involving rape, arson, armed robbery, and burglary the result of which is death. Speaking for proponents of the bill, Republican Representative C. William "Dub" O'Neill, of Columbus, declared that the death penalty should be enacted to "satisfy that cry from society for justice."[23] The bill passed 62 votes to 36 just six weeks after its introduction.

The legislation got a far different treatment in the Senate, however, where Democrats opposed to capital punishment kept the bill bottled up in the Judiciary Committee for months under the leadership of committee chairwoman Marigene Valiquette, of Toledo, a death penalty opponent. On November 29, 1979, frustrated Senate Republicans tried unsuccessfully to force the bill out of committee but failed in a vote of 18 to 15 along partisan lines. Valiquette defended her handling of the legislation, saying she wanted to draft as constitutional a statute as possible. But Republican Senator Richard Finan, of Evandale in suburban Cincinnati, perhaps the legislature's most outspoken supporter of the death penalty, criticized the argument made by Valiquette and others that the bill was being held up while the U.S. Supreme Court considered pending death penalty appeals. Such cases, he argued, will always be before the court. Three months later, on February 20, 1980, still-seething Senate Republicans tried again to force a vote, led this time by Senator Paul Pfeifer, a Republican from Bucyrus in the northwest part of the state, but failed again, 18 votes to 14. Months passed with no further action.[24]

The issue came to a head the following September, when the Judiciary Committee finally approved the bill, but not without first stripping the felony murder provision. In its place, Democrats proposed capital punishment for a murder determined to be "outrageously or wantonly vile, horrible, or inhuman in that it involved the physical torture of the victim." That was too much for Finan and Pfeifer, who despite their many months of frustration then led an unusual charge to oppose the bill and, combined with eight Democrats who crossed party lines, defeated the measure 23 votes to 10 on September 17. "Republicans Defeat Death Penalty Bill," read the next day's headline in Gongwer News Service, a widely read and highly respected statehouse daily news report, to the considerable amusement of anti–death penalty advocates. But Finan, a no-nonsense legislator whose nickname around Capitol Square, "Cementhead," reflected the strength of his convictions, defended his actions. Democrats, he charged, had tried to pass a law so restrictive that death sentences would be handed down in Ohio only under the most extraordinary circumstances. As he would reflect facetiously years later, only if the murder were committed "in the middle of Broad and High downtown on a Saturday when Ohio State was playing Michigan on a sunny day and the victim was a policeman." Others dubbed it a deathless penalty bill.[25]

The vote killing the legislation was a short-term victory for Democrats, who saw their inaction on the legislation used against them in the fall elections. Thanks in part to that campaign tactic, Democrats lost control of the Senate to the GOP in November 1980. The newly elected Republican majority, still furious at the bill's handling the previous session, made the death penalty their top priority by introducing a new bill, Senate Bill 1, on January 6, 1981, only the second day of the legislative year. As a winter storm dropped four inches of snow outside and temperatures fell to ten degrees, Pfeifer—now Senate Judiciary Chairman—predicted quick passage of the legislation, saying the philosophical issues had already been debated the previous session. Finan, the bill's sponsor, said it was time to give Ohioans what they wanted. "This is an issue that's very important and very vital to the people of this state, no matter what we think," he testified before the committee. "They're asking that the death penalty be reimposed."[26]

There was little doubt about the bill's fate in the Senate. Pfeifer had chafed under what he considered Valiquette's undisciplined management of the judiciary committee and now saw himself as the law-and-order technician of the process, who would guarantee a fair set of hearings. Finan was the ardent, almost evangelical proponent of capital punishment who was not going to be dissuaded or outmaneuvered this time, especially with control of the Senate in Republican hands. Both were at the beginning of long political careers—Pfeifer would later become a state supreme court justice while Finan would serve six years as Senate president. Although the two grew estranged over the years, they were a duo whose goals were difficult to derail at the time.

As they had in the past, opponents contested the idea that capital punishment was any more a deterrent than a less severe penalty, pointing to states whose murder rates surged after adopting the death penalty. (Data compiled by sociologist Thorsten Sellin had found no difference in homicide patterns from the 1920s through the 1950s in Ohio and Indiana, which had the death penalty, and Michigan, which did not.[27]) The American Civil Liberties Union led the charge against the bill, as its chief Ohio lobbyist, Ohio State law professor Lawrence Herman, testified several times in favor of eliminating capital punishment because of its history of uneven enforcement, especially when it came to the poor and minorities. But Herman also testified about the pros and cons of details of the bill, ultimately taking the approach that if a law were to pass, it should at least be narrowly written and offer as many protections for defendants as possible.

As committee hearings went on, the Ohio Catholic Conference argued that capital punishment reinforced a disregard for human life. The American Friends Service Committee, a Quaker-affiliated social justice group, said death sentences served no purpose but to compound the offense that led to the punishment. Rosina Maynard of the Ohio Coalition against the Death Penalty said there was no excuse for capital punishment in Ohio. "You can't give Ohio a death penalty that is uniformly, properly and indiscriminately enforced," she testified.[28]

Proponents argued their position just as strongly. The Ohio Prosecuting Attorneys Association said the state needed a strong death penalty statute, a stand backed by the testimony of several local prosecutors. The Fraternal Order of Police said lawmakers owed it to the citizens of Ohio to put capital punishment back on the books. Randy Walker, a Columbus police officer paralyzed when shot by a paroled murderer, said the death penalty would act as a deterrent. "If we want criminals to know we are serious about stopping violent crimes, we need to give them a message that the state will no longer tolerate them," he said.[29]

The Senate Judiciary Committee itself was deeply divided and, as previous committees had tried, very nearly took capital punishment off the table on January 28, 1981. Outside the hearing room that day, eight opponents quietly marched up and down the hall protesting the bill. "Death penalty is torture," read one sign. "The Death Penalty is a simple solution for simple minds," read another. Inside the room, Floyd "Buzz" Fay, a twenty-nine-year-old carpenter from Toledo, explained how he was imprisoned for a 1978 murder he was later found innocent of. "Could you live with yourselves if you vote for this bill and then an innocent person is electrocuted?" he asked. Fay's testimony moved even Senator Michael DeWine, a conservative Republican who would later serve two terms as a U.S. senator. "This is not something any legislator can take lightly," he said after the hearing. Seizing the moment, Senator Timothy McCormack, a Cleveland-area Democrat opposed to the death penalty, proposed an amendment to replace capital punishment in the bill with life in prison without the possibility of parole. It was a proposal that opponents would make again and again over the next few months, looking for a tough-on-crime compromise that would remove the death penalty from the bill, and often led to hours of legislative debate. When Pfeifer called the roll on the amendment, the measure failed by just one vote.[30] A week later, the legislation squeaked out of committee 5 votes to 4, then passed by a wide bipartisan margin of 23 votes to 10 in the full Senate on February 11, 1981. The version on the way to the House imposed the death penalty for felony murders, multiple murders, murders for hire, murders by repeat offenders, and murders involving the killing of a police officer.

The year before, annoyed by the way his Senate Democratic colleagues had watered his bill down after it left the House, Tranter helped Finan engineer the bill's defeat in the Senate. As sponsor of the new bill in the House, he set out to craft as constitutional a piece of legislation as possible to get a law on the books that would stay there. Fueling his concerns, and aiding death penalty opponents, were the long shadows cast by the U.S. Supreme Court's 1972 *Furman* decision and 1978 *Lockett* ruling. The state had already been through the ugly process of trying to respond to courts' rejection of the law twice, Tranter reasoned; surely a third time would suffice. As a result, advocates of the new law were relatively open to compromise as debate moved forward through the spring of 1981, first in a House Judiciary subcommittee and then in the full Judiciary and Criminal Justice Committee.[31]

In May, Representative Lee Fisher of suburban Cleveland inserted language that raised the minimum age for execution to eighteen at the time a crime was committed. Fisher—later a one-term attorney general, an unsuccessful gubernatorial candidate, and, in 2006, the first Democratic lieutenant governor elected in twenty years—also successfully proposed eliminating a provision that imposed the death penalty when the victim was under sixteen. Meanwhile, lawmakers went back and forth on whether to include life in prison without the possibility of parole as an option, and whether a jury or judge would be able to impose a death sentence.[32]

Though the outcome appeared clear, opponents continued to argue that the law would be ineffective and applied unevenly, especially against minorities. "Any system of justice has its flaws," Benson Wolman, executive director of the Ohio chapter of the American Civil Liberties Union, told the Judiciary Committee. "And when the chips are down, we cannot as a society allow life to be taken in a system that is not colorblind." Other opponents took a theatrical approach to make their point. In the Senate, Columbus Democrat Michael Schwarzwalder suggested an amendment that would require the governor to throw the switch on the electric chair. During House committee hearings, Representative David Hartley, a liberal Democrat from Springfield, proposed allowing condemned inmates to choose between drawing and quartering, hanging, and garroting. Randall Dana, then the state public defender and a bill opponent, warned that death penalty cases would cost the state millions of extra dollars in defense attorney fees because of the long appeals process. But prosecutors had little patience with that argument. "Protecting people is the issue, not money," testified Franklin County Prosecutor Michael Miller.[33]

On June 3, 1981, the Judiciary Committee approved the bill 13 votes to 5, but not before rejecting another attempt to substitute life in prison without the possibility of parole. A week later, the House passed the bill 67 votes to 31, including a provision that allowed juries to recommend death sentences. During the two-hour debate, both sides echoed arguments made by their colleagues at Ohio's constitutional convention more than a century earlier. Proponents argued that capital punishment was a just act by society that would help stem the nation's crime wave, while opponents said the death penalty was barbaric, unfair, and ineffective. Legislators spent an hour alone debating the life-in-prison option. Representative Bill Mallory, a black Democrat from Cincinnati, gave examples of innocent people wrongly convicted, triggermen who got lighter sentences than accomplices by cooperating with prosecutors, and the high number of minorities sentenced to death—two-thirds in 1978 before *Lockett* emptied death row. "Death sentences fall disproportionately on minorities and the poor," Mallory argued before the proposal was tabled by a 56-to-42 margin.[34]

In the joint House and Senate committee ironing out differences in the bill, the life-without-parole issue became tangled in the notion of whether Democrats or Republicans were going to take a harder line on crime. Ultimately, a compromise was reached that allowed for the possibility of parole after twenty years and after thirty years. The Senate approved the final version on June 30. The House dragged its feet for a few days longer, debating whether to use its vote as leverage on other bills, including the state budget, but in the end House lawmakers voted 71 to 28 on July 1 in favor of the legislation. Rhodes, who narrowly beat Gilligan in 1974 to return to the office he had held for eight years in the 1960s, signed the bill on July 19.

Enactment of the law marked both the beginning of a new era of criminal justice and the end of an important chapter of legislative history. In the ten years it took to pass a capital punishment bill after *Furman*, lawmakers set records for the length of their debates. Unable to take the pressure, some legislators took "a walk to the duck pond," as the expression went, leaving committee hearings to avoid key votes. At least three times—in March 1972, February 1979, and January 1981—committee proposals to eliminate capital punishment failed by just one vote. (Although it's tempting to debate a "what if" scenario had those votes gone the other way, the reality is that the death penalty would have been amended back onto the bill anyway once it reached the full House and Senate.) Compromises abounded: Republican Alan Norris, sponsor of the 1974 bill, and Democrat Harry Lehman, chairman of the House Judiciary Committee in 1979, were capital punishment opponents who felt their obligations as lawmakers overrode their personal convictions. Some Democrats voted for the death penalty, some Republicans agreed to less stringent versions of the bill. It was a time when a position against the death penalty, if reasoned, was not the end of the political world. "It was a different environment," Tranter, a Democrat who supported capital punishment, would reflect. "Today they'd hang your ass."[35]

Ohio's new legislation took effect October 19, 1981, and as after the 1974 law, it didn't take long to begin filling up the state's death row again. Just two days later, on October 21, Leonard Jenkins and Lester Jordan pulled up in a brown Cougar to the Harvard Avenue branch of National City Bank in Cleveland. Jenkins tucked a gun into his back pocket and they walked inside, where he used his gun to disarm the bank security guard and herd customers to the rear of the bank. Jenkins and Jordan then moved teller to teller, Jenkins holding each at gunpoint and threatening to shoot anyone who moved while Jordan removed money from the drawers.

Neither man was a stranger to crime. Jenkins, twenty-seven, had been paroled from prison two years earlier after serving time on a robbery charge. Jordan, fifty-six, had an arrest record going back thirty-eight years, including prison time for a 1970 robbery. Although Jenkins would later argue that he was forced into the robbery by Jordan, who threatened to hurt Jenkins's wife if he didn't cooperate, he clearly was in charge on this day. As they worked, employees activated silent alarms and police rushed to the scene. Cleveland officers John Myhand, an eleven-year veteran of the force, and Anthony Johnson, a rookie patrolman, arrived first. They parked their patrol car near the front of the bank and walked to the door. As Myhand looked inside and saw an armed Jenkins, he realized an actual robbery was underway. "This is a good one, take cover," he said.

Inside the bank, seeing an officer outside the door, Jenkins turned to Jordan and said he was going to "blow the mother fucker's head off." He then said, "We got to shoot our way out," and fired at the officers through the bank's glass doors. Running through the door, Jenkins exchanged fire with Johnson. Both were hit and taken to the hospital, where Johnson died of a gunshot to the head and Jenkins was treated for a bullet wound that severed his spinal cord and left him permanently paralyzed below the waist. Jordan surrendered without incident. At twenty-two, Johnson was just three months out of the police academy.

Following his arrest, Jenkins was indicted on several charges, including aggravated murder with the death penalty specifications that the murder be committed during an aggravated robbery, during a kidnapping, and during a course of conduct involving the attempted killing of two or more people. He was also charged with aggravated robbery, two counts of attempted murder, and eight counts of kidnapping. Before the trial began, prosecutors dismissed one kidnapping and one attempted murder count. Following a trial, the jury returned guilty verdicts on all counts on March 26, 1982. After a second hearing to decide the punishment, the jury recommended death, and on April 16, 1982, Judge David Matia of Cuyahoga County Common Pleas Court sentenced Jenkins to death, the first Ohio inmate sent to death row under the new law.[36]

Jenkins's attorneys raised multiple points on appeal, first and foremost challenging the statute's constitutionality. They argued to the appeals court for Cuyahoga County and then to the Ohio Supreme Court that the state must use the least restrictive means possible as punishment where a right as fundamental as life is at stake. The interests of society in stopping crime, Jenkins's lawyers continued, could be met by something less final than a death sentence. Jenkins's legal team also challenged his death penalty as a violation of protections against cruel and unusual punishment, and argued that Jenkins himself was not an appropriate candidate for death. His IQ of 63 was low, they said, and he had a mental age of just over nine years. Further, the argument went, his mother had testified during his trial that he was subject to abuse from an alcoholic father as a child, while his wife said he wasn't even capable of attending to his own personal hygiene as a adult.[37]

The state supreme court had little patience for these arguments and, on December 17, 1984, unanimously upheld Jenkins's conviction and death sentence. Chief Justice Frank Celebrezze cited the U.S. Supreme Court's decision in *Gregg* eight years earlier to emphasize that the nation's highest court had recognized that the death penalty, as a sanction or punishment, is proper in extreme cases. Capital punishment, he wrote, again quoting *Gregg*, "is not a form of punishment that may never be imposed, regardless of the circumstances of the offense, regardless of the character of the offender, and regardless of the procedure followed in reaching the decision to impose it."[38]

Like the trial judge, the state supreme court was also unswayed by the mitigating factors offered on Jenkins's behalf. "Despite a low I.Q., appellant demonstrated that he could disarm a bank guard and immobilize all of the tellers and patrons in the bank by threat of force," Celebrezze wrote. "He clearly intended to fire his weapon and was fully aware that the person at whom he directed his shots was a police officer."[39]

Though Ohio's 1981 law would be challenged numerous times in the future and numerous death sentences would be overturned for different reasons, Celebrezze's ruling marked the beginning of long string of court decisions that would uphold the fundamentals girding the new statute. The supreme court, as Celebrezze wrote, had thoroughly examined and discussed each argument Jenkins raised and had even agreed with him on some points, such as the fact that prosecutors improperly stretched four aggravating factors into five when charging him.

"Nonetheless," Celebrezze concluded, "we are completely satisfied that today's decision accomplishes the goal of all criminal cases—the fair and impartial administration of justice, i.e., justice from both the accused's and society's perspectives." He then added, "Finally, no person is capable of completely putting aside the full range of emotions encountered when considering a capital case. We are completely satisfied in this respect also that today's decision represents, to the best of our abilities, an objective, impartial, and unprejudiced review of the conviction and sentence given to this appellant."[40]

Celebrezze also tried to assure Ohioans that the new death penalty law would be implemented as impartially as possible in years to come. He pointed out that the law allowed the court to collect "a vast quantity of information," starting with capital indictments and ending with sentences, to ensure that the appropriateness of each death sentence could be weighed against other cases.[41] The message was clear. Not only was Ohio's new death penalty statute constitutional, it would also be fair.

THREE

The Volunteer

"What was the use in living?"

—*Convicted killer Wilford Berry, dubbed "the Volunteer" for his
refusal to appeal his death sentence*

THE TV satellite trucks got there first, some the night before, some starting at 6 AM that day in late February, at least twenty by the end, jockeying
for the best position in the long parking lot outside the Southern Ohio
Correctional Facility in Lucasville, a sprawling complex of brick and con-
certina wire and guard towers in the rolling Appalachian foothills at the
southern end of the state. Next came the demonstrators, hundreds of
them, bundled in blankets and quilts against the wind and temperatures
in the mid-thirties. Some were opponents of capital punishment and sang
protest songs and held signs that read things like "Killing is not the way
to healing." Some, a smaller group, supported the death penalty and held
a counterdemonstration about twenty feet away. "This is great," said
Robert Vallandingham, whose father, a Lucasville guard, was murdered in
the prison's nine-day riot in 1993. Last to arrive were the reporters bound
for the inside of the prison. Even though only a few were designated as
official witnesses, dozens had registered for credentials to attend media
room briefings, some from as far away as England and Germany.[1]

Wilford Lee Berry Jr. arrived at Lucasville shortly after 8 PM on Thursday, February 18, 1999, riding in a white van that brought him from the Corrections Medical Center in Columbus, the state prison system's main medical facility for sick or injured inmates. Riding down U.S. 23 with him were three guards and Rod Francis, the CMC warden. At 8:18 PM, Berry entered the prison's death house, a small brick building set apart from the other Lucasville units. He had a cup of black coffee at 8:29 PM, chatted with Warden Stephen Huffman and guards for a couple of hours, then went to bed at 10:56 PM, saying he was going to get some sleep.

The next day, he woke up ninety minutes before dawn and ate a breakfast of boiled eggs, cereal, and juice. The prison chaplain arrived about 7:30 AM to offer counseling, but Berry said he didn't want to meet with him. He took a shower, then met briefly with Huffman. Most of the morning he spent chatting with Cindi Yost, an assistant state public defender. He passed up an eleven o'clock lunch of fish and creamed potatoes, and when his afternoon meal arrived on a white foam plate—lasagna, garlic bread, and cheesecake—he picked at the lasagna and sipped a cup of Pepsi but ignored the other food. In the afternoon he began to suffer from diarrhea and endured four or five severe attacks; prison staff brought him Pepto-Bismol and crackers and 7UP for relief. At 4:30 PM he took another shower; when he was done, he cleaned his cell.

The thirty-six-year-old Berry, once a gangly six feet tall, was now a chubby 190 pounds, much of the weight put on during the last two years at the medical center. He sat on a metal cot bolted to the wall of a four-foot by ten-foot holding cell seventeen steps from the state's death chamber. His thick face was pale and unshaven. He was given a TV and radio but didn't turn them on, nor did he open a Gideon's Bible sent to his cell. The only things he read were six cards and letters that guards delivered to him late in the afternoon. He wore a white pullover smock-type shirt over a white T-shirt and navy-blue pants with a red stripe running down the legs. The outfit was the traditional clothing in Ohio for condemned inmates.[2]

In the eighteen years since the state's new death penalty law had been enacted, everything had changed, as the saying goes, and yet nothing had. The statute had been challenged numerous times in court and undergone significant revisions. Death row had filled to almost two hundred inmates. Condemned prisoners could now choose to die by electric chair or injection but had lost a significant step in the appeals process. No one had been executed, although a couple of prisoners, including Berry, had come close. On March 14, 1994, John Byrd, sentenced to die for killing a Cincinnati Proctor & Gamble executive moonlighting as a convenience store clerk, was spared five hours and twenty-five minutes before his scheduled execution. On January 25, 1996, Robert Buell, who had raped and killed an eleven-year-old girl, spent the day in the death chamber holding cell at Lucasville before the U.S. Supreme Court, by a 5-to-4 vote, allowed him to continue his appeals. And on March 3, 1998, guards were transporting Berry to Lucasville when they got word of a stay handed down by the U.S. Supreme Court. They pulled over on U.S. 23 just south of the small city of Circleville and turned around to come back to Columbus.

When Berry finally arrived in Lucasville, in 1999, the state's new governor, Bob Taft, had been in office thirty-eight days. Taft had been elected as a moderate Republican the previous fall. The death penalty had rarely come up as a campaign issue. If pressed, Taft said he supported capital punishment as an expression of the will of the voters. For the most part, the state's death statute remained an abstract concept, a stark possibility that nonetheless loomed far off on the horizon.

After Leonard Jenkins arrived on death row in Lucasville in 1981, the unit slowly filled up at the rate of about ten condemned inmates a year. Opponents of the death penalty carried on their battle to have the law thrown out, and in January 1987 the state's Roman Catholic bishops issued a statement opposing capital punishment. But by 1988, death row was at capacity with eighty prisoners, and officials announced plans to add an additional cell block. In the fall of 1992, the state approved a forty-thousand-dollar contract with Jay Wiechert, of Fort Smith, Arkansas, an expert in building and rebuilding electric chairs for states including Alabama, Georgia, and Virginia. No replacement parts were available for the seventy-year-old chair, so Wiechert built a new base and completely rewired it, adding an electrical control panel, a high-voltage transformer, cables and body electrodes, and a voltage and time chart recorder. Almost eleven thousand days had passed since the chair was last used. "We want to be ready, given that there are some people on death row who are close to exhausting their appeals," Sharon Kornegay, a prisons spokeswoman, said at the time the contract was announced.[3]

As far as Berry was concerned, sitting a few feet from the state's untested death chamber on February 19, 1999, he had given up his appeals the day he was arrested nine years earlier.

Berry was born in Houston on September 2, 1962, the son of Wilford Berry Sr. and Jennie Franklin. He arrived two weeks prematurely after his mother went into labor early because of a fall. When he was just a baby, the family moved to Cleveland. Berry's father, a Korean War vet, soon began suffering from bouts of mental illness and was ultimately admitted three times to the Lima State Hospital for the Criminally Insane, where he was diagnosed as "schizophrenic, paranoid type." An erratic man, he left the family for good right before Christmas Day of 1963 after walking back and forth in their apartment for several hours, threatening them with a knife. The police came to the apartment to check on the family; they had picked Berry Sr. up drunk on the streets, claiming he'd killed them all. Berry's mother often said how much he looked like his father.[4]

Berry—"Bubba" to his family—was born with strabismus, a severe cross-eyed condition, but his mother could not afford surgery to correct the problem until he was eight years old. Other children picked on him because of his appearance. He was often beaten up. He wet the bed until age seven and was not circumcised until he was eight. Berry also suffered from a speech impediment so severe that often the only person who could understand him was his older sister, Elaine, who would serve as a kind of interpreter. He also suffered from episodes resembling epileptic seizures as well as a condition called pneumothorax, a breathing disorder that caused his lungs to collapse and was not corrected until he was nearly an adult.[5]

As a young child, Berry was left in the care of a babysitter and her teenaged children, who repeatedly raped and sexually abused him. One girl would require him to suck her breasts, another to penetrate her vaginally with his penis. A boy anally raped him. Seeking escape, Berry would crawl between the couch and the wall to sleep. He cried when his mother went to work at various factory jobs, asking her not to leave, asking for a hug, but she would get angry and just walk out. She said he was too old for hugs. "So I started to lie," Berry said years later. "I kept the truth to myself." He tried to commit suicide around the age of nine, taking all of the tranquilizers he'd been given for his hyperactivity. His mother arranged for a Big Brother mentor, but Berry says the man made sexual advances towards him. His mother moved the family several times, from one apartment to another, requiring Berry to switch schools often, six times before third grade alone. Struggling to raise two children by herself, his mother once tied her belongings in a sheet and went to the welfare office with Berry and his sister to get help. A victim of childhood abuse herself at the hands of an alcoholic stepfather, Berry's mother occasionally beat Berry and his sister with an extension cord.[6]

As a child of nine or ten, Berry began dreaming about fighting a mysterious "lady in black," around the same time his mother was dabbling in witchcraft, including holding a séance. Berry believed the lady in the dreams was the daughter of the devil and imagined fighting her, going to hell, then to heaven, coming back down and decapitating her. He could not go to bed without a Bible and had begun hearing voices. When he was about eleven years old, he arrived home one night at 10 PM with no clothes on, saying he had walked seventy-seven blocks from downtown Cleveland. He said he had been hit and knocked down, and that he awoke in an alley. Reconstructing the bizarre event years later, his mother and sister surmised he'd been sexually assaulted. At thirteen, Berry went outside one night and stumbled on what he described as a parallel world in which the lady in black commanded creatures to try to kill him. But he was able to get a sword and kill her. He knew if he didn't find her, "eventually we'll run into each other or she'll kill me or I'll kill her and in the process a lot of people will die. That's her nature."[7]

At the age of fourteen, Berry brought a knife to school to use on a boy who had insulted his mother. That earned him a trip to the Child Study Center in Columbus, then to Buckeye Boys Village, a treatment center for delinquents, where he stayed for fifteen months. A psychologist noted that his "emotional condition was quite seriously severely unstable" and that he could be a danger to himself or others. He recommended further treatment, which Berry never received; he dropped out of high school at sixteen. At seventeen, he took about a hundred aspirins to try to kill himself, and on another occasion he took rat poison. In 1978 and again in

1980, Berry underwent surgery to repair damage to his lungs. One doctor told him that he was a "corpse looking for a place to die."[8]

When Berry was nineteen, he moved to Texas, hoping to find relatives of his father. Instead, he ended up stealing a car in Weatherford, a small community just outside Fort Worth, and was arrested and sentenced to prison for six years. Prison doctors diagnosed him as schizophrenic, gave him psychotropic drugs, and placed him in a prison psychiatric ward. He was raped during his first two years and tried to commit suicide several times, once cutting his forearms so deeply he required sutures. He began refusing the drugs, including Mellaril, an antipsychotic medication, out of fear that they slowed his ability to defend himself from attacks. Other times he would sell the drugs to other inmates. He was finally moved, at his request, to solitary confinement.[9]

After Berry was released from prison, he returned to his mother in Cleveland, but she soon kicked him out for irresponsible behavior, including burning a pentagram in the kitchen floor. He held a few odd jobs, then went west and ended up in California; he was living in San Francisco when the 1989 earthquake struck, destroying his apartment. He worked briefly as a Red Cross volunteer in the aftermath of the quake until his erratic behavior caused supervisors to have him briefly hospitalized. He became involved with a girl, Michelle, but she rebuffed him. Back in Ohio, staying with his older sister, Elaine Quigley, he seemed changed, secretive, often sitting alone in a room and staring. Quigley and her husband weren't sure what was wrong but assumed he'd been traumatized by the earthquake. On November 28, 1989, Berry started a job working under the table as a night handyman at an east side Cleveland bakery. The man who hired him, Charles Mitroff, told his father he thought the new employee would work out well.[10]

About 2 PM on February 19, 1999, the U.S. Supreme Court, in a one-paragraph decision without comment, denied a request by Berry's public defenders for an emergency delay of his execution. The court, without comment, also denied a request by David Bodiker, the state public defender, to hear an appeal of a decision by the Sixth U.S. Circuit Court of Appeals the day before refusing to block the execution. "This appears to remove the last barrier," said Ohio Deputy Attorney General Mark Weaver. Berry's attorneys agreed. "While we've always maintained that he's incompetent to waive his appeals, we do not feel we have a credible claim that he's too insane to be executed," said public defender Jon Woodman. "We have a policy of not presenting frivolous motions just to cause delays." The decision had little effect on Berry. He continued to bide his time in his cell, chatting with Francis and Yost, both of whom had befriended Berry over the years and had spent the most time with him. With Yost's help, Berry had written his own version of a psalm the day before. She asked him if he wanted to add any lines, and he said no. Late in the afternoon, Berry agreed to meet with his mother and sister. The three spent about an hour together, and the two told Berry they loved him. Pressed by his sister, Berry said he had asked God for forgiveness. He also said he had forgiven himself.[11]

Shortly before midnight each day, Charles "Chuck" Mitroff—like Berry, a "Junior"—said good-bye to his wife, Barbara, left their home in the Cleveland suburb of Pepper Pike, and drove the eleven miles to 6308 Fleet Avenue, the location of Charles Bakery, the traditional Polish-style bakery he had run for almost thirty years after inheriting the business from his father. Charles Mitroff Sr. was an immigrant from Macedonia in Eastern Europe who had crossed into the United States from Canada and worked in Cleveland's then-booming steel mills for a time. In Cleveland he had married Mitroff's mother, the daughter of Polish immigrants.[12]

Their son was a handsome man in his early fifties with grayish-blue eyes and a receding hairline, an avid golfer who worked hard to support his wife and three sons. He spoke to his father on the phone every day, updating him on things at the store. Not much of a drinker, he enjoyed an occasional martini with his wife. His days were long. Each night the bakery produced hundreds of loaves of pumpernickel and rye bread, as well as paczki—a type of jelly doughnut—kolaches, kuchen, poppy-seed rolls, Vienna rolls, custard and cream doughnuts, and many other pastries. In addition to the overnight hours, Mitroff also ran bakery stands at area flea markets to earn extra money. He came from the old school, his brother-in-law would recall. If you wanted something extra, you worked for it.

The bakery did a fair amount of street sales from a shop at the front of the store, but most of the business involved deliveries to wholesalers around the city. After arriving at the bakery each night, Mitroff picked up a load of pastries and set off on a route to deliver the goods across Cleveland. Most nights he'd arrive back after 2 AM, load up again, and head out on another route.[13]

With two days left in November 1989, Mitroff hired a gangly handyman with a mustache who gave his name as Ed Thompson. Mitroff put him to work as a porter, washing pans and cleaning the floor at the bakery at night. Mitroff told his wife the man looked like he needed a job. Thompson, an alias that Berry had adopted some time after returning from San Francisco, had other ideas. In the late morning or early afternoon of November 30, Berry, along with a young neighborhood acquaintance, eighteen-year-old Anthony Lozar, who had recently been released from a mental hospital, hatched a plan to rob and murder Mitroff, take the company van, and go to Kentucky.[14]

Before going to work that day, Berry bought an SKS Chinese model semiautomatic assault rifle and a sawed-off .22-caliber rifle and hid them in an alley next to the bakery entrance. At about 11:20 PM that night, Mitroff pulled out of his Pepper Pike driveway in his blue Chevrolet van to start his nightly round of deliveries. He arrived at Fleet Avenue, loaded the van, and drove off. After he'd gone, Berry let Lozar into the store and told him where to hide. When Mitroff returned, the baker came into the store and, seeing Berry, said, "Where's the key?"

At that moment, Lozar moved from his hiding place and without speaking shot Mitroff once in the chest with the assault rifle.

"You shot me," Mitroff gasped as he fell, speaking to Berry.

"I didn't shoot you," Berry said with a laugh. "Do I have a gun?"

"Call the police," Mitroff responded. A moment later he begged, "Call the ambulance."

Instead, Berry took the .22 rifle, walked up to Mitroff, and shot him once in the head. "I could see that he was dying," Berry said afterwards. "I just pulled the trigger. . . . If you kill the brain, rest of the body dies."

"I did it for the hell of it," Berry said. "Laughed right through it." A coroner's report would list the cause of death as both shots—the one fired by Lozar into Mitroff's torso and the one fired by Berry. Berry and Lozar mopped and washed the bakery floor as best they could, put Mitroff's body in the van, and drove to Lozar's sister's house. They got a shovel, then headed for a bridge at East Forty-Ninth Street and Chard Avenue, where they dug a shallow grave, took Mitroff's wallet, and buried the body. They switched plates from a 1984 Ford station wagon belonging to an East Forty-ninth Street resident, then drove the van to American Pride Car Wash to clean it, leaving behind the shovel, a pair of boots, and a piece of blood-stained fiberboard. They slept in the van that night, then went to a Kmart the next day, where they bought black spray paint to paint the van. They spent the night at a friend's house, then briefly went to see Berry's sister, Elaine, who told them police wanted to talk to them about Mitroff. Shortly thereafter they took off for Kentucky in Mitroff's van. The robbery netted them $32.55.[15]

Well before dawn the next day, bakery customers began calling Barbara at home to complain that they hadn't received their baked goods. Barbara called police, who met her and bakery employee Christina Blaut at the store, where they found the undelivered baked goods, unwashed pans, recently mopped floors, and the hint of a reddish residue on the floor that was dismissed as jelly from a doughnut. Officers assured the family everything was fine, that Mitroff had probably just gone off by himself for a while. Hardly satisfied with this explanation, the family hired private detective William Florio, an ex-Cleveland cop who visited the scene with Barbara's nephew, stuck his pen in the floor, and saw immediately that the reddish residue was blood, a suspicion confirmed when they found a bucket caked with blood. Florio alerted detective friends on the force that it looked bad. On December 3, as the search for Mitroff continued, Berry, still referring to himself as Ed Thompson, called Barbara and explained that he had reported for work at midnight on November 30 but left after waiting outside for half an hour.[16]

Around midnight on December 4, patrolman Stan Voorhees of the Kenton County, Kentucky, police department saw a van weaving and slowing on U.S. 25, about nine miles south of the city of Covington. Suspecting a drunken driver, he decided to follow the vehicle even though he was outside his jurisdiction, planning to stop it if it entered the city. As he followed, Voorhees saw the occupants leaning over as if placing something under the front seat. He also saw that the van had Ohio personal plates, though it appeared to be a commercial vehicle. He radioed the information in, and the report came back that the plates belonged to a station wagon. As soon as the van crossed into Kenton County, Voorhees pulled the vehicle over in the parking lot of Glen's Woodland Inn, a popular local restaurant.

Inside the van, Berry debated his options. Their plan was already going awry; they'd gotten off Interstate 75 a few minutes earlier only to find out what Kentucky county they were in and to look for gas. Berry told Lozar to shoot Voorhees with the assault rifle, but Lozar refused. At that moment a large German shepherd belonging to the restaurant owner started barking. Berry backed down, mistaking the animal for a police dog. Approaching the van, Voorhees noticed a dealer's sticker indicating the vehicle was new, yet observed that someone had just spray painted the van black. He asked Berry for his driver's license; Berry told him his name was Ed Thompson and gave him a piece of paper with a Social Security number. Running that information, Voorhees quickly learned that no one in Ohio had been issued a license under that name. He told both men to get out of the van. As Lozar got out, Voorhees saw the butt of a rifle sticking out from under the front seat. He pulled his gun, ordered the two to the ground, and handcuffed them. Inside he found a bag of marijuana, a rifle case, a .22 rifle, and a Chinese-style assault rifle. Lozar and Berry were taken into custody and arrested. Lozar, scared of Berry, began talking to Detective Matthew Rolfsen only after the officer agreed to keep them separated.[17]

On December 13, Kenton County deputy jailer Mark Carter was leading Berry into court when Berry began mumbling. What's the problem? Carter asked. Berry replied that he and his partner had shot a man in a Cleveland bakery, stolen his van, and left the man's body in a grave.

"Did you kill the man?" Carter asked.

"Yes, I did," Berry said.

After the court hearing, Carter took Berry back to his cell, but his fellow prisoners soon began complaining that Berry was discussing details of a murder. After jailer Michael Moran moved Berry to a new cell, Berry started telling him about the crime.

"Me and my partner, we're the ones that killed that guy in Cleveland and you didn't even get my shoes from it," Berry said.

When Moran asked him what he was talking about, Berry explained that there was blood on his shoes. Moran called the prosecutor, who called Rolfsen, who took a statement from Berry. Berry said he would talk to Cleveland police if he were guaranteed the death penalty. The same day, as the two awaited extradition, a Cuyahoga County grand jury indicted them on death penalty charges for Mitroff's death.[18]

Berry's trial began the following summer on Monday, June 25, before Judge Carolyn Friedland. After just over a week of testimony from eighteen separate witnesses, the jury deliberated three hours before deciding on July 3 that Berry was guilty of killing Mitroff. Under the provisions of Ohio's death penalty statute, the court then conducted a separate hearing at the end of the month to determine whether Berry should be sentenced to death.

Almost from the moment of his arrest, Berry maintained he had decided to kill his new boss "for no reason." As the trial's penalty phase got under-way, Berry's attorneys introduced a new story. Before Mitroff hired Berry, they said, he had nearly hit Quigley and her young daughter with the delivery van. Mitroff quickly apologized, and Quigley, who lived in the neighborhood and had seen the bakery for years, didn't think much of it. But Quigley told her brother about the incident, which his attorneys argued gave him a delusional sense of needing revenge. Berry's lawyers moved for a new trial, but Friedland wasn't convinced. "You can't discount the fact all of these things you are telling me are your client's self-serving statements or the self-serving statements of his family," she said.[19]

As the punishment phase continued, Berry's mother and sister testified about Berry's problems as a boy, his father's mental illness, and the bizarre incident when Berry arrived home without any clothes. Quigley also told the jury about the near accident with Mitroff's van. Two Boys Village employees, a psychologist and a counselor, testified about Berry's coping problems. Robert Goldberg, a psychologist who had tested Berry for competency to stand trial, told the jury of Berry's psychological problems and said his mother was responsible in great part for his personality dis-order. In a statement prepared for the court, Goldberg cast serious doubt on whether a man with such mental problems should be executed. During this testimony, Berry's mother learned for the first time the fate of her husband, Wilford Sr., who had died in a mental institution in 1979. Finally, Berry himself took the stand and recounted for jurors the story of his childhood and the rapes by his babysitter's children. He told of his nightmares, his health problems, the rape in the Texas prison, and the suicide attempt. He said jurors might as well sentence him to death. "Because by the time I finish 20 or 30 years, I will be so institutionalized that I wouldn't hesitate to kill you for just looking at me," he said. "It will be on your conscience, not mine, if any of you ever hear my name in the future. I have a mental problem. I need help, and the prison system won't give me that help."

George Lonjak, a Cuyahoga County assistant prosecutor, derided Berry's comments as a babbling, unsworn statement. He contrasted Berry with Mitroff, the hard-working baker who labored long hours to provide for his family. By contrast, Berry acquired things in a "callous manner." "He does it with greed and he does it in a vicious, violent act," Lonjak said.[20]

The jury agreed, recommending on August 1, 1990, that Berry be put to death. On August 13, Friedland followed their wishes and sentenced Berry to die. His execution date, she told him, would be December 1, 1991, the second anniversary of Mitroff's death.

Two days later, a three-judge panel spared Lozar, the man who had lain in wait for the baker to enter the business and fired the first, fatal shot. Although the judges could have sent Lozar to the electric chair, they instead sentenced him to fifty-three years in prison. Mitroff's brother-in-law, Richard Bowler, said after the verdict was announced that while the process seemed biased in Lozar's favor, the defendant would be out of society for a long time. "We're not unhappy with the sentence," Bowler said.[21]

His wish to be executed clear, Berry moved onto death row just as Governor Richard Celeste, a two-term Democrat from Cleveland and a staunch opponent of capital punishment, was winding up his last months in office. The death penalty and what Celeste saw as its inequities, especially where race was concerned, had long been on the governor's mind. Soon after taking office the first time, in 1983, he directed his staff to research the possibility of an execution coming before him and to prepare a system for reviewing such cases. But no executions seemed imminent, and by the mid-1980s the state's savings-and-loan crisis occupied much of the governor's attention. In the spring of 1989, House and Senate lawmakers approved a bill giving inmates the choice between the electric chair and injection, but Celeste vetoed the legislation. (A similar bill giving inmates the choice became law in 1993 with backing from prisons director Reggie Wilkinson. He argued, not in favor of inmates but on behalf of prison staff, that death by electrocution was such a gruesome process that it wasn't fair to the corrections' employees on whose shoulders the job would fall.[22]) Celeste's attorneys drafted a memo on the legalities of issuing a type of blanket commutation of all death sentences—taking the condemned inmates off death row, though not out of prison—but decided it was not an appropriate use of his clemency power.

Then, midway through his second term, Celeste began to take a look at the role domestic violence had played in the crimes committed by women prisoners in Ohio. After studying data collected by Ohio State sociologists, Celeste asked the state's Adult Parole Authority to create a process for women to appeal their cases based on factors of domestic violence that at the time of their convictions could not be used as a defense. More than a hundred women submitted appeals through this system, and on December 21, 1990, Celeste granted clemency to twenty-five women and asked the parole authority to take a close look at another thirty-two cases where the evidence of domestic violence wasn't entirely clear. Celeste's actions inspired dozens of other inmates to request clemency, and while he couldn't consider all those, he did decide to undertake a partial review of death penalty cases in his very last days in office. He focused on the women on death row and on men whose execution dates were approaching soon. What Celeste determined was that, more than anything else, "a profound racial bias cast doubt over virtually every death sentence," especially considering that all four women on death row at the time were black. Celeste was also troubled by the degree to which death row inmates suffered from low IQs, signs of mental illness, and chronic addictions. To be sure, they were heinous killers who should be removed from society. But they were also from the margins of society, those least capable of functioning in the world.[23] After weighing the cases, Celeste held a news conference on January 10, two business days before leaving office, to announce that he was commuting the sentences of eight inmates, four women, four men, six of them black. One of them was Leonard Jenkins, the first killer sentenced to die under the state's new law.

The governor told reporters that he felt that a blanket commutation of all death sentences would have created a backlash that would have hurt the chances of repealing the death penalty. But he also was deeply troubled by the role race appeared to play in sentencing, noting that, at the time, 54 of 101 of the men on death row were black. (By contrast, blacks make up about 11 percent of Ohioans.) "I don't think statistics alone prove racism, but I believe these statistics call for further study of Ohio's system of rendering decisions in capital cases," he said.[24]

The incoming Republican governor, George Voinovich, and the newly elected Democratic attorney general, Lee Fisher, immediately challenged the commutations, and a several-year court battle ensued. Beyond the legal wrangling that Celeste's decision initiated, however, his action struck at the heart of the state's fears over a growing crime rate and a frustration that, ten years after enactment, the death penalty was a toothless tiger. This frustration ultimately came to a head in Ohio in 1994, a year that saw one of the fiercest public debates over capital punishment since the state's 1912 referendum.

The U.S. Supreme Court had expressed similar concerns over death penalty delays and had already begun to place limits on state convicts' ability to turn to the federal constitution for relief. At issue was what is known as the writ of habeas corpus, literally, "you shall have the body," a right under federal law by which defendants convicted in state courts could appeal their cases to the federal system. The protections granted by habeas corpus originated in British common law in the seventeenth century as a way to shield the individual from abuses by the state. In the United States, Congress expanded the power in 1867 to protect ongoing Reconstruction efforts in the South. Over the next century the court required defendants to exhaust all their state appeals before seeking habeas corpus relief. But in 1963, in *Fay v. Noia,* the court, by a 6-to-3 vote, allowed inmates more access to the federal right, ruling to permit a state inmate the chance to pursue the relief even without exhausting his appeals to state courts. As a result, defense attorneys began using the law to challenge convictions in the federal courts and over the years became skilled at filing motions on their clients' behalf in a strategy that had the effect of vastly slowing down the capital punishment system.

By the late 1970s, the Supreme Court, under conservative chief justice William Rehnquist, began to restrict habeas relief out of a concern that inmates were abusing the writ by filing multiple claims over time. The court continued to place limits on the habeas writ, including a major decision in *McClesky v. Zant*, a 1991 case involving a second federal appeal by Georgia inmate Warren McClesky, sentenced to die for shooting an off-duty police officer during a 1978 robbery. The decision limited inmates to one habeas filing instead of repeated claims and put a heavy burden on the inmate to prove that a second habeas filing was not frivolous. Justice Anthony Kennedy lamented the cost and delays created by successive appeals. "Perpetual disrespect for the finality of convictions disparages the entire criminal justice system," he wrote in the April 1991 decision denying McClesky's claim.[25]

Congress acted in a similar fashion to limit death penalty appeals. The Antiterrorism and Effective Death Penalty Act, signed by President Clinton on April 24, 1996, set a one-year deadline for filing habeas corpus appeals and restricted the ability of federal judges to overturn state court decisions. In an unusual move, the U.S. Supreme Court quickly agreed to hear a challenge to the law, upholding it by unanimous vote just two months later. Senator Orrin Hatch, the sponsor of the legislation, applauded the ruling with comments that summed up the feelings of the day. "We've protected the rights of these people who have been convicted, but we are going to quit playing this game of incessant frivolous appeals at the cost of taxpayers paying unnecessary dollars and the pain for victims and their families," he said.[26]

In Ohio, politicians heard the cry for justice loud and clear. When Betty Montgomery, a Republican state senator from Bowling Green and former county prosecutor, was running for attorney general in 1994, she was guaranteed questions at every campaign stop about the death penalty. "The failure to impose the death penalty in Ohio was symbolically telling Ohio citizens that the justice system wasn't working," Montgomery would recall. "If we're going to have it on the books, we need to have it working and working fairly."[27] Voinovich, the former mayor of Cleveland, highlighted the delays in the first week of 1994 in his State of the State speech. Addressing lawmakers at the Capitol Theatre in the downtown Riffe Center in Columbus, Voinovich proposed a constitutional amendment for the following November that would eliminate state appeals courts from a death row inmate's process for appeals. "Justice in capital punishment cases has for decades been a prisoner itself, held captive by a system that's not working, a system that prolongs the suffering of victims and their families, wastes untold amounts of taxpayer dollars, and renders the death penalty anything but a deterrent," Voinovich said. "Justice delayed is justice denied."[28]

The legislature quickly followed suit, introducing House Resolution 15, sponsored by Representative Johnnie Maier, a Massillon Democrat, to take Voinovich's proposal and place it on the ballot. Emotional testimony flowed at legislative hearings that spring. Relatives of Monte Tewksbury, whose killer, John Byrd, came within five hours of death in March, complained of the delays in his case. "John Byrd has had 11 years to plead for his life, and I think he gave my father maybe 30 seconds," twenty-nine-year-old Kimberly Tewksbury-Wright told a criminal justice subcommittee of the Senate Judiciary Committee on April 7. Madge Burton, whose two daughters and granddaughter were stabbed to death by Rhett Depew in 1984, said the greatest tragedy in life is having your children murdered. "The next greatest tragedy is to see the criminal go through endless appeals," she said.[29]

Death penalty opponents warned that removing the appeals court from the capital punishment process would eliminate another safeguard against wrongful sentences. They also pointed out that much of what appeals courts did was compile trial transcripts and other records, a burden that would simply be transferred to the Ohio Supreme Court without shortening the process. On May 13, 1994, Robert K. Domer, of Canton, testified about his own experience with a wrongful capital punishment conviction. Domer was a down-and-out mortgage banker in 1963 when he was arrested for the murder of a man found in his burning car. Prosecutors said Domer murdered Howard Riddle to fake his own death so his wife could collect $288,000 in insurance payments. In fact, Riddle, a fruit peddler whom Domer had met in a bar in Akron, died of natural causes before Domer put the body in the car. Had the court of appeals not been available to review his case, "my death sentence could easily have been carried out," Domer testified.[30] Undeterred, the House and Senate both approved the measure. The issue would go to the ballot.

Three months later, on a related matter, the Ohio Supreme Court ruled unanimously that state appeals courts could no longer issue delays in executions after inmates had exhausted their round of appeals in the state courts. Many death penalty cases, wrote Chief Justice Thomas Moyer, were reaching a point of judicial saturation. "We have created a web of procedures so involved that they threaten to engulf the penalty itself," Moyer wrote in *State v. Steffen.* "Procrastination will not satisfy the soul." On November 9, voters overwhelmingly approved Issue 1 by a more than two-to-one margin, eliminating the state appeals courts entirely from the death penalty process. They also elected Montgomery attorney general, ousting Democrat Lee Fisher. Upon taking office in January, Montgomery would move quickly to further streamline the appeals process and to beef up the office's death penalty unit.

Around the country, 1994 had become a year of death penalty debate. In February, U.S. Supreme Court justice Harry Blackmun concluded that the death penalty could not be fairly implemented under the Constitution and announced that he would no longer "tinker with the machinery of death." In September, President Clinton signed a crime bill that created sixty new federal death penalty crimes. Kansas restored its death penalty, and three states, Idaho, Maryland, and Nebraska, carried out their first executions in more than three decades.[31] In Ohio, the year ended with a divided state supreme court voting to uphold the Celeste commutations, saying the state constitution supported his actions. The 4-to-3 ruling on December 30 did not sit well with justices on either side of the issue. Alice Robie Resnick, a tough-on-crime Democrat who voted in the minority, had no qualms about overturning the commutations, calling Celeste's actions a blow to the rights of crime victims. Celeste "intentionally bypassed established procedures and flouted the constitutional limits on his clemency authority," she wrote. Moyer, a moderate Republican who voted in the majority, said he did so with regrets but saw no other choice given the reading of the Constitution. Yet he noted, "The conduct of the death-penalty defendants that produced their convictions and death sentences is the lowest form of human behavior. If the death penalty is appropriate for anyone, it is appropriate for them."[32]

Meanwhile, Wilford Berry was doing everything he could to speed up his own execution.

His campaign began soon after the Eighth Ohio District Court of Appeals, in a fifty-nine-page ruling on October 21, 1993, upheld his conviction and death sentence by a 2-to-1 vote. The court methodically rejected the thirty-two objections Berry's attorneys raised to the conviction and imposition of death. "By his own pre-trial admissions, Berry began planning the crimes about ten hours before the Mitroff murder," Judge Joseph Nahra wrote. "Berry purchased weapons and hid them in an alley near the bakery. Berry also admitted shooting Mitroff in the head with the .22 rifle after Mitroff pleaded for help." Judge Sara Harper dissented, writing that, in her opinion, Berry's mental health and troubled upbringing were enough to spare him.

On March 29, 1994, Berry wrote Montgomery, telling her he was guilty of the crime, felt no remorse and would kill again. The "death penalty should be used as an [sic] form of capital punishment," he wrote. In handwritten letters full of misspellings but in a strong script, he pleaded with the supreme court to let his execution to proceed. "I know I am guilty of the crime I committed," he wrote Moyer on April 21, 1995. He followed up with an angrier letter on June 1, addressing Moyer as "Fuck Face" and urging him to end the appeals process.[33]

On June 28, 1995, the state supreme court ruled 6 to 1 to uphold Berry's conviction and death sentence. Justice Andy Douglas, writing for the majority, acknowledged Berry's troubled childhood, the fact that Lozar had not received a death sentence, and even the work Berry did for the Red Cross in California. He also touched on Berry's wish to be executed but said it wasn't enough to challenge Berry's mental state. "A professed wish for the death penalty (as opposed to a lifelong term of imprisonment) does not, by itself, call the defendant's competence into question," Douglas wrote. Justice Craig Wright dissented, saying that in his opinion Berry belonged in an institution for the criminally insane.

A month later, Berry filed a one-page, handwritten motion again asking for his appeals to end. In October, he asked that the state public defender be dismissed as his attorney. He wanted only to be represented by Cindi Yost because she had agreed not to file any appeals paperwork on his behalf.[34]

Berry had always been a loner, shunning society to escape abuse, whether playground bullies as a child or prison rapists in Texas, and the same held true after his imprisonment for Mitroff's murder. He again refused medication, fearful it would slow him down. He spent his time listening to soft rock—Fleetwood Mac was a favorite—reading, writing poetry, and drawing. He acted up at times, setting off a sprinkler system to guarantee a move to solitary confinement where he felt less stress. He went out of his way to portray himself as psychologically healthy. Although he kept to himself, his desire to end his appeals was well known and won him enemies on death row. His mother and sister visited him at Mansfield in the fall of 1995 and pleaded with him for over three hours to drop his pursuit of his own death and allow his appeals to go forward. But he would not agree. He said he didn't want to talk about it. When the Ohio Parole Board, at the request of Governor George Voinovich, undertook consideration of clemency for Berry that same year, Berry refused to talk to the board's representative during a prison visit. The board voted 10 to 0 against clemency on September 15, 1995.[35]

In January of 1996, Montgomery made good on her promise to speed up death penalty cases in the state by forcing a sudden showdown with Robert Buell, the rapist-killer of eleven-year-old Krista Lea Harrison. Up to that point, the case of Buell, on death row since 1984 for the 1982 killing, was the epitome of a drawn-out death penalty appeals case. After the state supreme court upheld his sentence in 1986, he filed his habeas appeal just five days before his first scheduled execution date. Later, he withdrew that appeal to pursue an ineffective assistance of counsel argument in the state courts, then chose to delay his habeas appeal after that argument was rejected. In October 1995, the state supreme court set an execution date for January 25, 1996, but by now Buell had fired his public defenders, citing an irreparable rift, and brought on new attorneys who asked U.S. District Judge Paul Matia for a routine delay in the execution. Instead of granting it, Matia deemed that Buell had engaged in inexcusable behavior by his delays and denied the request. After the U.S. Court of Appeals for the Sixth Circuit overturned Matia and granted the stay, Montgomery seized the opportunity and appealed immediately to the U.S. Supreme Court, drawing criticism from Buell's attorneys, who said she was trying to short-circuit his federal appeals; after all, they argued, his habeas request had not yet begun. "I find her tactics cruel," Cleveland attorney Jeffrey Kelleher said on January 25. "She's trying to literally bring this guy to death's door."[36]

Protesters were marching in Lucasville and TV trucks were parked outside the Rhodes tower in downtown Columbus when the U.S. Supreme Court voted 5 to 4 just after midnight on January 25, 1996, to delay the execution. Justice Antonin Scalia, in a scathing three-page dissent, questioned whether Buell was trying to develop a legitimate claim or just engaging in delaying tactics. "If this is sufficient to outweigh the State's interest in proceeding with its judgment, executions could be stayed indefinitely," he wrote. Montgomery defended her aggressive handling of Buell's case, saying she was going to keep playing hardball. "We did what we wanted, and that's to send a message that we will squeeze and slow down the gaming of the system," she said later in the day on January 26. True to her word, she began calling county prosecutors asking if they needed help with their cases, particularly the requesting of execution dates from the state supreme court. Her zeal earned her bitter criticism. "Why is Betty Montgomery in such a hurry to kill people?" one defense attorney asked. The day after Easter of 1996, the *Akron Beacon Journal* published a political cartoon of Montgomery snapping at a cross-carrying Jesus to hurry it up. Whether the criticism was warranted is up for debate, given the long delays in appeals at that point. But with the zeitgeist on her side, Montgomery, undeterred, pushed on. Buell wasn't the end of things, she promised. Next up was Wilford Berry.[37]

In November 1996, the Ohio Supreme Court ordered Friedland, the judge who had presided over Berry's trial, to determine whether Berry was competent to waive his appeals and pursue his execution. Friedland held a three-day hearing during which three doctors who had previously evaluated Berry were called to testify. Forensic psychiatrists Phillip Resnick and Robert Alcorn and psychologist Sharon Pearson all agreed that Berry was suffering from a schizotypal (mixed) personality disorder with antisocial features. Pearson, based on three interviews with Berry in the summer of 1995, concluded that "Mr. Berry's cognitive and emotional deficits, in combination, establish that he is not competent to make the decision to end his appeals at this time." But Resnick and Alcorn, based on their own review of the case and interviews with Berry, came to the opposite conclusion. "Berry has the mental capacity to understand the choice between life and death and to make a knowing and intelligent decision not to pursue further remedies," Resnick wrote in an April 1996 report submitted to the Ohio Supreme Court. Significantly, he reported that Berry was also clear that he preferred freedom over death, but had no interest in lingering for years or decades in prison. "Do it or let me go," Berry told Resnick.[38] On July 22, 1997, Friedland ruled that Berry was competent to pursue an end to his appeals.

Just over a month later, around 5 PM on September 5, 1997, a handful of inmates rioted on death row unit number four—the cellblock where Berry lived—and freed all thirty-seven inmates on the unit. During the riot, some inmates began attacking others, including those they believed were prison informants. When they got to Berry's cell, the inmates, their identities hidden as they covered their heads with T-shirts and towels, told him to come out. As Berry emerged, the inmates attacked him, beating him and repeatedly smashing his face with a heavy padlock attached to a chain. The assault crushed his facial bones and jaw so badly he would need metal implants. The beating also pulverized his right hand, broke several ribs, and bruised his internal organs. Guards retaking the unit at first thought Berry was dead. "I feel like my face is falling off," he said after the attack. The attackers told Berry "he was being beaten because of not filing appeals on his death sentence."[39]

Three weeks later, Berry was still recovering in the Corrections Medical Center in Columbus when the state supreme court heard arguments in an appeal by the public defender's office of Friedland's decision finding Berry competent. Greg Meyers, head of the public defender's capital crimes division, argued that Berry had had a death wish from the moment he was arrested and was too sick to be executed. But Simon Karas, an assistant attorney general under Montgomery, said Berry acknowledged his guilt, had accepted his fate, and wanted to die. Further appeals, he said, were delaying the inevitable.[40] The court issued its unanimous decision on December 3, 1997, agreeing with the past experts and other reviews and rulings. While Berry was mentally disturbed, the court found, he understood his position and was capable of deciding whether to continue or drop his appeals. "Berry is not using his death sentence to fulfill a death wish produced by his disorder, as the Public Defender argues," the court said in an unsigned opinion. "Instead, he prefers freedom to death, but prefers a speedy execution to incarceration on death row during a prolonged legal struggle."

The opinion concluded by setting an execution date of March 3, 1998. The public defender's office immediately appealed to the federal courts. As that fight waged, the Ohio Parole Board met on February 13 to weigh a new request for clemency for Berry from his lawyers. In its report, issued that day, the board concluded that Berry carefully planned Mitroff's murder, that he was more guilty than Lozar because he hatched the scheme and bought the guns, and that he was not currently mentally ill. By an 8-to-0 vote, the board denied clemency. On February 19, Berry's sister and mother filed an appeal in U.S. District Court asking for a delay and a new hearing. "My son is mentally ill and needs a guardian," his mother, Jennie Franklin, said in an affidavit. On February 27, the two visited Berry at the prison medical center, but the trip did not go well. Berry swore at them, told them they'd get over his death in a week or two, and threatened to slit his mother's throat if she prevailed in stopping his execution.[41]

But the same day, U.S. District Court Judge Algenon Marbley agreed to a delay, ruling that the state supreme court hadn't properly determined if Berry was competent to volunteer to die. Montgomery immediately appealed, but Marbley's order was upheld by the federal appeals court in Cincinnati. On March 3, prison staff drove to the Florentine, an Italian restaurant on the west side of Columbus, and bought Berry a dish of lasagna for his last meal, the only time a death row inmate's last meal was purchased at a restaurant and not prepared in the kitchens at Lucasville. Berry, meeting with public defender Cindi Yost, ate the lasagna and a slice of strawberry cheesecake, then got into the van for Lucasville and his scheduled execution. But the U.S. Supreme Court upheld the delay and the van was called back.[42]

The odd legal battle—Berry, helped by the state, fighting his own family for the right to die—continued through the spring and summer. On May 22, a three-judge panel of the Sixth Circuit appeals court ruled that Marbley made a mistake in delaying the execution. Three months later the full Sixth Circuit upheld the decision. A week later the U.S. Supreme Court refused to hear a new appeal on behalf of Berry, and two weeks after that the Ohio Supreme Court set a new execution date of February 19. At the request of Taft, who had been in office little more than a month, the parole board revisited its decision on Berry and on February 2 again voted to deny clemency. The Sixth Circuit in Cincinnati denied another request to delay the execution, and on February 17 Berry met with William Klatt, Taft's top lawyer, to ask that his execution be allowed to proceed. On the afternoon of Friday, February 19, the U.S. Supreme Court turned down Berry's last appeal.

Outside the Lucasville prison walls, the parking lot was now overflowing with a combination of protesters and reporters. As the crowd grew, prison officials decided around 7:45 PM to erect extra snow fencing around the parking lot to help control the numbers. Inside, inmates ate dinner and then were locked in their cells to avoid any disturbances created by the scheduled execution. In the death house, Berry requested a sedative; he took one dosage of Valium at 6:30 PM and another at 8:02 PM. Eight minutes later he ate his cheesecake from earlier. At 8:20 PM he met with Yost for the last time. They prayed, and she read from the Bible to him. Weeping, Yost asked Berry to change his mind, but to no avail.

In the prison yard, Rehabilitation and Correction staff escorted Berry's sister and mother to the death house, unwittingly walking them past the van from D. W. Davis Funeral Home parked just outside. Ninety miles north, Taft retired to the governor's residence in the east side Columbus suburb of Bexley to await the outcome with Klatt and Brian Hicks, Taft's chief of staff. They sat in the dark in the residence's dining room because curtains had not yet been installed and protesters were just outside holding a candlelight vigil. Montgomery and her staff waited in offices on the seventeenth floor of the Rhodes Tower in downtown Columbus. Both Taft and Montgomery kept open phone lines to the prison. In Garfield Heights in suburban Cleveland, Mitroff's sister, Eleanor, her husband, and a daughter waited by the phone.[43]

A few minutes before 9 PM on the evening of February 19, 1999, guards opened the door to Berry's cell. Lucasville warden Stephen Huffman approached with the death warrant in hand. With Rod Francis standing outside the cell, Huffman read the warrant to Berry. The Supreme Court having upheld Berry's conviction and sentence, Huffman was commanded "to carry into execution the sentence of death."

Escorted by six guards, Berry walked into the death chamber at 8:59 PM. Though he made no resistance, under prison regulations he was still strapped to the gurney. Berry had always disliked the idea of dying by injection, fearful it would reproduce the awful feelings of suffocation he had suffered from his lung problems. Instead, he preferred electrocution because he felt it would create the same brain-numbing feelings he had experienced undergoing several EKGs. Prison officials tried to convince him that injection would be like going to sleep, with no effect on his lungs. Eventually, a year earlier, with no fanfare, he had quietly changed his mind and agreed to submit to the needle and the $88.42 in fatal chemicals used in lethal injections: sodium pentothal to put him to sleep; pancuronium bromide, a paralyzing agent; and potassium chloride, which stops the heart and causes death. Even so, the night before, he asked again about the effect the execution would have on his breathing.[44]

A delay now ensued as members of the execution team had trouble inserting the IV into Berry's right arm. Twenty minutes passed. Finally, the problem resolved and the tubing in place, Yost and Berry's mother and sister were escorted into the viewing chamber at 9:24 PM. They were joined on the other side of a partition by William Florio, the private investigator hired by the Mitroff family, Kentucky police officers Stan Voorhees and Matthew Rolfsen, and reporters for the *Cleveland Plain Dealer,* the *Cincinnati Enquirer,* and the Associated Press.

At 9:26 PM, Huffman gave a signal to begin the flow of chemicals, placed his hand on Berry's chest, and patted it softly. Berry lay on the gurney reciting the Lord's Prayer. After a minute had passed, Berry took three heavy breaths, then sighed. He was pronounced dead at 9:31 PM. Voorhees called it the end of a ten-year funeral. At a postexecution briefing in Lucasville, prison system director Reggie Wilkinson told execution team members the state was proud of what they had done to make the process go well. In Cleveland, Richard Bowler, Mitroff's brother-in-law, said the family felt tragic relief that it was over. In Columbus, Montgomery had been prepared to battle any last-minute appeals. Now she said a few words to her staff before dismissing them, then issued a short statement. The justice system, she said, had implemented its solemn responsibility. Her thoughts and prayers were with both Berry and his victims. "There are no winners here tonight," she said.[45]

The following Wednesday, about eighty people attended a funeral for Berry's cremated remains at Broad Street Presbyterian Church on the outskirts of downtown Columbus. Mourners sang songs and said prayers during the hour-long service. Yost read the psalm she had helped Berry write the day before his execution. "Praise be to the All Mighty for his forgiveness of me as a sinner," it read. "He has power to comfort and sooth [sic] my soul that cries in pain." Berry's remains sat on a small wooden pedestal at the front of the church. To the right of the pedestal was a wooden table holding five photographs from the time Berry was a child through adulthood, and four pots of flowers and plants. Berry's sister and mother, wary of publicity, did not attend. Instead, they collected Berry's remains and held a private family memorial service, scattering his ashes in the open air. They hoped somehow the gesture would give Berry the freedom he had sought most of his life. "I figured that was probably what he wanted all along," his sister would recall. "He just didn't know how to find it."[46]

FOUR

The Role of Race

"Why should these guys be spared?"

—*Sandra Craig, on her frustration at the plea deals offered the killers of her son, Jeffrey, stabbed to death over an ounce of cocaine*

THE ORNATE courtroom of the Ohio Supreme Court, on the first floor of a renovated Art Deco building of gleaming limestone, is literally something out of a movie: in 2000, when the building was in the midst of its $86 million reconstruction, Steven Soderbergh filmed portions of his drug war epic, *Traffic,* in the chamber, even building a makeshift bench for Michael Douglas and his fellow movie judges. The real courtroom is even more cinematic: justices sit at a high wooden bench overlooking a long, carpeted room of polished wood panels, tall windows, long white curtains, and row after row of burgundy-upholstered chairs. Murals depicting scenes from early Ohio history encircle the upper walls. Overhead, ornate paintings of half-naked figures—classical renditions of American Indians and Grecian-style luminaries—cover the ceiling and provide a visual respite during days of less-than-gripping legal testimony.

In this chamber, on March 19, 2005, assistant state public defender Robert K. Lowe stood at a podium before the court's seven justices and explained why his client, Gregory McKnight, should not have been sentenced to death. By itself, the scene was not unusual; the court regularly hears death penalty appeals as part of its docket. But this was not your ordinary capital punishment case. McKnight had been convicted three years earlier in a trial that drew national headlines after a judge in the rural county where McKnight shot and killed a Kenyon College student dismissed the capital elements of the case, ruling that McKnight's due-process rights could be violated given the cost of a death penalty trial. The facts of the case were also unusual. McKnight, a black man, was accused of kidnapping white college student Emily Murray, taking her 125 miles away to his trailer after they finished a shift at a campus pizza restaurant, shooting her in the head, and rolling her body in a rug. The investigation into Murray's disappearance led to yet another twist in the case: the unexpected discovery of a second body, eventually identified as Gregory Julious, an acquaintance of McKnight who was also black.

The supreme court hearing was also unusual because the only attorney present was Lowe. The Attorney General's office had missed a deadline to file its argument in the appeal and so was banned from participating.

Midway through Lowe's presentation, Justice Paul Pfeifer interrupted to ask additional questions, while making it clear he wasn't happy about the state's blunder. Twenty-four years had passed since Pfeifer led the charge to enact a new death penalty law, and over the years he had become increasingly skeptical of the capital punishment system he had helped to create. In particular, he had come to believe that prosecutors often attached qualifications to aggravated murder charges to raise the penalty to death in ways that weren't always justified. In McKnight's case, the indictment charging him with kidnapping included language that he "did not release the said Emily S. Murray in a safe place unharmed." On this day, Pfeifer wanted to know more about the kidnapping charge against McKnight and whether other factors may have played a role in the decision to bring that charge.

"So the evidence of kidnapping in the Murray case is that she left work a few minutes after the defendant," Pfeifer asked Lowe.

"Correct," Lowe responded.

"And she and her car next surface in Vinton County."

"Correct," Lowe said.

"And with respect to Julious the evidence was he and the defendant were last seen together."

But McKnight, Lowe pointed out in response, had not been charged with kidnapping Julious.

"I understand that," Pfeifer responded sharply. "My question is why?"

"That would be a question for the state," Lowe responded.

Letting that comment pass, Pfeifer then zeroed in on what he saw as the crux of the case before him: one man, two victims, but only one of the deaths carried a capital charge.

"What was the race of the defendant?" Pfeifer demanded.

"The race of the defendant?" Lowe said. "Black."

"What was the race of Murray?"

"White."

"What was the race of Julious?"

"Black."

Satisfied that he'd made his point, Pfeifer moved on, soliciting from Lowe the information that the state had not offered evidence to justify the kidnapping charge. Lowe quickly added that the evidence that was presented found that two separate people, a neighbor of McKnight and a park ranger, saw Murray driving in the area in the past and on one occasion riding with McKnight and McKnight's wife. "She was familiar with the area," Lowe said.

Pfeifer then inquired whether that would be evidence against kidnapping, and Lowe responded in the affirmative.

"So in both cases there's really no evidence offered of kidnapping," Pfeifer said. "In both cases the victims are last seen in a county other than Vinton County and they surface deceased on the defendant's property in Vinton County?"

"Correct," Lowe said.[1]

Eight months later, by a 6-to-1 vote—with Pfeifer dissenting—the court upheld McKnight's conviction and death sentence.

Race has long played a role in the death penalty system, dating back to the earliest years of the country, when slave states enacted laws permitting capital punishment for a wide range of crimes committed by blacks only. During the colonial period, black slaves who killed whites in Georgia, even if in self-defense or in defense of another, were automatically executed.

An 1856 treatise summarizing slave laws in the southern states counted more than sixty capital crimes for slaves in Virginia, compared to only one, murder, for whites. Even in death, blacks were treated more harshly: executed slaves often had their heads displayed on poles.[2] In the 1940s, researchers found a stronger likelihood in selected North Carolina counties for killers of whites to be sentenced to death than killers of blacks, while a similar study of death sentence commutations in nine southern states in the 1920s and 1930s found whites on death row were more likely to have their sentences commuted than blacks.[3]

Historically, blacks have been executed at far higher rates than whites. Of all recorded executions between 1608 and 1972, for example, 7,084 blacks were put to death in the United States and the American colonies, or 49 percent of the total of 14,634 executions, according to the Espy file, a list compiled by researchers M. Watt Espy and John Ortiz Smylka and first made available through the Inter-University Consortium for Political and Social Research. (This compilation is generally considered an estimate and not a completely accurate totaling.) A 1965 study by the Kentucky Legislative Research Commission found that the majority of people put to death in that state were black. And according to data compiled by the Death Penalty Information Center, a Washington, D.C.–based organization opposed to capital punishment, by the end of 2007, 374 blacks had been executed since 1972, or 34 percent of all executions, a rate almost three times higher than the proportion of blacks in the U.S. population.[4]

In Ohio, similar racial disparities have been noted for decades. In 1961, the state's Legislative Service Commission, a bipartisan arm of the General Assembly, found that of sixty people sentenced to death between 1950 and 1959, twenty-three, or 37.3 percent, were black ("Negroes" in the language of the commission's study), far above the then-6.5 percent proportion of blacks in the population but just below the number of blacks represented in the prison population overall. This latter fact, the study concluded, proved a lack of racial discrimination in the sentencing of blacks to death. But the commission also noted that nearly twice as many whites had their death sentences commuted as blacks. "From these figures it appears that a Negro murderer, once sentenced to death, is much less likely than a white murderer to be saved by commutation," the study said.[5]

Of the estimated 437 people put to death in Ohio between statehood in 1803 and 1963, when Donald Reinbolt went to the electric chair in the last execution for thirty-six years, 29 percent of those executed were black in a state where African Americans typically made up less than 10 percent of the population. From the time the state's current law took effect in 1981 through early 2008, Ohio sent 296 offenders to death row. Of those, 143, or 48 percent, were black. Over the years, 109 of those inmates have been removed from death row, either because courts overturned their sentences, they died in prison, or they were executed. Of the 187 inmates still on death row in early 2008, just over half were black. Of the 26 inmates executed since 1999, 9 were black.[6]

As we have previously seen, death penalty opponents in Ohio argued that the law would be used disproportionately against minorities and the poor. Although the statistics bear this out to a degree, there is a more deeply ingrained bias in the capital punishment system when it comes to race, and that relates not to the defendant's skin color but that of the victim. In fact, some argue that the death penalty system as enacted in Ohio and across the country discriminates not against minority killers but against their black victims. In other words, since blacks tend to be killed most often by other blacks, the system is actually more lenient on African American killers than on white offenders once the race of the victim is considered.

Proponents of capital punishment have seized on this issue as an example of reverse discrimination. Walter Berns, in his classic book in favor of the death penalty, *For Capital Punishment,* says that most black people, like most white people, are not criminals. "What distinguishes them," he writes, "is that the law-abiding black population supplies a disproportionate number of the victims of crime; and it would be a cruel victory indeed if, having struggled so long and so hard, and, finally, so successfully against all the forms of injustice imposed on them by the white population, they were now to be exposed to what may be—in part, at least—preventable black crime because of the reluctance of white liberals to allow black criminals to be punished as they deserve to be punished."[7]

The issue of race and the death penalty, in the courts for decades, came to a head in three major court rulings over the past half century. In 1965, lawyers arguing on behalf of William Maxwell, a black man from Arkansas convicted and sentenced to death in 1962 for raping a white woman, engaged criminologist Marvin Wolfgang to assemble data on rape convictions in a representative sample of nineteen Arkansas counties during the years 1945 through 1965. Wolfgang's survey was conducted in the summer of 1965 as part of a study of the application of the death penalty for rape in eleven southern states. The data found that a black man convicted of raping a white woman had about a 50 percent chance of receiving a death sentence, regardless of the facts and circumstances surrounding the crime, whereas a man who was convicted of raping a woman of his own race stood only a 14 percent chance of receiving the death sentence. In addition, a U.S. Bureau of Prisons study submitted on Maxwell's behalf concluded that 90 percent of the 455 men executed for rape in the United States between 1930 and 1972 were black. (Not until 1977, in *Coker v. Georgia,* did the U.S. Supreme Court permanently ban the death penalty in cases of the rape of an adult woman.) These facts failed to persuade courts that discrimination had occurred in Maxwell's situation. Judge Harry Blackmun, then a judge on the Eighth U.S. Circuit Court, acknowledged in the appeals court decision upholding Maxwell's sentence that in states allowing the death penalty for rape, the punishment may have been discriminatorily applied over the years. "We do say that nothing has been presented in Maxwell's case which convinces us, or causes us seriously to wonder, that, with the imposition of the death penalty, he was the victim of discrimination based on race," Blackmun wrote.[8]

In 1970, the U.S. Supreme Court returned Maxwell's case to the lower courts on procedural grounds not involving the race argument. But two years later, in *Furman,* disparities based on race were cited as part of the decision overturning capital punishment. "The Negro convicted of rape," Justice Douglas wrote in his concurring opinion, "is far more likely to get the death penalty than a term sentence, whereas whites and Latins are far more likely to get a term sentence than the death penalty."

In 1987, the high court again considered the role of race in the death penalty in a landmark decision that largely settled the issue for good, at least from the perspective of the courts. The case involved the conviction and death sentence in Georgia of Warren McClesky, a black man tried for killing a white police officer investigating the robbery of a furniture store on October 12, 1978. (A follow-up decision in 1991 on a different appeal by McClesky led to the previously discussed restrictions on federal habeas appeals.) As with the case of William Maxwell twenty years earlier, attorneys argued a pattern of discrimination in sentencing based on the race of the victim. This time, they believed, the evidence was overwhelming. At the core of their argument was a pair of highly detailed studies, led by Iowa State researcher David Baldus, of more than two thousand Georgia murders in the 1970s. The study examined cases by the race of the offender and victim and also factored in 230 variables, such as aggravating or mitigating circumstances. It concluded that defendants charged with killing white persons were 4.3 times more likely to receive the death penalty than those accused of killing blacks. Combining the race of the defendant and the race of the victim, Baldus also found that in cases involving black defendants and white victims, death sentences were handed out in 22 percent of the cases, compared to 8 percent of cases involving white defendants and white victims, 3 percent of cases involving white defendants and black victims, and 1 percent of cases involving black defendants and black victims. Baldus also noted that prosecutors were far more likely to seek death sentences in cases in which blacks killed whites.

Proponents of the death penalty countered that the statistics were misleading because many of the murders involved circumstances, such as domestic violence or fights between acquaintances, that are the least likely to warrant a death penalty to begin with and that often involve killers and victims of the same race. Mary Beth Westmoreland, a Georgia assistant attorney general, argued before the court in October 1986 that blacks were more often killed in family disputes, lovers' quarrels, and barroom fights. By contrast, whites were more often killed in robberies and other situations more likely to provoke "the moral outrage of the community" and of the jury.[9]

Taking Baldus's data under consideration, the U.S. Supreme Court, by a 5-to-4 vote, upheld McClesky's conviction and sentence on April 22, 1987, determining that broad statistical conclusions could not be used to challenge the appropriateness of an individual death sentence. Writing for the majority, Justice Powell said that McClesky could not argue that the death sentence he received was disproportionate to the sentences in other murder cases. "The likelihood of racial prejudice allegedly shown by the study does not constitute the constitutional measure of an unacceptable risk of racial prejudice," he wrote. "The inherent lack of predictability of jury decisions does not justify their condemnation." Powell also said that McClesky's claim, taken to its logical conclusion, would throw into serious question the principles that underlie the entire criminal justice system. "His claim easily could be extended to apply to other types of penalties and to claims based on unexplained discrepancies correlating to membership in other minority groups and even to gender," he wrote. McClesky, forty-four, died in Georgia's electric chair in September 1991.

Although the Supreme Court decision largely ended the debate in the courts, subsequent studies of the effect of race have reached similar conclusions to those of the Baldus analysis. In 1990, the U.S. General Accounting Office reviewed twenty-eight studies done to date that looked at capital punishment and the effects of race. The GAO analysis concluded that in 82 percent of the studies, the race of the victim was found to influence the likelihood of being charged with capital murder or receiving a death sentence. In 2000, the U.S. Justice Department released the results of a study requested by President Clinton that found U.S. attorneys were almost twice as likely to recommend seeking the death penalty for a black defendant when the victim was nonblack as when the victim was black. In January 2003, a study commissioned by the State of Maryland found that race played a major role in how the death penalty was applied. The author of the study, Ray Paternoster, a University of Maryland criminologist and longtime student of the death penalty, concluded that killers whose victims were white fared the worst. Significantly, the study of 1,311 homicide prosecutions found that prosecutors were more likely to file for a death sentence and refuse to drop those charges when the victim was white.[10]

Ohio analyses have reached the same conclusion. In 1980, Rosina Maynard, an independent researcher and death penalty opponent, studied the 105 individuals sent to Ohio's death row under the 1974 statute. Of those, 66 were black, or almost two-thirds. She also found that while blacks were overwhelmingly sentenced to death for killing a white person, not a single white person was sent to Ohio's death row for killing a black victim between 1974 and 1978, when the law was declared unconstitutional.[11]

In 1977, death penalty researchers Glenn Pierce and William Bowers began collecting and analyzing death penalty data from Florida, Georgia, Ohio, and Texas, states whose prosecutions involved 70 percent of the nation's capital cases in the first five years after *Furman*. The results, published in 1980, once again found that killers of whites were far more likely than killers of blacks to be sentenced to death. In 173 cases where a black person killed a white person in Ohio, for example, 44 were sentenced to death, or 25 percent of all cases. By contrast, in 1,170 cases in which blacks killed other blacks, death sentences were handed out just 2 percent of the time. In 2004, Bowling Green State University criminologists analyzed 5,976 Ohio homicides between 1981 and 1997 and determined that murders involving white victims and female victims were significantly more likely to result in death sentences than homicides involving, respectively, black victims or male victims. The Bowling Green study went beyond most analyses to conclude that the combination of being white and female surpassed race alone as a factor in who is sentenced to die.[12]

David Doughten, a veteran Cleveland defense lawyer who has handled dozens of capital cases, says there has always been a race element to the death penalty in Ohio. "I'm not saying judges or prosecutors or anybody is overtly racist—I don't think they are—but you see it happen," he explains. "You see it in deals. You see it in negotiations. You see it in how things are reviewed."[13]

Although Pfeifer was not highlighting new allegations about the fairness of the death penalty when it comes to race, the *McKnight* case underscored the fact that much was unknown about the state's twenty-year-old death penalty law. Opponents had argued for years that prosecutors in smaller and less-wealthy counties were selective about death penalty indictments because of the cost of a capital trial. But *McKnight* brought the issue to the wider public's notice for the first time in Ohio after a judge initially dropped the case's capital charges, determining that the cost of the trial could hurt the county financially. Moreover, the concerns about race raised by Pfeifer, architect of the death penalty law turned skeptical enforcer, brought up new questions about the law's disparities.

As a result, the Associated Press decided in 2002 to undertake a study of the state's death penalty system that no one else, particularly the state, seemed willing to do. As the lead researcher and reporter, I turned first to the only available baseline of statewide data (beyond totals of death sentences and executions): the annual reporting by counties to the state supreme court of capital indictments. Assisted by colleague Liz Sidoti, I gathered the data from 1981 through 2002, then merged the information with a database of prison records. Almost immediately, we were presented with a series of challenges that underscored the difficulty of studying the death penalty in Ohio or any other state. To begin with, many of the indictments reported to the supreme court were inaccurate. Over the years, well-meaning county clerks, with no guidance from the state, had occasionally submitted aggravated murder indictments with a specification for carrying a weapon, in the mistaken belief that that charge was equivalent to a death penalty specification such as kidnapping or robbery. In addition, clerks submitted dozens of cases involving juveniles, who under Ohio law cannot be sentenced to death. Cuyahoga County, for example, submitted indictments for 972 individuals during the two decades I studied. But 260 of those were non-death cases, including 44 juvenile indictments. In Muskingum County in eastern Ohio, clerks regularly submitted all murder cases to the state supreme court, assuming the inaccurate indictments would be weeded out. Unfortunately, there was no provision in law to analyze the incoming indictments in any way, other than to file them with the court. As a result, the state's highest court slowly accrued two decades of partially inaccurate data about the state's capital punishment system. (The problem continues today: as recently as 2004, Stark County submitted indictment data for two juveniles, who by law cannot be executed.) In the end, I removed 455 murders from the database that never carried a death sentence, as well as an additional 152 indictments against juveniles. I also added 18 capital cases that had slipped through the cracks and were not reported to the court. The final tally: 1,936 indictments over twenty-two years.

Even when cleaned up, however, the data were sorely lacking in two vital areas: the race of the victim and the race of the defendant. Even though prison records provided the defendant's race in many cases, it was missing in many other instances, specifically when an offender was initially charged with a capital crime only to have the charge reduced or even dismissed— a frequent occurrence in Cuyahoga County, for example. And other than race-of-victim data collected by the state public defender's office for those individuals on death row, victim information was nonexistent for the vast majority of those charged with death penalty crimes. Gathering both those categories of data involved months of correspondence and phone calls to county prosecutors, coroners, health departments, and prison officials. It was October 6, 2004, two years after the project began, when I reached a

Cleveland homicide detective who confirmed the race of the final victim in the database, a black man from Cleveland killed during a 1988 robbery.

The results, published in May 2005, were consistent with decades of similar research around the country: under Ohio's 1981 capital punishment law, offenders facing a death penalty charge for killing a white person were twice as likely to go to death row than if they had killed a black victim. In 1,081 cases in which the victim or victims were white, 193 offenders, or 17.9 percent, were sentenced to death. In 800 cases where the victim or victims were black, 68 offenders, or 8.5 percent, were sentenced to death. Moreover, in 693 cases where the victim or victims were white and the offender was white, 127 offenders, or 18.3 percent, were sentenced to death. By contrast, in 752 cases where the victim or victims were black and the offender was black, 63 offenders, or 8.4 percent, were sentenced to death.

On the surface, the results were clear: color matters in capital punishment cases, and most significantly, the color of the person killed. These are incontrovertible facts, available to anyone willing to examine the data. But as the court rulings in *Maxwell, Furman,* and *McClesky* have shown, the reasons for this disparity are far less clear-cut. Viewed through those lenses, the question is not so much "Does race play a role?" as, more significantly, "What is the role of race compared to numerous other factors in the criminal justice system?"

There is no doubt, based on numerous studies over the years, including the Associated Press review in Ohio, that the likelihood of receiving the death penalty increases for offenders whose victims are white. It is a pattern acknowledged even by some on the pro–death penalty side. As John Murphy, executive director of the Ohio Prosecuting Attorneys Association, puts it, "There does seem to be a disparity there."[14] But the reasons for this disparity are not as obvious as just the role of skin color. Most murders in the United States are intraracial, meaning people of the same color killing other members of the same race. Moreover, for a variety of historical and sociological reasons, crime rates are higher among minorities, meaning—as Berns reflected—that blacks are disproportionately represented both among murder victims and among those charged with committing murder. In 2005, for example, 48.6 percent of all people arrested for murder and nonnegligent manslaughter in the United States were black, close to four times the number of blacks as a percentage of the population.[15] As the State of Georgia argued in the *McClesky* case more than twenty years ago, because blacks are more likely to die at the hands of blacks, likely people they know, the aggravating circumstances surrounding a particular crime may not be as great as those involving a black or white person killing a white stranger. As a result, differences in the severity of crimes are one possible explanation for the different treatment of capital cases for black and white victims.

This is not an entirely clear-cut explanation, however. On the one hand, it is possible to apply such an argument to the type of study that I undertook for the Associated Press, which was a relatively simple analysis—though unprecedented, at least in Ohio—achieved by counting up the number of black and white defendants and black and white victims. On the other hand, Baldus and other academic researchers used the statistical technique known as multiple regression to account for all other factors that might influence a sentence, including the severity of the crime. This approach isolates the role that race plays and so is not susceptible to the types of argument the State of Georgia made to the Supreme Court. Hence, one of the most disturbing patterns in the Baldus study, which formed the basis of *McClesky*, was the conclusion that prosecutors were more willing to add aggravating circumstances to murders involving white victims than blacks.

Just as the Supreme Court in *McClesky* said that a pattern of general discrimination was not enough to prove racial bias in a particular case, so too have proponents of the death penalty argued that allegations of societal racism obscure the guilt of individual offenders. The late Ernest van den Haag, a law professor and researcher, proposed that to regard the death penalty as unjust because it is unequally distributed confuses inequality with injustice.

> The guilt of any one murderer (and the justice of imposing the death penalty on him) is not diminished if other, equally or more guilty, murderers are not convicted or executed, whether because of racial discrimination, accident, or sheer capriciousness. Guilt is personal. That others were spared punishment is no reason to spare you the punishment your crime deserves. Others got away with murder; they were not caught, convicted, or executed, for whatever reason. If these were grounds for not punishing those caught and convicted, we could never punish.

Or, as Marquette University political science professor John McAdams puts it, "It is not the case that, because some taxpayers find a way to cheat the Internal Revenue Service (IRS) and get away with it, everybody has the right to cheat. And it's certainly not required that the IRS be abolished."[16] Rather than being too harsh on black offenders, Van den Haag and others argue, the death penalty system, if anything, is too soft on them, to judge by the number of black killers of black victims who don't receive the death penalty.

Take the case of Jeffrey Craig and Keith Johnson, two young black men murdered in Columbus in the summer of 1995 after a drug deal soured. One of the killers, Gregory Stamper, who was white, was indicted on death penalty charges in November 1995. After refusing to cooperate for more than a year, on November 19, 1996, Stamper gave a jailhouse statement to prosecutors and agreed to testify against a codefendant, James White, who was black, in exchange for a guilty plea to avoid the death penalty. Police arrested White later that day. The next day, Stamper pleaded guilty to the deaths of Craig and Johnson and was sentenced to twenty years to life. White's trial in September 1997 was in only its second day when a neighbor testified that he could identify White as being outside the house where the murders occurred. White also knew that Stamper was scheduled to testify against him. Faced with these facts, White decided to plead guilty and, as with Stamper, prosecutors dropped the death penalty charges in exchange. White, sobbing quietly, was sentenced to twenty years to life, along with an additional ten to twenty-five years for robbing the two men. Relatives of the slain men were convinced that the combination of Craig and Johnson's race and their involvement in drugs lessened their worth in the eyes of prosecutors. "It was just another black person dead," said Sandra Craig of her only son. "They could just do this and move on to the next thing."[17]

Doug Stead, a veteran Franklin County assistant prosecutor, strongly disputed this. Decision making was driven not by race but by the goal, given the facts of the case, to put two killers behind bars for as long as possible. "If I believe the person committed this crime, my first responsibility is to take him off the streets," he said. "And if I have any doubt at all about my ability to do that, that might encourage me to take a plea." Indeed, his position was borne out in a similar case less than two years later, in which two black men, both small-time drug dealers, were shot by Kareem Jackson in a robbery that netted him a small bag of marijuana and forty-five dollars. "They know my name, I have to kill them," Jackson said before he put a pillow over each of his victims' heads and executed them. Like Stamper and White, Jackson was offered a plea deal before the trial began—in his case, life without parole—but unlike them decided to reject it. Prosecutors offered three other plea bargains to codefendants, including to a man also charged with the death penalty in the case—Jackson's childhood buddy, Derrick Boone—who testified against his friend at trial. A Franklin County jury quickly recommended a death sentence for Jackson on January 28, 1998. After the verdict, Stead said, "This is the kind of man for which we have a death penalty." A month later, Judge Michael H. Watson sentenced Jackson to death, and the mother of one of the victims, Leslie Walker, said the decision restored her faith in the criminal justice system.[18] Based on lawmakers' original intentions when crafting a death penalty law, Stead's posttrial statement is true, though one could argue it also applies to Gregory Stamper and James White. And while Jackson's death sentence runs counter to allegations of bias against killers of blacks, the fact remains that had he accepted the plea deal offered him, the outcome would have buttressed, not challenged, those allegations.

In early 2000, twenty-year-old Gregory Julious was living with his girlfriend, Dana Bostic, at her home in Chillicothe, a small city about an hour south of Columbus. Julious, from Cincinnati, had initially moved in with Bostic because he needed a place to stay; over time their relationship turned romantic. He worked briefly at a Rally's restaurant and cleaned houses but had trouble holding down jobs and spent most of the time watching Bostic's two young children. He got to know Gregory McKnight after McKnight, who was married, started an affair with Lisa Perkins, a friend of Bostic, often visiting Perkins at Bostic's home. McKnight, twenty-four, had grown up in New York City but moved to Columbus as a teenager. He also had a past: before he was twenty-one he'd served time in a juvenile detention facility for gunning down a man in 1992 when he was just fifteen years old. He married his wife, Kathy, in

May 1998 and supported her and their young son and daughter with a variety of jobs, from selling cars to being a delivery person.[19]

Julious, McKnight, and the two women hung out together that spring of 2000, including a trip to Columbus in April to hear a reggae band. Late in the afternoon of May 12, Bostic got home from work and found McKnight, Julious, and her daughter in the kitchen. She left with her daughter to pick up her son; when she got back an hour later, McKnight and Julious were gone, though the door was unlocked and candles they had lit were still burning. Later, when Julious didn't come home, she called his pager. McKnight returned the call and put Julious on the line, who explained that he was in Columbus at the home of one of McKnight's friends and they were going to a party at Ohio State University. Bostic found the conversation unusual because Julious wouldn't let her ask him anything and abruptly ended the call. She never saw him again. When she encountered McKnight a couple of days later, he said he had taken Julious to Cincinnati to see some friends.[20]

The following month McKnight and his wife, Kathy, bought a trailer in rural Vinton County, an Appalachian county among the state's poorest. They moved their belongings in but went to live with Kathy's ill mother in the tiny town of Gambier, home to Kenyon College, a leafy campus of sixteen hundred students atop a wooded hill overlooking miles of farm fields about an hour northeast of Columbus. Two or three months later, McKnight got a job working at the Pirate's Cove restaurant, a longtime student hangout. He was friendly with his co-workers, who often gave him a ride home to his mother-in-law's house on Met-o-Wood Lane.[21] One of those co-workers was a young woman named Emily Murray.

Life was looking up that fall for Murray, a philosophy major from Cold Springs, New York, and, like Gregory Julious, just twenty years old; their birthdays were only a week apart. She had attended Kenyon for two years, then taken time off to recover from a bout of severe depression that included a suicide attempt, an overdose of Tylenol, the previous May. After a trip to Japan with an older stepsister, she returned to Kenyon in the fall rejuvenated. She lived on campus while getting ready to start classes again in the winter semester. Murray was outgoing and friendly, with a spiritual bent. She attended a conference on religious vocations in the middle of the fall and talked with excitement about her lifelong dream of becoming an Episcopal priest. She stayed in close contact with her friends and her family, e-mailing her father or talking with her parents on the phone almost daily.[22]

Like others, Murray got along with McKnight. At times she had given both McKnight and his wife rides in her green Subaru, including down to Vinton County. McKnight was friendly to Murray, which was no surprise given that he made a habit of propositioning women whenever he could, whether the affair with Perkins in the spring—after Julious disappeared, he claimed he was going to leave his wife for Perkins—or the woman he hit on at a restaurant in nearby Mount Vernon, where he worked before he started at the Pirate's Cove.[23]

On Thursday, November 2, 2000, Murray went shopping at the Mount Vernon Wal-Mart with friends to prepare for a party to celebrate her last day at work. She bought a blender for a daiquiri party and an alarm clock to help her get up on the weekend; she set it for 10 AM Sunday morning. That night, shortly before 10 PM, she started her shift at the Pirate's Cove, just a few hundred feet from her Watson Hall dormitory. Several friends came by to help celebrate her last night on the job, though they left before she finished her shift. McKnight was working that night too. He clocked out at 2:59 AM on Friday, November 3; Murray clocked out eight minutes later. They weren't seen leaving together. Shortly afterwards, Murray's roommate heard the door open and someone come into the room. She didn't get up, assuming it was Emily.[24]

Murray's friends realized something was wrong the next day when she didn't show up for the daiquiri party and they couldn't find her car. She also hadn't left a note on the dry-erase board she would often fill up with details of her whereabouts. After looking for her in vain, her friends called campus security and her parents. A friend searching the dorm room found her wallet, including her driver's license, credit cards, and bank cards. All her toiletries, including toothbrush, hairbrush, and makeup, were also still there. Asked about Murray on Sunday night, a curt McKnight said he had no idea where she was. But he told the Pirate's Cove bartender that he thought Murray was "probably dead." He continued working at the restaurant and continued to proposition women. "We could have a quickie," he said to a co-worker one night in the weeks after Murray disappeared, coming up behind her and making the proposal while her boyfriend, also a Pirate's Cove worker, was out of earshot.[25]

A month later, on December 9, two Vinton County sheriff's deputies serving a warrant to McKnight for an unrelated robbery indictment saw a green Subaru behind his trailer. A computer check linked the car to Murray, listed as a missing endangered person. After requesting a search warrant, police, including the FBI, entered the trailer and found bloodstains on the carpet near the front door. A trail of blood down the hallway led them to Murray's clothed body rolled up in a carpet. A search of the surrounding property the following day turned up a bone, which led to further digging and the discovery of the remains of Gregory Julious.[26]

McKnight was arrested and in March 2001 indicted for Murray's death on an aggravated murder charge with four death penalty specifications: murder to escape detection, kidnapping, aggravated robbery—alleging the theft of the Subaru—and murder as a "course of conduct" in which two or more people were killed. He was also indicted on a charge of simple murder for the death of Julious since prosecutors felt they couldn't prove premeditation or add an aggravating factor such as kidnapping or robbery.[27] More than a year passed as McKnight's attorneys prepared for the trial, including a February 2002 motion to dismiss the death penalty charges on constitutional grounds.

Six months later, as McKnight's autumn trial date approached, Judge Jeffrey Simmons of Vinton County Common Pleas Court threw out the capital elements of the case. The "potential impact of financial considerations could compromise the Defendant's due process rights in a capital murder trial," Simmons wrote on August 8. "The court finds that this risk is unacceptable in this case." The decision caused an uproar that attracted the attention of the national media. The *New York Times* reported that it was the first time a U.S. judge had dismissed death penalty charges because he feared the county couldn't afford a proper defense. CNN and *Time* magazine sent reporters to cover the trial. Vinton County Prosecutor Timothy Gleeson flew to New York to appear on the *Today* show with Murray's parents. The state objected strongly to the ruling, saying Simmons's decision usurped Ohio's authority to prosecute a death penalty case. With the death penalty off the table, McKnight's attorneys unsuccessfully pressed their client to consider pleading guilty to aggravated murder. On August 23, the point became moot when Simmons reversed himself, saying he had been responding to possible violations of McKnight's due process rights instead of any proof of actual violation. After a three-week trial, McKnight was convicted of Murray's death on October 10. The jury recommended the death penalty four days later. Despite pleas from Murray's family to spare them the long-term pain of the death penalty process, including a sworn statement by her sister, Kathleen Murray, that further court proceedings might tear the family apart, on October 25, 2002, Simmons sentenced McKnight to die.[28]

Although the case was over, a troubling set of facts remained, especially weighed against the long history of racial inequities in Ohio's death penalty system. An upper-class, twenty-year-old white woman attending a private liberal arts college is killed by a working-class black man. The murder of a second victim, a twenty-year-old black man, does not warrant a death penalty charge despite the similar circumstances. Like Murray, Julious was on friendly terms with McKnight. Like Murray, he had given no sign that he expected to be gone long the night he vanished; he left all his belongings at Bostic's house, including his clothes and identification card. Like Murray's body, Julious's body then turned up at McKnight's trailer in Vinton County. Pfeifer wasn't the only one who noticed the similarities. Emily's parents, Tom and Cynthia Murray, were also concerned about the disparity and questioned Gleeson about the difference in charges. Unlike Murray, her parents would recall, Julious had no one to raise an alarm when he disappeared. Murray had a cadre of friends who noticed immediately when she didn't come home. Her parents were so attentive they jokingly called themselves "stalker parents." Her father was a nationally known bioethicist who was comfortable talking to reporters. By contrast, Julious was a convicted drug dealer who had recently served time in prison. Uneducated, he was practically homeless when he met Bostic. His belongings fit in one suitcase. He had a state identification card but no driver's license and walked everywhere.[29]

Gleeson, the Vinton County prosecutor, says race was not an issue in the indictment process; there was simply not enough evidence to bring an aggravated murder charge in Julious's death, let alone death penalty specifications. "While I respect Justice Pfeifer," he would recall, "the insinuation that we were guided by race—nothing could be further from the truth." As he would argue in a court filing, the evidence proved beyond a reasonable doubt that McKnight kidnapped Murray. McKnight, Gleeson asserted, was trying to make an issue out of race without any regard for the quality of evidence in the Julious case or the differences in the murders' circumstances, and "without any review of the character, history, or background of that other defendant." The jury did not lose its way, Gleeson said. "The trial court did not lose its way. No manifest miscarriage of justice occurred."[30]

Three years and one month after McKnight was sentenced to death, the state supreme court upheld his conviction and sentence, rejecting out of hand his argument that he shouldn't have faced a death sentence because there wasn't enough evidence to elevate the murder to a capital crime. Writing for the majority, Justice Alice Robie Resnick said all evidence pointed to a kidnapping, including the facts that Murray and McKnight left work at about the same time, that her car was found parked behind his trailer, that she did not have her wallet, driver's license, and credit cards when she disappeared, and that her murdered body was found rolled up in a carpet inside his trailer. "Here, circumstantial evidence, forensic testimony, and appellant's own statements proved beyond a reasonable doubt that appellant kidnapped and murdered Murray," Resnick wrote. Five of the remaining justices agreed, although three of them— Pfeifer, Judith Ann Lanzinger, and Chief Justice Thomas Moyer—said prosecutors had failed to prove Murray and Julious were killed as part of a continuing course of conduct. Moyer made it clear that he didn't find enough evidence for a capital charge for the death of Julious, though he noted the similarities in the two deaths. "Both Murray and Julious were shot in the head," he wrote, "and their bodies were disposed of on McKnight's remote homesite."

For his part, Pfeifer also disagreed with the death sentence for Murray's murder, saying there was no evidence beyond a reasonable doubt that McKnight kidnapped the young woman. He scoffed at the argument that sought to link McKnight's penchant for extramarital affairs as evidence he forced Murray home with him. "That McKnight sought lovers seems a thin reed on which to base a kidnapping conviction," Pfeifer wrote. He continued, "Based on the evidence in the record, it is as likely that Murray voluntarily drove McKnight home and voluntarily entered his home. Sadly, there is no doubt that McKnight committed a brutal murder. Nevertheless, because of the lack of evidence of the aggravating circumstances, McKnight should not be sentenced to death, and I dissent from the portion of the majority opinion that upholds the death sentence."

Emily Murray was opposed to the death penalty, and her parents honored her wishes by opposing it themselves. The only reason they argued against the decision by Judge Simmons to throw out the death penalty elements of the case was that they wanted to make certain McKnight, a vicious killer of at least three people, would end up in prison for life. At the time, the only way under Ohio law to press for life without the possibility of parole was to begin with a death penalty charge. The Murrays continue to oppose McKnight's death sentence and are hoping to see it reduced to life without parole. To this day, they agonize over the differences in the criminal justice system's treatment of the disappearances and murders of Julious and their daughter. Regardless of the details of those cases, they are haunted by a single, stark fact about Julious. "If they'd taken his disappearance seriously, and they caught McKnight," Tom Murray would recall, "then Emily would be alive."[31]

The Bargaining of Death

It's almost the lazy way to do this.

—*Hamilton County prosecutor Joe Deters, on the proliferation of plea bargains in capital cases*

LATE IN the day on July 8, 1999, Michael and Julie Hensley pulled up to the Sidney, Ohio, home of Brett Wildermuth, a computer programmer and Bible study teacher with whom Julie was familiar. Wildermuth met them at the door, telling them he'd heard there'd been shootings at Hensley's house earlier in the day and that people had been hurt. Michael Hensley started to leave, but Wildermuth suggested he come in and pray. Hensley agreed but only after retrieving a gun from his car. Wildermuth was not alarmed; he was familiar with Hensley's fear of a mysterious cult that Hensley claimed wanted to harm him. Once inside the house, however, Hensley took the gun and shot Wildermuth in the back. "Mike," Wildermuth said as he fell. Hensley shot him again. It was his fourth murder of the day.[1]

Hensley, sometimes known as Iron Mike, a large man with tattoos of a snake and a skull on his arm, had left three bodies at his home hours earlier. First to die was Amy Mikesell, a fourteen-year-old girl Hensley beat and stabbed to death before stuffing her body in a basement crawl space. Next were cousins Sherry Kimbler and Tosha Barrett, both sixteen, shot in an upstairs bedroom pleading for their lives after running from Hensley, who was beating them with a baseball bat. Hiding in the basement was twenty-two-year-old Amy Eagy, a coworker of Hensley's at a local janitorial service. Searching for her through the house, Hensley fired shotgun blasts into the closet, wounding Eagy, before leaving the home. Investigators eventually determined Hensley killed the three in a rage over his belief that they had told authorities he was selling LSD. Friends of the slain teenagers said Hensley, who had several citations for public indecency, had been paying the girls to watch him masturbate. After killing Wildermuth, Hensley drove off by himself and disappeared, possibly driving into Kentucky. Five days later, he shot at a driver, fired into the house of another Bible study teacher, then took three hostages at a Speedway gas station in Sidney before finally surrendering to authorities.[2]

Shelby County prosecutor James Stevenson, first elected in 1993 and a veteran of the office dating back a decade before that, charged Hensley with four counts of aggravated murder with a death penalty specification of kidnapping. Sidney is a small city of about nineteen thousand, and surrounding Shelby County is a largely rural area. The killings shocked the community and dominated local news coverage. People were so frightened after the murders that as long as Hensley was on the loose, police provided round-the-clock protection in the neighborhood where the shootings had happened. Stevenson threw himself into the case, working closely with members of the victims' families to decide how to proceed—whether to go to trial and push for a death sentence or to cut a deal to spare the families the ordeal of a capital case.

Ultimately, two themes emerged. First, Stevenson correctly pointed out that even if he secured a death sentence against Hensley, it could be a minimum of twelve years and perhaps longer before that sentence might be carried out. "Cases just go on and on and on," Stevenson would recall. "In the Hensley case, that was a big, big factor in the victims' decision. They indicated they wanted me to resolve the case in a way that it would be over and done in a way they could get on with their lives." Secondly, just three years earlier, state lawmakers had approved a change in law that for the first time allowed for life in prison without the possibility of parole (LWOP, in the sterile language of the criminal justice system), which would guarantee a true sentence of life behind bars. After a final meeting with family members of Hensley's victims, Stevenson authorized the deal. On March 7, 2000, Hensley signed the plea agreement, writing his name in a clear but slightly sloppy script, the handwriting like that of a child who has just learned cursive. He pleaded guilty to four counts of aggravated murder, three counts of kidnapping, and three counts of attempted aggravated murder and is serving a life sentence at the Southern Ohio Correctional Institution in Lucasville. Despite Hensley's fate—secure behind bars for life—the outcome did not offer everyone among the aggrieved the finality they sought when discussing their options. Mark Kimbler, the father of sixteen-year-old Sherry, later regretted the decision to accept the plea bargain and believes too much attention was paid to the potential cost to the county if they proceeded with a trial. (Stevenson estimated the trial would have cost a minimum of sixty-four thousand dollars; as it was, the county received nine thousand dollars in federal funds distributed by the Ohio Office of Criminal Justice Services to cover the cost of overtime for sheriff's deputies investigating the murders.) "There shouldn't even have been a choice in the matter," Kimbler said. "He should have been straight for death row and put to death as far as I'm concerned, with the type of crime he's done." But Stevenson said the cost of the trial was not a factor in his decision. "That's the cost of doing business. That's what we get paid to do."[3]

The role of plea bargains in the criminal justice system, and especially capital punishment cases, is a feature of law most people oppose personally but end up having to tolerate because the entire system would likely collapse without such an option. By most estimates, nine out of every ten criminal prosecutions in the United States are resolved with a plea bargain of some kind.[4] There simply aren't enough prosecutors and courtrooms to proceed to trial with the rest. But the plea bargain is not just a tool to ease the job of prosecutors, defense attorneys, and judges. A multitude of factors can lead to the necessity of a plea, not all of them pretty, but few of them unnecessary. In cases with multiple defendants, for example, the plea bargain is a time-honored tool for winning convictions—offender A gets something as a reward for testifying against offender B. In addition, the evidence available when an indictment is brought often changes by the time a trial approaches, perhaps weakening as witnesses' statements change, or taking on a different perspective as details about a defendant's motives or upbringing emerge. Moreover, despite what TV tells us about gleeful victims hugging in courtrooms after a verdict is announced, not everyone affected by crime, whether burglary, robbery, or murder, wants to undergo the ordeal of a trial.

When it comes to capital punishment, the value of plea bargaining as a tool and the validity of reasons for choosing it over a trial don't diminish just because the charges include a possible death sentence. As Franklin County assistant prosecutor Doug Stead noted in the last chapter, his first responsibility is making sure a guilty offender is taken off the streets. Before the Franklin County prosecutor's office makes any decision about a plea bargain, it consults with the victim's family and with the police department that investigated the crime. If Stead is comfortable that he can put the offender behind bars one way or the other, "then usually it comes down to what the family wants me to do," he said. "If they want me to go for it, I go for it. If they want to take a plea, we take a plea."[5] In Clark County in west-central Ohio, prosecutor Stephen Schumaker expressed a similar sentiment when discussing a plea bargain offered to Thomas DeWitt, convicted of killing his seventy-year-old grandmother and three others in 1983. In the *DeWitt* case, the county faced a legal battle over forcing a minister to testify about conversations he had had with the suspect. "If we hadn't pled that case, he may be on death row or he may be walking the streets a free man," Schumaker said.[6]

In *Gregg v. Georgia,* the 1976 decision that restored the death penalty, the U.S. Supreme Court considered and then rejected the argument that plea bargains in death penalty cases were somehow responsible for an unconstitutional system by contributing to a random application of justice. As Justice Byron White wrote in his concurring opinion, "Petitioner also argues that decisions made by the prosecutor—either in negotiating a plea to some lesser offense than capital murder or in simply declining to charge capital murder—are standardless, and will inexorably result in the wanton and freakish imposition of the penalty condemned by the judgment in *Furman.*" Such an argument, White said forcibly, is untenable. Without evidence to the contrary, White wrote, it can't be assumed that prosecutors will be motivated in their charging decisions by factors other than the strength of a case and the likelihood that a jury would impose the death penalty if it convicts an offender. "Thus, defendants will escape the death penalty through prosecutorial charging decisions only because the offense is not sufficiently serious; or because the proof is insufficiently strong," White concluded. "This does not cause the system to be standardless any more than the jury's decision to impose life imprisonment on a defendant whose crime is deemed insufficiently serious or its decision to acquit someone who is probably guilty but whose guilt is not established beyond a reasonable doubt."

The prevalence of plea bargains is one of the factors the Associated Press's study of Ohio's death penalty system analyzed, in part to test whether the 1981 law was accomplishing what lawmakers intended: punishing the worst of the worst with the ultimate penalty. What the study showed was that prosecutors often agreed to plea bargains that took execution off the table. Of the 1,936 capital indictments filed statewide from 1981 through 2002, the study found, just over half ended in plea bargains. Cuyahoga County led the way; 56 percent of its 712 capital indictments concluded with a plea bargain. Close behind was Franklin County, which indicted 334 individuals with capital crimes during the two decades of the analysis period. Of those indictments, 183, or 55 percent, ended with plea bargains. By contrast, the county sent just sixteen individuals, or 5 percent, to death row during the same time. In the rest of the cases, juries or three-judge panels sentenced offenders to nondeath punishments, charges were dropped, some offenders were found incompetent to stand trial, and a few were acquitted. In 1999, for example, Carlo Owens pleaded guilty to killing Patrick Pryor and Loretta Young, a young couple shot to death in a burglary at their apartment near Ohio State University on January 14, 1998. Prosecutors and defense attorneys agreed to the plea with the recommendation that Owens receive life in prison. Despite the arrangement, Owens narrowly escaped a death sentence when a three-judge panel rejected the agreement and deadlocked 2 to 1 in favor of death. A unanimous vote was required. (Owens was black and Pryor and Young were white.) Pryor's grandfather, Fred Aukeman, said he was satisfied with the life sentence Owens received, saying the murders were a violent act but Owens did not seem like a violent person. Franklin County Prosecutor Ron O'Brien said the 1996 law permitting life without the possibility of parole was a factor in Owens's plea deal.[7]

Ohio and other death penalty states have always permitted a high percentage of plea bargains. As the *Hensley* case proved, even a particularly violent murder is not a deterrent to seeking a deal. The AP study also found that 131 people charged with killing multiple victims escaped death row over the years by pleading guilty. That subset included twenty-five people accused of killing three or more victims. By contrast, the majority of people sentenced to death row during the same time were convicted of killing just one person. Of 274 death sentences, 196 involved single-victim killers.

Ohio's experience with capital punishment plea bargains is not unique. In California, 47 percent of 2,866 capital cases were resolved without a trial—almost all through plea bargains—from 1977 through 1989, according to the most recent data compiled by the state public defender's office. In Nebraska, a study commissioned by the Nebraska Crime Commission and published in 2001 found that prosecutors in the counties home to the big cities of Omaha and Lincoln were 2.1 times more likely to take death penalty cases to their conclusion rather than accept a plea bargain compared to their counterparts in the more rural parts of the state. In New York, plea bargains were offered in twenty-six of the fifty-four capital cases between 1995 and 2003, according to the state's Capital Defender Office. The high percentage of plea bargains in New York even inspired a constitutional challenge to the state's law by attorneys arguing that the plea-bargaining provisions were forcing defendants to plead guilty rather than risk execution. At issue was a part of the law that prohibited the death penalty if an offender reached a plea deal with prosecutors; such a provision violated the constitutional rights, the argument went, of those offenders who demanded a jury trial. In federal death penalty cases, 105 of 429 cases, or about one in every four, have ended with plea bargains since 1988, according to the Federal Death Penalty Resource Counsel Project. (Margaret O'Donnell, a Kentucky attorney involved with the project, noted that the percentage dropped after attorneys general under President Bush ordered federal prosecutors to limit the use of plea deals.[8])

Although the use of plea bargains in capital punishment cases is hardly new, its prevalence gained national attention in 2003 in Washington state when Gary Ridgway, one of history's most prolific serial murderers, pleaded guilty to forty-eight killings in exchange for escaping the death penalty by providing information about the whereabouts of several bodies. Ridgway, known as the Green River Killer, identified locations for additional victims, many of them prostitutes; he is currently serving forty-eight consecutive life sentences. Prosecutors were aware that the deal looked unorthodox given the killer they were dealing with. As Dan Satterberg, chief of staff in the King County prosecutor's office in Seattle, put it, "The prosecutor's initial reaction was, 'No way, because if not Ridgway, who?'" He continued: "In the end we thought that the principle of seeking the truth and seeking answers for families who were hurting was a sufficient principle to set aside seeking the death penalty. Every case has to be tested on its own merits and the strength of its evidence. I don't believe it's a legal precedent in any way." Satterberg's boss, the late Norm Maleng, the prosecutor who cut the deal, remained at peace with the decision. "I did then, and I do today," he said weeks after the 2003 deal was reached.[9]

The merits and strength of each case are a common theme when prosecutors talk about the use of plea deals. Stevenson, the Shelby County prosecutor, would recall of his decision in the *Hensley* case: "There are probably persons around the state of Ohio who meet the criteria to be on death row who aren't on death row. Hensley is a good example of that. He meets all the criteria to be eligible to be on death row. But on the other hand, the very system in Ohio takes into consideration that you have to look at each case individually."[10]

Take another case of a multiple killing in a county unaccustomed to a large docket of criminal offenses. Before dawn on March 19, 2000, in New Boston, Scioto County, in southern Ohio, forty-two-year-old James Curry attacked his ex-girlfriend, Lana Spradlin, and stabbed her to death in her apartment. When her nine-year-old son Daniel woke up, he said, "Please don't kill me,'" but Curry stabbed him to death anyway. Several hours later, Curry drove to the home of Spradlin's sister, Pam, and Spradlin's mother, and killed them both. During the second pair of murders, Curry ordered Dwayne Spradlin, the family's mentally retarded brother, to leave the room or be killed. Despite the wanton slaughter of four people, including a nine-year-old boy who begged to live, it was the ordeal that Dwayne Spradlin underwent that day and might have had to relive during a trial that persuaded the family to accept a plea deal for Curry, who is now serving life in prison with no chance of parole. Pam's father, Eugene Chamberlain, said he wanted Curry to live to be ninety and pay for his crimes every day through his prolonged imprisonment. "To me that's more punishment," he said. "If they execute you, it's over with." Pam's sister, Roberta White, said she wished she could have seen Curry put to death, to be able to smile at him and have the last say as he was executed. But in the end, she said, "But I also hope that we made the right decision in him going to jail and living every day." Lynn Grimshaw, the prosecutor at the time, echoed others' comments when he said that there are many factors in a criminal justice case that make it difficult to paint the topic of plea bargains with a broad brush. Still, even Grimshaw acknowledged, "If there's ever a guy that deserved death, he was it."[11]

One of the few prosecutors opposed to accepting plea bargains in death penalty cases and willing to talk about it publicly is Joe Deters, of Hamilton County, where Cincinnati is located. Deters, a Republican, started his career as an assistant prosecutor in 1982, then was elected prosecutor for a four-year term in 1992. After serving two terms as state treasurer, he returned to the office in 2004. Deters is blunt about the state's obligation to prosecute capital indictments to their conclusion. "There's a lot of lazy lawyers out there," he said in a 2003 interview. "You're not here to take pleas. You're here to try cases." Or, as he put it even more facetiously, "I can send my ten-year-old daughter to take a plea." He also takes judges to task, saying he believes some are more willing to look favorably on plea agreements because of the reduction in their workload. "It's a very frustrating situation when down here we take that whole area of law so seriously and apparently there's others in this state who are pretty cavalier about it," Deters said. He also raised the point that a plea bargain in a death penalty case is not exactly a fair use of the law when it comes to the defendant. He called it unethical to seek a death sentence in the form of a capital indictment and then to use it as a bargaining chip. "It's wrong to put someone in jeopardy of losing their life and then negotiate a plea," Deters said. He continued, referring to criminal defendants: "You're at such a poor negotiating posture that it's wrong to do that."[12] As a result of this approach, Hamilton County has the highest proportion of men on death row—20 percent in May 2007, or 38 out of 186 death row inmates—despite the lowest indictment rate of any of Ohio's large metropolitan areas.

Deters's approach is all the more striking given the prevalence of plea bargains in Ohio's other big cities, such as Columbus and Cleveland. Very often, especially in the early years of Ohio's death penalty law, the choice to die was often in the hands of the defendants themselves. Lewis Williams, the inmate executed in 2004 after struggling and pleading for his life, refused to bargain for his life even as several other defendants in the courts at the same time did so. In 1983, Cuyahoga County had fifty-four capital indictments, including the one against Williams for killing Leoma Chmielewski in the January 20, 1983, robbery at her home. Thirty of those indictments, or 55 percent, ended in plea deals cut for prison terms in exchange for escaping a death sentence. The county prosecutor's office argued that Williams's case embodied the complications of death penalty prosecution. As Timothy Miller, criminal division chief for the office, explained, death sentences can be avoided at many stages of a capital case based on decisions made by a judge, the jury, or the accused, as well as prosecutors. Those decisions can include a defendant's willingness to discuss plea bargains and to take responsibility for a crime, neither of which Williams did. "If these 30 other defendants had not exhibited some level of accepting responsibility, they very likely—if the jury had agreed that the death penalty was appropriate—they'd be on death row also," Miller said. Williams was also a textbook case of a defendant not trusting his own attorneys despite their best intentions to represent their client. One of his lawyers was also a law director in a Cleveland suburb, a position of authority that made Williams suspicious. Cleveland attorney David Doughten estimates that many inmates on death row today were offered plea bargains that they turned down because they didn't trust their attorneys, either because of racial overtones—black defendants uneasy with white lawyers—or because the attorneys didn't take the time to visit their clients and put them at ease. As David Stebbins, a veteran capital crimes defense attorney based in Columbus, puts it, "Many times a good relationship can overcome a client's reluctance."[13]

As Stevenson, the Shelby County prosecutor, worked on the *Hensley* case, an unusual possibility arose as part of the plea deal discussions. Family members of Hensley's victims wanted the chance to know what had happened to their loved ones, to know more about why Hensley did what he did. Hensley's attorneys, pointing out that a trial would provide no such opportunity, offered to make their client available as part of a possible plea deal. Although the interaction was not a deal breaker, Stevenson agreed to the idea as part of the terms he ended up offering Hensley. Some families opted for a jailhouse interview with Hensley himself. Others watched a video interview with Hensley that was filmed by Dave Clark, the Sidney Police Department's lead investigator, immediately after Hensley pleaded guilty and was sentenced on March 7, 2000. Later the same day, over a boxed lunch of ham sandwiches, chips, and sodas, police officers, sheriff's deputies, and the families of Hensley's victims crowded into a training room in the police department and watched the video. Hensley spared little in the interview and in some cases appeared to go out of his way to include lurid details about the killings. Some family members were silent, some wept, some shouted at Hensley's video image. A few had to leave, the process too painful. On the one hand, Sidney police chief Steve Wearly would recall, the family members wanted to know what the truth was. They wanted to know what caused Hensley to commit such a terrible act. "But when they did hear it," he said, "it was worse than they expected."[14]

Hensley's attorney, Kort Gatterdam, says the death penalty indictment against his client was entirely appropriate. He says he expects a jury would have convicted him, but he questions whether, because of Hensley's mental health issues, Hensley would have received a death sentence in the penalty phase of the trial. (Among other things, Hensley had a sexual addiction and studied satanism.) Gatterdam says there's no question that plea bargains keep the criminal justice system afloat. "Plea bargaining is absolutely essential to capital cases because of how long the litigation is after a capital trial and how expensive it is," he says. "If all these cases got tried, the system, which is already overburdened—it would stop."

Stevenson, now a Shelby County judge, has no regrets about the case. He says his concerns about the relitigation of death penalty cases and its effect on families was vindicated years later when the county's only death row inmate, Kevin Yarbrough, had his sentence overturned on the grounds he was mentally retarded. Here was a defendant convicted in a murder-for-hire scheme whose sentence had been upheld at every stage of his appeal by state and federal courts and presumably been made final, awaiting only the actual execution. Yet after the U.S. Supreme Court ruled in 2002 that executing the mentally retarded was unconstitutional,

Yarbrough's case was once again splashed across the front of local newspapers. "With that little bit of history," Stevenson said, "I'm comfortable with the way we handled Hensley."[15]

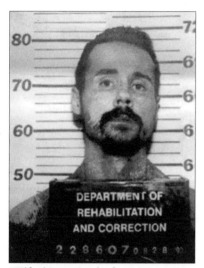

Wilford Berry Jr., the first inmate executed under Ohio's new death penalty law, sought death from the day he was arrested and fought all attempts to keep him alive. *Reprinted by permission of the Ohio Department of Rehabilitation and Correction*

Charles Mitroff Jr., the hardworking son of immigrants, had just finished a late-night delivery of baked goods when he was shot by Anthony Lozar and Wilford Berry Jr. *Reprinted by permission of the Mitroff family*

Known as Iron Mike, Michael Hensley avoided the death penalty by pleading guilty to charges of killing three teenage girls and a Bible studies teacher. *Reprinted by permission of the* Sidney Daily News

Sherry Kimbler and her cousin Tosha were among Michael Hensley's four victims in a 1999 killing spree in western Ohio. *Reprinted by permission of the Kimbler family*

Gregory McKnight received a death sentence for shooting a white Kenyon College student but not for his earlier killing of a black acquaintance. *Reprinted by permission of the Ohio Department of Rehabilitation and Correction*

Gregory Julious, a poor ex-felon when he was befriended by Gregory McKnight, was never seen again after leaving with McKnight for a Columbus party. *Reprinted by permission of the Ohio Department of Rehabilitation and Correction*

Kenyon student Emily Murray, shot by McKnight in his rural Ohio trailer, aspired to be an Episcopal priest. She disappeared after her last shift at a college pizza shop where she worked with McKnight. *Reprinted by permission of the Murray family*

As attorney general, Betty Montgomery sought to break what she considered a logjam of unwarranted delays created by defense lawyers. *Reprinted by permission of Betty Montgomery*

State senator Richard Finan helped create Ohio's current death penalty law, calling it spinach the state had to eat. *Reprinted by permission of the Ohio State Senate*

Donald Reinbolt's 1963 execution for killing a grocer was routine, but grew in significance as he became the last person executed in Ohio for almost forty years. *Reprinted by permission of the Ohio Department of Rehabilitation and Correction*

Leonard Jenkins killed a policeman during a bank robbery and became the first inmate sentenced to death under the new 1981 statute. Governor Richard Celeste commuted his sentence in 1991. *Reprinted by permission of the Ohio Department of Rehabilitation and Correction*

Governor Harry L. Davis questioned disparities in the handing out of death sentences but nonetheless allowed twenty executions to go forward during his years as governor in the 1920s. *Reprinted by permission of the Grandview Heights Public Library*

Governor Michael DiSalle, who commuted six death sentences and let six others proceed during his single four-year term, reflected on his "temporary Godlike power." *Reprinted by permission of the Grandview Heights Public Library*

Governor James Rhodes allowed two executions after being elected, then quietly put capital punishment on hold while the federal courts debated its constitutionality. *Reprinted by permission of the Grandview Heights Public Library*

Governor Richard Celeste, troubled by what he saw as a deep racial bias in the death penalty, commuted eight death sentences as his term expired. *Reprinted by permission of Richard Celeste*

Governor Bob Taft presided over the resumption of Ohio's death penalty, allowing twenty-four executions to proceed during his eight years as governor. *Reprinted by permission of the University of Dayton*

Governor Ted Strickland calls the death penalty the law of the land but has acknowledged the exonerations of numerous death row inmates across the country through DNA testing. *Reprinted by permission of the office of Gov. Ted Strickland*

Chief Justice Thomas Moyer upheld many death sentences but also expressed concerns about the aggressive behavior of county prosecutors in capital trials. *Reprinted by permission of the Ohio Supreme Court*

Justice Paul Pfeifer helped write the state's death penalty law but grew concerned that prosecutors were pushing the boundaries of the act beyond the scope intended by its drafters. *Reprinted by permission of the Ohio Supreme Court*

Akron pawnbroker Sydney Cohen had operated his shop for more than thirty years without a robbery before being shot and killed in a botched holdup in 1974. *Photo by Ted R. Schneider Jr. Reprinted by permission of the* Akron Beacon Journal

Sandra Lockett was a twenty-one-year-old recovering heroin addict when she masterminded the plan to rob Cohen to help friends she'd met on a weekend trip to New Jersey. *Reprinted by permission of the Grandview Heights Public Library*

Hamilton County prosecutor Joe Deters criticizes plea deals in death penalty cases, calling it a lazy approach that is also unfair to defendants. *Reprinted by permission of the Hamilton County Prosecutor's Office*

Lewis Williams ended up on death row after refusing a plea deal, then made headlines around the world when he struggled in the death chamber, pleading to God for help. *Reprinted by permission of the Ohio Department of Rehabilitation and Correction*

Jerome Campbell's death sentence was commuted by Governor Bob Taft after questions arose about blood on Campbell's shoes and what a jury knew about police witnesses. *Reprinted by permission of the Ohio Department of Rehabilitation and Correction*

Mindful of the spectacle public hangings had become, lawmakers moved executions to the Ohio Penitentiary in Columbus in 1885. *Reprinted by permission of the Grandview Heights Public Library*

SIX

Geography as Judge

Their attitude was, "Get the conviction first and worry about reversal afterwards."

—David Doughten, Cleveland defense attorney, on the approach to death penalty cases by Cuyahoga County prosecutors in the 1980s

"OHIO," GOES the tourism slogan of the nation's seventh-most populous state: "so much to discover."

To begin with, it's a state of big cities, first and foremost the "Three C's" of Cincinnati in the southwest corner, Columbus in the middle, and Cleveland on the shores of Lake Erie. But the list of big urban centers goes on, including Akron and Youngstown in the northeast, Dayton in the southwest, and Toledo in the northwest. That tally is followed by a litany of slightly smaller cities synonymous with the history of manufacturing in the country and now embodiments of rust belt survival: Canton and Warren in the east, Mansfield in the middle, Springfield in the southwest.

Increasingly, Ohio is also a state of suburbs. As urban problems mount, the population is fleeing for regions of booming growth—Delaware County in central Ohio, one of the country's fastest-growing counties; Warren in the southwest, absorbing residents of Cincinnati and surrounding Hamilton County like a sponge; Medina and Euclid in the northeast, similarly draining Cleveland and Cuyahoga County, which in 2006 lost more residents than any county in the United States outside Katrina-battered New Orleans Parish. (Ohio's suburban growth is all internal, city residents fleeing to bigger lawns and houses; the state's growth is statistically static, as the population would actually be shrinking without the slight annual influx of international immigrants and the fact that births are still outstripping deaths.)

Ohio is also a state of farms, with large swaths of land given over to everything from soybean fields to corn and wheat to giant megafarms with thousands of cows and hogs. Holmes County in northeast Ohio, an hour's drive or so from Cleveland, boasts one of the country's largest populations of Amish. And Ohio is also a state of rural poverty; twenty-nine southern and southeastern counties are officially within the federal designation of Appalachia. It was here, in tiny towns with crumbling schools and few job prospects, where Ohio's long-running lawsuit over inadequacies in school funding began and where residents still struggle with high unemployment.

Cities, suburbs, farms, and Appalachia. Like the country itself, Ohio is a patchwork of regions, peoples, and ethnicities collected under a common flag and constitution. Perhaps because of its diversity, Ohio has long prided itself on being a state of home rule, with decisions involving the lives of its citizens originating on the local level with minimal interference from the state. Although this is increasingly an illusion as state government takes over everything from the running of schools to the regulation of oil and gas drilling to behavior in strip clubs, the perception continues that a community's beliefs and morals are paramount, trumping whatever views outsiders might have on a subject. Nowhere is this more true than in the imposition of the death penalty, where the simple act of passing across a county line can drastically change the outcome of a murder and criminal trial.

In 2003, when Darrell Ferguson was sentenced to death in Montgomery County for fatally stabbing three people with their own kitchen knives, he became the seventh county resident sent to death row in twenty-one years. (A volunteer, he waived his rights to appeal and was executed three years later.) Yet during the same time period, neighboring Butler County, with a third fewer residents, also sentenced seven people to death. Moreover, prosecutors in Butler County filed thirty-two death penalty indictments during the same period. Contrast that to the eighteen filed by Montgomery County prosecutors; that in a county whose urban center, Dayton, is the state's sixth-largest city. Butler County has a population of about three hundred and forty thousand, compared to about five hundred and forty thousand in Montgomery County. Far more telling is the difference in the county's political makeup. In 2000 and 2004, Butler residents voted for George W. Bush for president. In Montgomery, one county away, residents voted for Al Gore and John Kerry.

Like race, the effect of geography on capital cases has long been observed, starting with the multiplicity of capital crimes available for slaves in the South compared to those for whites. Even as southerners were executing slaves for everything from theft to assault (and in some cases placing the heads of those put to death on pikes as a warning to other slaves), abolitionists in Pennsylvania managed to reduce the crimes for which death was punishment to first-degree murder alone. The inclusion of rape as a death-eligible crime was largely a southern phenomenon and by itself contributed to the disparities in death sentences across the country. Tellingly, the last public execution in the United States took place in Owensboro, Kentucky, when thousands watched Rainey Bethea hanged for rape in the summer of 1936.[1]

The Justice Department's 2000 analysis of the death penalty system, in addition to its findings of racial bias, also found evidence of geographic differences. For example, the study concluded that from 1995 to 2000, 287 out of 682 capital cases submitted to the Attorney General for review, or 42 percent, came from just five of the country's ninety-four federal districts. Further, the study found that forty of those districts did not recommend seeking the death penalty for any defendant during that time period. As previously noted, prosecutors in the big-city counties of Omaha were more likely to push for death sentences than their counterparts in more rural areas. And in Maryland in 2003, researcher Raymond Paternoster found differences in how prosecutors approach capital cases from county to county. Baltimore County, an area that does not include the City of Baltimore itself, was more likely to file for a death sentence than any other county, even though the county had the fewest death-eligible cases of any in the state. In Texas, Harris County, which includes Houston, has the distinction of having not just the highest number of executions of any county in that state but of any similar jurisdiction in the country. By the end of 2007, 102 offenders from Harris County had been put to death since the state resumed executions in 1982, more than the post-*Furman* executions in many entire states, including Virginia, Oklahoma, Missouri, Florida, North Carolina, Georgia, and Ohio.[2]

Disparities from one county to another are common in Ohio as well, as we have seen in the process of plea bargaining. In 1983, for example, prosecutors around the state bringing death penalty charges indicted forty-eight defendants with two or more factors, known as specifications, that elevate a case to a capital crime—such as murders committed during a robbery or burglary or while committing rape. Yet despite the severity of those indictments as reflected by the multiple specifications, just ten of those offenders were sentenced to death.[3] The basic difference in prosecutorial approach in the counties of Cuyahoga and Hamilton alone has created sharp distinctions in the outcomes of crimes punishable by death. In those cases, the discretion of prosecutors weighed heavily on the outcome, assisted in part by the willingness of families to cooperate—or not—and by the nature of the crime itself.

In the case of geographical bias, other factors come into play, including the reaction of juries in one county as compared to another to a possible death sentence. Take the differences between more conservative Butler County and its more liberal neighbor, Montgomery County. Butler County Prosecutor Robin Piper said the county indicts all offenders whose crimes meet the requirements for a death sentence, but also wants the cases to be strong. He also acknowledged that outcomes in capital cases vary by region, but said that jurors take an oath to represent their own community, not someplace they don't live. "It's an injustice for readers to maybe get the impression that there's some kind of unfairness or inequity to that," Piper said in a 2005 interview. "I don't think there is. I just think it has to do with the difference in geography." In Montgomery County, a spokesman for prosecutor Mathias Heck said that Heck reviews all murder cases carefully before deciding to seek a death sentence, and has chosen not to seek capital punishment several times as a result. The spokesman, Greg Flannagan, said the close scrutiny could explain the county's relatively low number of indictments and high death sentence rate.[4]

Even when prosecutors appear to have the upper hand in directing a county's approach to the death penalty, in reality they are, as elected officials, representing the wishes of the people who elected them. Franklin

County, whose largest employers include state government, Ohio State University, and hospitals, is a moderate, largely-white collar community where for years defense lawyers had a relatively easy time persuading prosecutors to go along with plea bargains or juries to sentence their clients to a punishment other than death. In 2007, the county had thirteen men on death row, less than half the figure for Cuyahoga County and less than a third the number of death row offenders from Hamilton County. The late Don Schumacher, a longtime Columbus defense attorney, called the county an oasis for defending capital cases in the early years of the law. Prosecutor Ron O'Brien concedes the demographics of the county as one factor in the relatively low number of death sentences, but says that when it comes to the worst of the worst, for the most part Franklin has done as well as any jurisdiction in the state.[5]

Sometimes there's no easy explanation for a county's approach to capital punishment. In eastern Ohio, in the adjoining counties of Mahoning and Trumbull, both manufacturing centers and union strongholds, prosecutors brought nearly identical numbers of capital indictments from 1981 through 2002, forty-five and forty-six, respectively, with identical outcomes: 22 percent of the cases resulted in a death sentence. Similarly, Lucas County in northwest Ohio, another manufacturing area and home to Toledo, with its glass factories and Jeep facility, also saw 22 percent of its capital indictments end with a sentence of death. Yet Stark County in eastern Ohio, which shares with those other counties a manufacturing history, has sent far fewer people to death row. In 2007, as prosecutors moved forward with a death penalty case against Bobby Cutts Jr., a police officer accused of killing his pregnant girlfriend, I examined the county's death penalty history using the Associated Press's original database along with four years of updated figures. I found that just one in ten death penalty indictments in Stark ended in a death sentence from 1981 through 2007. Frank Beane, a veteran county defense attorney, suggested one factor was the attractiveness of the state's 1996 law allowing for life without the possibility of parole as an option to a death sentence. "When it comes to taking a person's life, I think that jurors are reluctant to do it," Beane said.[6] (In February 2008, a jury convicted Cutts of the murders of his girlfriend and her nearly full-born child but declined to sentence him to death.)

On the other hand, twelve of the state's eighty-eight counties chose not to indict anyone on capital charges during the first two decades of the state's new death penalty era, including largely rural and in some cases poor jurisdictions such as Adams, Darke, and Meigs counties. Where the state's poorest counties are concerned, it's hard not to draw the conclusion that authorities take the cost of a capital trial into consideration when deciding whether to proceed with a death sentence. Yet, as we have seen, few judges or prosecutors will ever speak about the topic publicly. Judge J. David Webb in Paulding County, a rural farming area in northwest Ohio, hinted at the issue in a 2007 interview with the *Crescent-News* in Defiance when he said a capital case could cost a county as much as one hundred thousand dollars in attorneys' fees and expenses. Webb sat on a three-judge panel in nearby Auglaize County in 2000 that convicted a man of murder who had originally faced a death penalty. Webb said he didn't think the cost would ultimately be a factor deterring a small county prosecutor from seeking a death penalty indictment. "But it's one where I think the prosecutor would think long and hard as to, 'Is this really a death penalty case and is that what I really want?'" he said.[7]

The reality of capital costs to counties is what made the case of Gregory McKnight so significant; an elected official, Judge Simmons, went on record with concerns about the price tag of the death penalty law. Reflecting on that episode several years later, prosecutor Timothy Gleeson acknowledged the amount of money at stake was on his mind. "The cost was a concern because our county finances are limited, but it didn't guide the thought process as to how to proceed with the case," Gleeson would recall. "But because the case proceeded the way it did, my office and other county offices had to be that much more mindful of budgetary issues." Ultimately, the *McKnight* trial cost Vinton County, which has an unemployment rate that regularly tops 9 percent, about one hundred thousand dollars, about half of which the state and a criminal justice grant covered.

The U.S. Supreme Court ruled in 1932 in *Powell v. Alabama* that poor defendants have a constitutional right to representation, but that decision didn't take into account the resources that might be available to those offenders depending on where the crime was committed. In Ohio, the limits for attorneys' fees range from three thousand dollars per case in largely rural Coshocton County to seventy-five thousand dollars in Montgomery

County. Cuyahoga County pays a maximum of twelve thousand, five hundred dollars per attorney, a figure unchanged for decades. Hamilton, Clermont, and Warren counties pay up to forty thousand dollars per death penalty case, and Franklin County reimburses up to fifty thousand dollars. Although this can seem like a lot of money, it's usually a fraction of what attorneys would bill at an hourly rate in their private practice. Perry Ancona, a veteran defense attorney in Hamilton County, charges three hundred and fifty dollars an hour in his private practice but makes just forty-five dollars an hour for appointed capital cases, a small figure, he points out, when you begin to factor in the costs of paying rent, hiring secretaries, and maintaining copy machines. Typically, the money defense lawyers receive is not even close to what's needed to gather the evidence and conduct the investigations necessary in a capital case, especially when faced with the law-enforcement capabilities of a large, relatively well funded prosecutor's office.[8]

The cost of the public defender system has long been a concern for counties in Ohio. The County Commissioners' Association of Ohio calls the requirement to provide attorneys for indigent defendants "one of the truly pure forms" of federal unfunded mandates. This mandate stems from a 1972 U.S. Supreme Court decision that required states to fund the defense of indigent people accused of crimes that could result in their loss of liberty. In response, Ohio's 1976 public defender law provided for the state to commit 50 percent of these costs to counties. Yet a change in state law three years later allowed the legislature to reduce that amount to counties if the budget appropriation wasn't sufficient to provide the full 50 percent reimbursement, a process known as "proportional reduction." As a result, the amount of money available to counties from the state to defend poor offenders, including those charged with capital crimes, has fallen from a high of 48 percent in the 2000 fiscal year to 30 percent and below in more recent years. As a 2005 memo to lawmakers from the county commissioners association explained, "Counties continue to have an undue financial burden placed upon them through the state's failure to fulfill its partnership in sharing the cost of indigent offense."[9]

The difference in outcome by geography dates back long before the current law, however, and even then the counties of Cuyahoga and Hamilton showed disparities in how they approached the death penalty.

Today Hamilton boasts both the highest number of men on death row as well as the highest percentage of death sentences out of capital indictments of any county. But even in the nineteenth century, Hamilton had the greatest number of offenders put to death of any county in Ohio. Historical records list sixteen offenders hanged in the county between statehood in 1803 and 1885, when executions moved to the state penitentiary, and another seven between 1885 and the turn of the century. As under the current death penalty law, the next closest was Cuyahoga County, which put nine offenders to death in the county until 1885 and afterwards sent an additional three to be hanged at the state pen.

Hamilton County has always had the reputation of being the state's most conservative region. This is where prosecutors battled Larry Flynt over his adult bookstores and put the Cincinnati Contemporary Arts Center on trial for pornography over the center's 1990 Robert Mapplethorpe exhibit of male nudes. The movement that led to Ohio's gay marriage ban began with the Cincinnati-based Citizens for Community Values. It's the home of Ken Blackwell, a former city councilman and mayor later elected state treasurer and secretary of state and one of the most well-known black conservative Republicans in the country. Richard Finan, creator of the state's current death penalty law, hails from the Hamilton County suburb of Evandale. Cincinnati is also the home of the Taft family, perhaps the preeminent Republican name in the twentieth century, whose leading political figures included President William Howard Taft; his son, Robert A. Taft, a U.S. senator from 1939 to 1953 known as "Mr. Republican"; his grandson, Robert Taft Jr., also a U.S. senator; and his great-grandson, Bob Taft, governor of Ohio from 1999 to 2007, during which time he oversaw the resumption of executions in the state and allowed twenty-four to proceed. Just across the river from Cincinnati in Kentucky sits the new $27 million Creationism Museum, whose exhibits show dinosaurs and humans coexisting, to demonstrate that the earth is of very recent origin. The early wave of German immigrants flooding into Cincinnati in the 1830s and 1840s may help account for the region's conservatism, as may its strong Roman Catholic background and the area's southern location: Cincinnati is sometimes described as America's northernmost southern city.

Cuyahoga County, by contrast, is a largely Democratic stronghold whose base of votes has always been crucial for any politician running statewide.

A common political maxim is that a Republican running for statewide office must capture at least a hundred thousand votes from Cuyahoga County to be successful. This is the home of Dennis Kucinich, the former "boy mayor" of Cleveland voted out of office under a cloud after the city defaulted in the 1970s, then elevated to prominence as a liberal congressman who regularly runs for president promoting, among other initiatives, a U.S. Department of Peace. Another mayor of Cleveland, Carl Stokes, was the first black mayor of a major American city. State Senator Shirley Smith, of Cleveland, while serving in the House, unsuccessfully sponsored legislation four times attempting to study the state's death penalty system. Richard Celeste, the Democratic governor who opposed the death penalty and commuted the sentences of eight death row inmates in his last days of office, graduated from suburban Lakewood High School. For decades the region was a manufacturing powerhouse whose skies were darkened by belching steel mills and where unions were a strong and vital presence. It was the state's largest city at the beginning of the twentieth century, its population bolstered by waves of immigrants from eastern Europe as well as by blacks moving up from the South in the great northern exodus.

From the beginning of the state's new death penalty law, the two counties took a different approach to processing offenders through a capital indictment. In Cuyahoga County, prosecutors essentially attached death specifications to almost every murder case that came before them, then set about winnowing out those they planned to proceed with to trial and actually prosecute as capital cases. Part of this was sheer crowd control: Cleveland had one of the country's highest murder rates in the 1970s, and it was all prosecutors could do at times to keep up. As veteran capital crimes prosecutor Carmen Marino put it, interviewed after his retirement in 2007, "We tried homicides pretty much like most prosecutors try burglaries nowadays."[10]

Take this typical multiple indictment from February 1984. After a man named James Brown was killed in a robbery of an illegal after-hours club on February 17, prosecutors charged five people with his death, all of whom faced the possibility of the electric chair if convicted. Over the next few weeks, however, the charges against one defendant were dismissed, were lowered to murder for a second offender, and were reduced to involuntary manslaughter for the remaining three, whose sentences ranged from five years' probation to fifteen years in prison. As this and dozens of other Cuyahoga County cases reveal, the death penalty specification in the early years of the new law was the ultimate bargaining chip: frequently put on the table but rarely cashed in.

This shotgun approach to capital indictments, begun under the oversight of longtime prosecutor John T. Corrigan, began to change with the election of Stephanie Tubbs Jones, the county's first black prosecutor, for two terms in the 1990s. The county created a capital indictment review committee that attempted to better screen the death penalty cases before the prosecutor's office. The result was a more scientific approach to the process. Defense attorneys were allowed to present potentially mitigating evidence beforehand, while the views of victims' relatives on the death penalty were also considered early on. The committee also consisted of black and white prosecutors from within the office to guarantee a more representative reflection of the community. Whether because of the screening committee or for other reasons, the number of death sentences fell in the county, from thirty-three in the 1980s to twenty-two in the 1990s, including just two death sentences between 1995 and 1999. Despite these changes, the legacy of the aggressive approach taken by Cuyahoga County prosecutors in the 1980s lives on today in ongoing challenges to some of those early prosecutions, especially under Marino. In March 2006, in granting the habeas petition of death row inmate Joseph D'Ambrosio, U.S. District Judge Kathleen O'Malley highlighted cases where Marino appeared not to follow rules for providing evidence to death attorneys, and referred to a Sixth U.S. Circuit Court of Appeals ruling on another death sentence in which the federal appeals court described Marino's "shameful track record of breaking rules to win convictions." In 2003, the Washington, D.C.–based Center for Public Integrity included Marino among U.S. prosecutors with a high number of convictions overturned due to prosecutorial misconduct. For his part, Marino has no regrets about his career and stands by his work on several high-profile cases, including *D'Ambrosio.* Sipping coffee and eating biscotti in his large Cleveland home in the spring of 2007, Marino said the accusations that people were leveling at him were absurd. "I gave open discovery," he said of his interactions with defense attorneys. "The policy of the office was, you give discovery entitled by law."[11]

As the high rate of death sentences in Hamilton County reveals, the approach there was far more focused than in Cleveland. In the early years of the new law, the office under prosecutor Arthur Ney Jr. carefully sifted through its murder cases before deciding to approach the grand jury with possible indictments. Prosecutors looked at the nature of the crime, the type of victim, and above all, the strength of the evidence. "You don't go after an individual defendant with a death penalty unless you're sure you have the sufficient evidence to start out with," Ney would recall. "We didn't go after somebody unless we had the evidence. A lot of people would go after them without the evidence."[12]

This philosophy was clear in the case of the April 17, 1983, stabbing death of Monte Tewksbury, a Procter & Gamble employee moonlighting at the King-Kwik convenient store on Pippin Road in Cincinnati to earn extra money. Two men wearing masks entered the store about 11 PM and demanded money. Tewksbury handed over $133.97, as well as his watch, wallet, and wedding ring. Despite his cooperation, he was stabbed in the side, resulting in a large puncture wound to his liver. Severely hurt, Tewksbury still managed to get to a phone and call his wife, Sharon, to ask her to call the police and an ambulance. He stayed conscious until his wife and police arrived and was able to tell them what happened, including the fact that he did not resist the robbers. Nevertheless, Tewksbury was too badly injured to survive and died at the hospital early the next morning.

At almost exactly the same time that Tewksbury passed away, police in suburban Forest Park were following a large red cargo van as it drove into and out of a nearby Kmart parking lot with its lights out. Finally they stopped the van by a United Dairy Farmers store and questioned the occupants. The three men were arrested and eventually charged with Tewksbury's death. All three—the two alleged to have gone into the store and the man police said waited outside King-Kwik in a van—were charged with aggravated murder and aggravated robbery. But tellingly, and in contrast to the approach Cuyahoga County prosecutors were taking at the same time, only one man, John Byrd, was also charged with two death penalty specifications. Prosecutors never looked back, despite later claims that Byrd, while a participant in the robbery, was innocent of killing Tewksbury. (John Brewer, the second man alleged to have entered the store, later said he was the one who stabbed Tewksbury.) After a protracted series of appeals, and despite his claim of innocence, Byrd was executed on February 19, 2002, the third man put to death in Ohio under its new law.[13]

In the law's early years, Hamilton County was so successful in prosecuting offenders in capital cases, and juries were so willing to sentence those offenders to death, that avoiding a death sentence was news in and of itself. In August 1985, a Hamilton County jury recommended a sentence of thirty years to life for John Lawhorn, convicted in the stabbing death of Carlos Hall in April of that year. At the time, the *Cincinnati Enquirer* noted, Lawhorn was just the sixth person in the county to be spared execution since the law went into effect in 1981. This was not a surprising observation: just four years after the law's enactment, Hamilton County had already sentenced fourteen people to death. By contrast, Franklin County had yet to send a single person to death row.

Although Hamilton County prosecutors took a different approach to pursuing death sentences than Cuyahoga County, they were not immune to some of the same charges that have dogged Marino and others in the early Cleveland prosecutions. In 1999, for the second time since the new law took effect, the Ohio Supreme Court raised concerns about prosecutorial misconduct in death penalty cases, this time focusing on a fatal shooting in Cincinnati's violent Over-the-Rhine neighborhood. The defendant, Angelo Fears, was convicted of shooting Antwuan Gilliam during a crack cocaine–related robbery and sentenced to death. The court upheld Fears's conviction and death sentence, but not without a rebuke from Justice Francis Sweeney: "For the reasons that follow, although we find no reversible error, we express our deep concern over some of the remarks and misstatements made by the prosecutors involved in this case." Those remarks included belittling Fears's defense attorney, introducing past evidence of other misdeeds by Fears in violation of trial procedure, and giving the jury false information—such as wrongly alleging Fears pistol-whipped a robbery victim. Chief Justice Thomas Moyer found the Hamilton County prosecutors' behavior so egregious he voted against the death sentence for Fears. In his dissent, Moyer also noted several other instances of death penalty cases in the past decade where the court had rebuked prosecutors for misconduct, including three additional cases in Hamilton County.

Over the years, the U.S. Supreme Court has not been unmindful of geographic disparities in capital cases. But the court has also been clear—

with strong dissents, to be sure—that the discretion available to prosecutors and the variance by community standard does not by itself violate the Constitution. In 1968, in *Witherspoon v. Illinois,* the court ruled that jurors who expressed doubts about capital punishment, while not saying specifically they would vote against a death sentence, could not be struck as prospective jurors. A jury that must choose between life imprisonment and capital punishment, Justice Potter Stewart wrote, "can do little more—and must do nothing less—than express the conscience of the community on the ultimate question of life or death." Twenty years later, Justice Lewis Powell observed in *McClesky v. Kemp* that numerous factors may influence the outcome of a trial and a defendant's ultimate sentence, even though those factors may be irrelevant to the offender's actual guilt. "Finally," he wrote, "sentencing in state courts is generally discretionary, so a defendant's ultimate sentence necessarily will vary according to the judgment of the sentencing authority." That is a sentiment expressed time and again by prosecutors in Ohio.

In September 2001, twenty-one-year-old Brandon Moccabee used a shotgun to kill his wife, Lisa, and a man from Virginia named Shaun Williams after an evening of drinking beer and watching a movie at Moccabee's home in tiny Bloomingburg in Fayette County in the southwest part of the state. Rejecting the strong wishes of the victims' family members, prosecutor Steve Eckstein offered Moccabee a plea bargain to put him behind bars for the rest of his life. One of the toughest things a prosecutor must do, Eckstein reflected afterwards, is achieving the overall balance of justice, including what's right for the victims' family members but also what's best for the community. "It's the community that sets the tone for what they want to see in their community. The county is allowed to be the kind of county it's allowed to be," he said in 2004. "People in Hamilton County are free to push the way they want to go forward, and people in Fayette County are free to push the way they want to go."[14]

SEVEN

Diminishing Mercy

Surely society did not need to take the life of a mentally defective individual in order to protect itself.

—Governor Michael DiSalle, on his 1959 commutation of Lewis Bishop Niday's death sentence, as quoted in Wilford Berry's clemency request

NO ONE seriously thought Jerome Campbell was an innocent man. The evidence was overwhelming that some time on the evening of December 23, 1988, during a burglary of Henry Turner's Cincinnati apartment, Campbell stabbed Turner twice in the chest with one of his own kitchen knives, then plunged the knife all the way through Turner's right wrist, where police found the weapon when they discovered Turner's body the next day. Campbell had lived in the same apartment building recently and had been in Turner's apartment in the past. His fingerprint and palm print were found on the outside of Turner's kitchen door, as well as on a light bulb on the floor outside the kitchen. Donna Roberts, a woman who knew Campbell from the neighborhood, saw him late that night standing near the apartment building holding what appeared to be a bottle. During a police search of Campbell's sister's apartment, they found an empty bottle of Bacardi rum bearing the same label code number as a bottle found in Turner's apartment. Sitting in Hamilton County Jail, Campbell told his girlfriend, Estella "Niecy" Roe, that "he did it." He also wrote her a letter postmarked January 23, 1989, giving Roe a detailed alibi on his behalf.

Most damning of all, two jailhouse informants testified at trial that Campbell had admitted to the crime. And the same search of his sister's apartment turned up a pair of white Pony sneakers with human blood on the right shoe, a fact prosecutors tried to make the most of. "You talk about unlucky," Patrick Dinkelacker, an assistant Hamilton County prosecutor told jurors at the conclusion of Campbell's trial. "Did it just so happen that six days after this occurred when he got picked up he happened to have blood on his gym shoes? Human blood on his gym shoes. And the best excuse that you've heard is back in August somewhere he was involved in an incident where he got blood on his shoes." Faced with these facts, a Hamilton County jury in 1989 convicted Campbell of Turner's murder and then recommended the death sentence based on the aggravating circumstances of a felony murder committed during a burglary. The blood on the shoe had been powerful evidence, and at least one juror said she found Campbell guilty because "Turner's blood was found on Mr. Campbell's gym shoe."[1]

More than ten years passed, during which time state and federal appeals courts reviewed and upheld Campbell's conviction and death sentence. Then, in September 2002, Campbell became the first death row inmate to take advantage of a new law allowing inmates to request DNA tests at the state's expense when such tests weren't available at the time of the original crime and conviction. The results in Campbell's case were startling: the blood on the sneaker, so important to the prosecution, turned out to be Campbell's own blood, not Turner's. Then came a second important discovery. Lawyers researching Campbell's case for his federal habeas corpus claim uncovered police reports that strongly indicated the two informants who testified against Campbell, Ronys Clardy and Angelo Roseman, had obtained deals from prosecutors in exchange for their testimony, contrary to what jurors had been told about the evidence they heard. In the case of Roseman, a March 27, 1989, report said prosecutors intended to "work something out" for Roseman after his testimony. Roseman ultimately received a sentence of time already served. In Clardy's case, he said at trial he was testifying only because Campbell was evil. But a March 17, 1989, police report indicated that Clardy initially held back information on

Campbell because he wanted a deal. After Clardy's testimony, prosecutors dropped charges for lack of evidence, including an affidavit that said the victim of his robbery could not be found. But defense attorneys, in their motions a decade later for a new trial, submitted their own affidavit from the victim, who said he was never contacted by prosecutors despite the fact he worked and lived at the same place and was in the phone book. He also pointed out that after the charge was dismissed, he had even served on a Hamilton County grand jury.[2]

Suddenly there were serious questions about the conclusion the jury might have reached had they had the new information about the gym shoe and the informants. Faced with this new evidence, the Ohio Parole Board voted in favor of clemency for Campbell on May 2, 2003, the first time the board had voted to spare an inmate under the state's new death penalty law after rejecting nine previous requests. The board said its decision should not be seen as diminishing the nature of Campbell's crime. But it also said the DNA evidence and the revelation that prosecutors hid a deal with informants had tainted the final outcome of the trial. "The imposition of the death penalty should demand a greater certainty, confidence and reliability as to the proper weighing and balancing of credible evidence than was submitted to the triers-of-fact in this case," the board concluded.[3] Following this decision, attention shifted from the parole board's actions in a former electronics store turned state office building on the east side of Columbus to the thirty-one-story Riffe Building downtown. Campbell's execution was scheduled for June 27, and his life was now in the hands of Governor Bob Taft.

Lawmakers created the statutes that Ohio and thirty-seven other states use to bring death penalty charges against alleged murderers. Judges and juries determine whether those charges were merited. But it is governors in most of those states who have the ability to let an execution proceed or to stop it based on an ancient, extrajudicial right of appeal, the plea for clemency. In the more politically charged post-*Furman* atmosphere in the United States, the use of clemency has shriveled to the point of being an almost irrelevant afterthought. Governors use it rarely and almost always because of claims of innocence or gross errors at trial. But that was not always the case, and not all that long ago.

Like the right of habeas corpus, the power of clemency has old roots. The Greeks and Romans exercised clemency, the best-known example under Roman law being perhaps the pardon granted by Pilate to Barabbas. In England, the ability to grant clemency was vested in the crown, and its use can be traced back to the eighth century. Like any human institution, clemency under English law was subject to arbitrary use, and kings and other authority figures used it not just to soften the harshness of a brutal criminal justice system but also as a rewards process to win the favor of rivals. These pardons also had a practical effect: England used them to help fill the new colonies and man the British navy. Clemency was also the only recourse for convicted criminals to diminish punishment or proclaim innocence in the centuries before appeals became part of the judicial process. "The clemency power is something of a living fossil, a relic from the days when an all-powerful monarch possessed the power to punish and to remit punishment as an act of mercy," says Capital University law professor Dan Kobil, an expert on executive clemency. "It is the oldest form of release procedure, and it survives in some form in every state in the union and in every country of the world except China."[4]

Wary of the English model vesting clemency with the crown, lawmakers early on in the United States created advisory panels such as parole boards to participate in the process, resting the power of clemency either with governors or such boards. In 1993, in *Herrera v. Collins,* the U.S. Supreme Court emphasized the importance of the clemency process to the capital punishment system when it denied an appeal by a Texas inmate claiming he was innocent of the crime that sent him to death row. The court pointed out that the inmate was not without additional remedies, especially in the form of executive clemency, which Chief Justice William Rehnquist called the traditional fail-safe remedy for claims of innocence based on evidence that emerged after a trial. "Clemency is deeply rooted in our Anglo-American tradition of law," he wrote, "and is the historic remedy for preventing miscarriages of justice where judicial process has been exhausted."

The court further clarified its view of clemency's role five years later in a historic case arising from an Ohio murder. On the evening of June 20, 1990, in Cleveland, Eugene Woodard was one of four men prowling the city's east side for victims of what they called "gaffling," or carjacking. After a failed attempt in which they shot at a driver who escaped, the four men were riding in a stolen Oldsmobile Delta 88 when they spotted a man named Mani Akram driving a gray Oldsmobile 98 with custom wheels. John Woods, the driver of the Delta, pulled in front of Akram's car and slammed on the brakes, causing Akram's car to crash into the Delta. Woodard and another member of the gaffling party, Curt Thompson, got out of the Delta and approached Akram's car. Woodard opened the door and shot Akram. Thompson then pulled Akram out of the car, got in, and drove away. Woodard and the others followed in the Delta. After his arrest, Woodard was indicted on aggravated murder charges, convicted by a jury, and sentenced to death. The Ohio Supreme Court upheld his conviction and death sentence in 1993.[5]

The following year, the state's Adult Parole Authority informed Woodard that he could have a clemency interview on September 9 followed by a clemency hearing on September 16. Woodard balked, objecting to the short notice about the interview and asking that a lawyer attend both the interview and the hearing. When it appeared neither option was possible, Woodard sued in federal court, charging that Ohio's clemency system violated his rights to due process and his Fifth Amendment right to remain silent. The Court of Appeals for the Sixth Circuit granted some relief to Woodard, finding that he faced a "Hobson's choice" between participating in the clemency process and asserting his Fifth Amendment rights that raised the possibility of an unconstitutional procedure. But upon review, the U.S. Supreme Court reversed the appeals court in 1998 and found, in *Ohio Adult Parole Authority v. Woodard,* that the clemency process was separate enough from the normal judicial system that it required only minimal safeguards of due process. That might include, for example, intervention by a judge in the face of a system where a state official flipped a coin to determine whether to grant clemency, or where the state was arbitrarily denying prisoners any access to its clemency process. The court was clear that clemency itself does not violate due process. "Despite the Authority's mandatory procedures, the ultimate decision-maker, the Governor, retains broad discretion," Chief Justice Rehnquist wrote. "Under any analysis, the Governor's executive discretion need not be fettered by the types of procedural protections sought by respondent."[6]

Under current law in Ohio, prisoners petition the Ohio Parole Board, which schedules hearings, accepts evidence, and then issues a recommendation to the governor. In the distant past, the process was far more fluid, with offenders or their families making emotional, last-minute appeals to governors to spare their lives or those of their loved ones. In 1825, thousands gathered in the city of Newark to watch Peter Diamond hang for the killing of a man named Mitchell who tried to intervene in a fight at work. Diamond was on the scaffold, the noose around his neck, when the jailer galloped up on a horse announcing a commutation from Governor Jeremiah Morrow to ten years in prison. (The reprieve pleased many in the crowd who believed Diamond's sentence was too harsh given the accidental nature of the killing. But one observer was so disappointed by the outcome that he suggested at least hanging a dog.) In December 1871, Governor Rutherford B. Hayes announced he was granting convicted killer Andrew Brentlinger, sentenced to die for killing his wife, a hundred-day reprieve, pushing his execution from January 20, 1871, to April 7 of that year, when he was finally hanged at the Allen County Jail in Lima. In late May 1880, Governor Charles Foster granted George Price, a black man convicted of killing his former employer in Cincinnati, a six-week reprieve to determine whether he was insane. No evidence is found that the analysis was done, and Price was hanged on July 9, 1880, on a scaffold in the Hamilton County jail yard. Just a few weeks earlier, lawyers and relatives of three Canton boys scheduled to hang came to Columbus to plead, to no avail, to spare the lives of the condemned. The three teens, one aged sixteen, then two others seventeen, were executed on June 25, 1880.[7]

Other entreaties were more successful. Isaac Smith, of Pike County in southern Ohio, was sentenced to hang on August 23, 1889, for the murder of Stephen Skidmore. Before the sentence could be carried out, Governor James E. Campbell allowed a series of reprieves as lawyers attempted to introduce new evidence questioning Smith's guilt. Finally, on April 29, 1891, two days before Smith's latest date with the gallows, Campbell announced he was commuting Smith's sentence to life imprisonment. In his statement, Campbell professed to be left with few options. His first choice, a law that would allow prisoners such as Smith to be returned to court for a new trial, had not been enacted despite his entreaties. As a result, he had to choose between allowing Smith to be executed even though he might be innocent, or letting him go free despite the fact that the evidence that appeared to exonerate him might not withstand the scrutiny of cross-examination. Campbell noted that, as governor, he believed that pardons were meant for clemency or as relief from improper verdicts. "I am therefore constrained to commute his sentence to imprisonment for life, and let time do its work in disclosing the truth," Campbell announced. Smith took the news calmly, observing that he still hoped for a full pardon.[8]

In his 1922 treatise on the death penalty, *Death by Law*, Governor Harry Davis maintained that it was dangerous to give governors unchecked clemency powers. No single human being should have such power vested in him, he wrote. "In fact," he continued, "I am a strong believer that even the chief executive's unchecked authority to grant freedom to prisoners should be radically restricted, especially in the case of life prisoners, so as to obtain only in cases where clear proof of innocence is produced, or in the event of mortal sickness. For unwise and indiscriminate use of the pardon and parole power is one of the really serious elements contributing to crime conditions." Of course, Davis had nothing to worry about on his own account. Despite the questions he raised about capital punishment, records show as of the writing of that essay he had let sixteen men be executed without a single commutation; records show a total of twenty put to death during his administration.

Historically, one of the reasons governors have given clemency in capital cases is to correct what they see as imbalances in sentencing. Governor Thomas Herbert, governor from 1947 to 1949, commuted the death sentence of Charles Ames because the triggerman in the 1947 murder, Julius Emerick, received a life sentence from a different jury. Herbert made his decision, he said, not out of sympathy for Ames, "but in order that it may not be said that Ohio failed in comparative justice." Similarly, Governor C. William O'Neill commuted the death sentence of Cleo Eugene Peters in the 1950s after his codefendant, Michael G. Dumoulin, received a life sentence. Explained O'Neill, "under the law they are equally guilty."[9]

Michael DiSalle, a Democrat who served as governor from 1959 to 1963, commuted the death sentences of five men and one woman while letting an additional six executions of male offenders proceed. In his 1965 book, *The Power of Life or Death*, DiSalle reflected on the responsibility he faced. "No one who has never watched the hands of a clock marking the last minutes of a condemned man's existence, knowing that he alone has the temporary Godlike power to stop the clock, can realize the agony of deciding an appeal for executive clemency." Those were years when executive clemency was not the surefire political poison it's become today, but DiSalle still paid a price for his actions, and attributed his 1962 loss to Republican James Rhodes in part to those commutations. "You left yourself wide open when you could have ducked," one reporter charged following DiSalle's defeat in November of 1962. "So you saved the lives of six nonentities," said another reporter. "And who cares? If you'd kept your mouth shut, the world would be no poorer, and you'd be around for another four years to fight for the underdog."[10]

Consider the case that came before DiSalle in the spring of 1960. Frank Poindexter had been sentenced to die for his role in the shooting death of Marie Hires, of Hamilton, Ohio, one year earlier. Hires had been killed when Poindexter, Robert Leigh, and Sam Decker set out to rob her and her husband, Herschel, of thirty-seven thousand dollars they kept in a safe in their home—they preferred not to store the cash, profits from their family business, in a bank. Decker, one of the Hires's employees, heard about the money and enlisted the other two to rob the couple. The three entered the home on the evening of April 10, 1959, at which point things immediately went awry. As soon as Leigh and Decker came inside, Mrs. Hires went upstairs; when she returned, she was carrying a shotgun. Leigh was holding a gun on Mr. Hires, who shouted to his wife, "Marie, shoot this son-of-a-bitch!" Mrs. Hires fired, hitting Leigh in the shoulder and left ear. Herschel Hires jumped Leigh, and as they struggled, Leigh's gun went off, wounding Hires. Poindexter, who had been waiting outside, stepped in and fired his .38 caliber through a glass pane that formed the upper part of the half-open door, fatally wounding Mrs. Hires. Then he fled, leaving the wounded couple and Leigh lying in the house.

Butler County prosecutors charged all three men with first-degree murder, but only Poindexter went to trial. Decker, the plot's instigator, pleaded guilty to second-degree murder and received a sentence of life imprisonment with parole possible after ten years. Leigh, who had pulled the gun and fired first, pleaded guilty before a three-judge panel after prosecutors threatened him with the electric chair unless he named his accomplices. The same three judges tried Poindexter and sentenced him to death.

When Poindexter's request for clemency reached DiSalle, the governor undertook a personal investigation of the robbery and murder that is almost unimaginable today. He researched several cases of disparate sentences for people found guilty of similar crimes. He visited the Ohio State Penitentiary to talk to the offenders. He flew to Hamilton to tour the crime scene. "You cheap politician," one neighbor of the Hireses shouted as DiSalle arrived at the house. "Why don't you go back to Columbus where you can do some good?" On Easter Monday, the day of Poindexter's scheduled execution, DiSalle issued a four-day reprieve. On April 22, after further review, he commuted Poindexter's sentence to life imprisonment. "Thank God," Poindexter said, falling to his knees at the penitentiary and beginning to weep. "My prayers have been answered."[11]

In his approach to clemency, DiSalle drew on a statement that William Howard Taft, the former president from Cincinnati, made when he was chief justice of the U.S. Supreme Court. "Executive clemency exists to afford relief from undue harshness of evident mistake in the operation or enforcement of the criminal law," Taft wrote. "The administration of justice by the courts is not necessarily always wise or certainly considerate of circumstances which may properly mitigate guilt."

In his statement granting Poindexter clemency, DiSalle made reference to Herbert's earlier decision on Charles Ames. His decision, DiSalle said, was made in "view of the disparity in the punishment meted out to two men that I feel, in the eyes of society and the concept of our law, are both equally guilty."[12]

This notion of correcting a sentencing imbalance persisted into the administration of Rhodes, some of whose commutations cited the same concern. On November 30, 1966, he commuted the death sentences of two men, Curtis A. Bellamy Jr. and Elmer G. Miller Sr., both convicted in the beating death of Emma Austing three years earlier in Cincinnati. Austing survived the attack by the men, who were trying to elicit the combination of a safe, but died several weeks later. Prosecutors contended she died as a result of the beating, while the defense said she had nearly recovered from her injuries when she died of a blood clot. In Bellamy's case, Rhodes took into account his age (nineteen at the time of the crime), the fact he didn't plan the robbery, and the fact that Bellamy was easily influenced by two older accomplices. In the case of Miller, he said "the same doubts justify mercy in sentencing." The same day, Rhodes granted a reprieve to the third man convicted in Austing's death, Lester Eugene Swiger, then commuted his death sentence to life imprisonment on October 12, 1967, citing both the recommendation of the parole board and that of Hamilton County Common Pleas Judge Gilbert Bettman. Among the factors Rhodes considered were Swiger's lack of intent to kill anyone, doubt that the victim's injuries contributed to her death, "and the requirement of justice that sentences of accomplices be equaled."[13] Rhodes' death penalty decisions were strongly influenced by the advice of his executive assistant, John McElroy, a lawyer and World War II veteran whose military experience made him leery of capital punishment. In an interview with the *Columbus Dispatch* late in his life, Rhodes credited McElroy with putting a stop to executions in the 1960s. "McElroy was in charge," Rhodes told the paper shortly before Wilford Berry's first scheduled execution in March 1998. "He stopped it. I gave him total responsibility for electrocutions."[14]

Although DiSalle and Rhodes were very different politicians, both reflected the historical reality that governors up until the 1970s saw executive clemency as a tool within their rights to use regardless of the greater political atmosphere. In Ohio, for example, more than a third of sixty-seven offenders sentenced to death between 1950 and 1959 had their sentences commuted by governors. On December 7, 1970, in the midst of a strike by the two daily papers in Columbus, Rhodes commuted the death sentence of Ellis Vails, who thus achieved the distinction of receiving the last full commutation of a death sentence in Ohio until the eight commutations by Dick Celeste two decades later.

Describing that experience in a law review article in 2003, Celeste said it was important to live in a society that reflects people's best instincts and higher nature. "I believed then and I believe now," he wrote, "that to show mercy is a sign of our strength as a community, not a sign of our weakness. It is also, in a way, a reminder of our shared pain. For whatever punishment we impose, we can never replace the victims."[15] In later years, Celeste did not regret his decision in January 1991, although he acknowledged the mistake of not consulting more deeply with prosecutors and family members of the victims of the killers he freed from death row. "I would have had stronger grounds on which to make the case to the public," Celeste would reflect. "I don't think it would have changed my decision, but would have helped make my case that this was not an uncaring act."[16]

Such a mass commutation would have been newsworthy no matter when it occurred. But in exercising clemency as a form of mercy, independent of the legal status of the condemned, Celeste followed a path taken by several governors in decades past. In Oklahoma, Governor Lee Cruce commuted every death sentence that came before him during his tenure from 1911 to 1915, as did Oregon governor Robert D. Holmes from 1957 to 1959 and Massachusetts governor Endicott Peabody from 1962 to 1965. Governor Winthrop Rockefeller commuted all death sentences in Arkansas, and in New Mexico, Governor Toney Anaya commuted the state's five death row inmates before leaving office in 1986.[17]

In Illinois, separate investigations by the *Chicago Tribune* and Northwestern University journalism students in 1999 into the fairness of the state's capital punishment system found some death penalty cases flawed by faulty evidence and incompetent lawyers. The findings led former Governor George Ryan to halt executions and set up a commission to study problems with the system. Ryan ultimately commuted the sentences of all 167 death row inmates, calling the state's death penalty system arbitrary, capricious, and immoral.

In California, Edmund "Pat" Brown, governor from 1959 to 1967, considered fifty-nine death penalty cases during his eight years in office and commuted twenty-three of them. In his 1989 book *Public Justice, Private Mercy,* Brown sounded some of the same themes as DiSalle. During his life, Brown wrote, he had done many things that gave him pleasure and pride and a few he wished he could forget or try again. "But the longer I live, the larger loom those fifty-nine decisions about justice and mercy that I had to make as governor," he wrote. "They didn't make me feel godlike then: far from it; I felt just the opposite. It was an awesome, ultimate power over the lives of others that no person or government should have, or crave. And looking back over their names and files now, despite the horrible crimes and the catalog of human weaknesses they comprise, I realize that each decision took something out of me that nothing—not family or work or hope for the future—has ever been able to replace."[18]

As dramatic as Ryan and Celeste's pronouncements were, however, they were exceptions to the post-*Furman* rule that clemency would be handed down far less frequently than in the previous decades. Since the U.S. Supreme Court reinstated the death penalty in 1976, governors have granted clemency to 229 inmates, including the mass commutation granted by Ryan. As lawyer and death penalty researcher Austin Sarat of Amherst College notes, the use of clemency by governors since 1976 is a mere fraction of that in the decades previous. Governors in Florida, for example, commuted 23 percent of the state's death sentences between 1924 and 1966 and just 9 percent after 1976. Nationally, once the Ryan commutations are removed from the formula as a one-time event outside the normal reason for commutations, governors have granted clemency in only 5 percent of death sentences in the modern capital punishment era. By contrast, Sarat's research found about one in every five death sentences was commuted from 1930 until 1975. In the past, governors might commute a death sentence because they felt it was inappropriate based on the crime, to show mercy to a rehabilitated inmate, or to correct mistakes, including questions of innocence. Today, correcting an error is the most common reason for granting clemency. More importantly, clemency has shifted from an opportunity for a governor to show mercy to functioning as a quasi-judicial element of an inmate's legal process, a sort of superreview of the case once the courts have finished their job, but done without straying from the same facts the courts considered.[19] One result is that it is now virtually impossible to be elected governor without supporting the death penalty. Even Virginia governor Tim Kaine, who took office in 2006 despite personally opposing capital punishment, agreed to uphold the law and let executions proceed.

Taft and Rhodes, two of the best-known Republicans in state history, embody the approach of governors to clemency before and after *Furman*. Rhodes was willing to consider factors outside the strict elements of a case when examining a clemency request. In the case of Ellis Vails, Rhodes said the inmate had been properly convicted of first-degree murder. But, Rhodes continued, reaching a conclusion that reads like science fiction in today's political environment, "mercy is appropriate because inmate was incapable of removing himself from a life pattern inevitably inducing such a crime as he committed."[20] In fairness, Rhodes had history on his side; by that time federal courts had established a de facto freeze on executions nationally as the question of capital punishment's constitutionality made its way to the U.S. Supreme Court. As a result, a commuted death sentence didn't carry the same political weight it had a decade earlier. But despite all the attention that DiSalle's commutations drew in the early 1960s and Celeste's attracted in 1991, Rhodes showed himself as capable of mercy as either man.

In contrast, Taft was very much the modern governor when it came to clemency. Although the death penalty had not been an issue in his 1998 campaign against Democrat Lee Fisher, Taft took the reins of a state ready to see the state's almost two-decade-old law implemented. Public sentiment was on his side, and the parole board was not favorable toward mercy in capital cases. Reflecting the new territory of an active death penalty law, Taft's early clemency announcements were lengthy and revealed a substantial amount of consideration of the condemned inmate's record. In his four-page report denying clemency to Wilford Berry, for example, Taft reviewed at length the court action in the case and the study he had done of Berry, his crime, and his wish to die. For Berry and the next two inmates whose requests Taft denied, he described clemency as the most solemn duty of all for a governor. He dropped the "most solemn" superlative by the fourth request, from serial murderer Alton Coleman in April 2002, and said simply that he was once again faced with the responsibility of responding to clemency. He revived the word "solemn" in denying Robert Buell's request on September 23, 2002, then began adding the words "constitutional duty" the following year. By mid-2003 he had eliminated any reference to duty and the Constitution and began issuing short, one-page denials with the template phrase "Governor Bob Taft today issued the following statement . . ." Consistent in all his denials was a phrase at the end that began, "May God bless the family and friends of . . ." followed by the name of the murder victim.[21]

Up until Jerome Campbell's request, all Taft's decisions reached the same conclusion as the parole board, which had yet to recommend mercy.

On Monday, June 16, 2003, Annie Shockley, the daughter of Campbell's victim, Henry Turner, held a teleconference with Taft during which she urged him to allow Campbell's execution. Two days later she held a news conference to announce that Campbell deserved to be executed for the murder of her father. She told reporters she had decided to go public because she was tired of seeing only Campbell's relatives quoted in connection with the case. Shockley tried to counter the image of Turner as a bootlegger selling bottles of Bacardi rum from his apartment, painting a picture of a good man who worked for years in an iron mill yard. The public defender's office said it respected Shockley's opinion and felt for her loss, but pointed out that no one from Turner's family had shown up at Campbell's clemency hearing.[22]

By this time, Campbell was not just proclaiming the injustice of a death sentence but also professing his innocence of the crime, a point he continued to press in the courts. He didn't just want off death row: he wanted a new trial. In May, a Hamilton County judge denied that request, and on Friday, June 20, the state appeals court for Cincinnati also turned him down. "While it is obvious that the state wanted the jury to believe that the blood on the gym shoes was Turner's, even if a jury were presented with evidence that it was Campbell's blood on the shoe, we agreed with the trial court that there is not a strong probability that a new trial would result in an acquittal," wrote Judge Mark Painter of the First Ohio District Court of Appeals. With time running out, Campbell appealed to the Ohio Supreme Court on Monday, June 23, 2003, asking for a delay of his execution and an order for a new trial.

On Thursday, June 26, 2003, the day before Campbell's scheduled execution, anticipation was growing. On death row in Mansfield, Campbell packed two boxes and two laundry bags of belongings, including a ten-inch portable TV, a radio, a fan, a lamp, family photographs, and clothes. In Cincinnati, TV station WLWT was with Campbell's mother and niece as they awaited final developments. Also in Cincinnati, Turner's relatives, including his daughter and a grandson, David Houze, waited for any word from Taft. In Columbus, the governor was preparing for a news conference.

About noon, Campbell's family got a call from the state public defender's office, where lawyers had just been informed by Taft's legal counsel that the governor was granting Campbell's request for clemency and would remove him from death row. Elated, family members jumped up and down and hugged. In Mansfield, Campbell got the news from state public defenders Joe Wilhelm and Pam Prude-Smithers. He let out a couple of yells loud enough to startle a prison caseworker and guard standing near his death row cell. In Columbus, standing in the governor's ceremonial office in the Statehouse, Taft made it official: he would spare Campbell from death despite strong evidence that he was guilty of killing Turner. "Although the new evidence does not exonerate Mr. Campbell," Taft said, "it does contradict an impression that was left in the minds of some jurors during the trial." Taft also expressed sympathy for Turner's family and said the announcement was not meant to diminish Campbell's responsibility for the murder. The governor said the decision was difficult but not necessarily any worse than other death penalty cases to come before him. "They've all taken a considerable amount of time," he said at the time. "It's something a governor must take very seriously."[23]

The decision didn't sit well with Turner's relatives. Houze said Campbell's tactics and profession of innocence were nothing but a ploy. One of the original prosecutors on the case, Patrick Dinkelacker, now a Hamilton County judge, spoke out to deny he'd done anything wrong by introducing the shoes as evidence. "There was never any effort on our side to hide anything [from the jury]," he would recall. In an interview immediately after the commutation, Campbell continued to profess his innocence of the crime itself and said his next step was to keep pushing for a new trial. His appeals never got far on the state level: the state supreme court turned down his request for a new trial the day Taft commuted his sentence.[24]

For Taft, the mercy he showed Campbell was an isolated occurrence that would not be repeated. In his remaining four years in office, Taft would allow an additional seventeen executions to proceed, including seven in 2004, when Ohio was second only to Texas in the number of offenders put to death. The men executed under Taft included some of the most notorious killers in modern Ohio history: Alton Coleman, who was sentenced to death in Ohio for killing a suburban Cincinnati woman and a fifteen-year-old Cincinnati girl, was suspected in at least eight murders nationwide, and was also under death sentences in Indiana and Illinois; Willie Williams, who gunned down four men execution-style in a Youngstown public housing unit in a dispute over drug territory; and Jeffrey Lundgren, a cult leader who orchestrated the massacre of a family of five, including three children, in Kirtland in northeast Ohio in 1989. (Taft also denied clemency to Akron double-killer Richard Cooey, who raped and murdered two female University of Akron students in 1986 after giving them a ride. Cooey was in Lucasville awaiting execution in 2003 when the federal courts agreed he had been inadequately represented for a portion of his appeals and allowed his new attorney's request for a delay.)

Some of those put to death on Taft's watch claimed they were innocent of their crimes, among them John Byrd, Ernest Martin, and Robert Buell. Six of those executed were volunteers who waived their appeals and whose clemency applications were filed against their wishes by state public defenders. One of those was Stephen Vrabel, of Youngstown, who killed his girlfriend and their three-year-old daughter, then stuffed their bodies in a freezer and continued living in the same apartment for a month. Vrabel appeared to be so mentally ill that the Ohio Supreme Court split 4 to 3 in upholding his death sentence, including a dissenting vote by Republican chief justice Thomas Moyer.

Although Taft spared Campbell's life, he also put off the execution of another inmate, John Spirko, on a temporary basis. Spirko, convicted of killing the postmistress of tiny Elgin in northwest Ohio in 1982, has long maintained his innocence, saying he was a suspect because of his criminal background. Taft granted Spirko five successive reprieves while the state continued to conduct DNA tests on evidence found at the scene, and new governor Ted Strickland continued the delays at the request of Spirko's attorneys with the blessing of the attorney general's office. Spirko received two additional reprieves from Strickland in 2007, and in January 2008 the attorney general's office concluded there was no DNA match linking Spirko to the crime scene. On January 9, 2008, Strickland commuted Spirko's sentence to life without the possibility of parole.

In October 2006, Taft was facing a possible twenty-fifth execution on his watch, that of condemned inmate Jerome Henderson, one of the highest tallies of any governor nationwide. He said at the time that he was surprised so many requests for capital clemency had come before him but was satisfied with the law and the state's procedures for handling capital punishment cases. "I'm comfortable that the people have, through their elected representatives . . . decided that there should be a death penalty in Ohio for the most horrible kinds of crimes, that we have a process in Ohio that is a fair process," he said. "I have not seen evidence to the contrary, and in fact now with DNA we have another safeguard in place to make sure that there is no error in certain facts that causes someone to be subject to the death penalty."

It's what the people of Ohio still support today, he continued. "It obviously should be reserved for certain kinds of crimes and offenses," he said. "It should be something that's imposed by a jury of peers with a very high standard of proof, and something that should continue to be subject to a wide series of appeals, to make certain that it is appropriately and fairly administered." Although Taft never disagreed with the parole board on clemency in his eight years as governor, he said, adamantly, "We didn't rubber stamp the parole board. We did our own analysis and write-up and weighed all the factors independently."[25]

Like Rhodes, Taft had history on his side when it came to clemency. But in Taft's case, the tide of history was going in the other direction. Although executions peaked in 1999 nationally and began a gradual decline, there was still plenty of support for the death penalty during his years in office and many executions occurring across the country during the same time period. Putting inmates to death had become commonplace and rarely merited the front page of the paper or the lead story on the nightly news.

At the last moment in the fall of 2006, the federal courts gave Jerome Henderson permission to join a lawsuit challenging the constitutionality of lethal injection and delayed his execution. Although the parole board denied Henderson's request, Taft had yet to issue his own decision by the time Henderson received his temporary federal reprieve. Attention then turned to Strickland, the first Democrat elected in twenty years after a state government scandal swept most GOP statewide politicians out of office. Almost immediately upon taking office, Strickland announced he was delaying each of three upcoming executions by about a month to give himself time to review the cases. This action set off alarms for death penalty opponents as well as the law enforcement community, who each saw the inklings of a possible moratorium on the horizon. Strickland dismissed such talk. While saying he was conscious of the numerous examples of exoneration through DNA testing around the country, Strickland was assuredly a death penalty supporter. "If I were to decide I was going to have a moratorium on executions, I would just say so," he said at the time. "People are reading between the lines, and there's nothing written there." True to his word, Strickland allowed two of the three executions to proceed after taking time to review the case files; a federal judge delayed the execution of the third inmate, Kenneth Biros, to allow him to join the injection lawsuit.[26] Moreover, Strickland's commutation of Spirko was not exactly a cry for justice. He rejected Spirko's request for a full pardon and made it clear that problems with the evidence and the "slim residual doubt" about Spirko's responsibility for the crime drove his decision. He also criticized Spirko's claim that his own lies had led to his conviction, calling those arguments unpersuasive. "At times, when he wasn't denying having committed the murder," Strickland's commutation announcement said, "he appears to have admitted doing so."[27]

Only eight years separated Celeste's extension of mercy to eight condemned inmates and the beginning of Taft's streak of twenty-five denials (including Cooey) out of twenty-six requests. But the gulf could hardly be wider and is not likely to be bridged anytime soon. Strickland's long-term approach to clemency remains to be seen, but as his initial actions predict, and as Taft's approach confirmed, the use of clemency as a tool of mercy in capital punishment cases has all but disappeared in Ohio. Its replacement, pro forma requests for executive intervention followed by pro forma rejections of those requests, is far removed from the flexibility that marked the pre-*Furman* decisions by Republicans and Democrats alike.

Last Day

States it was hard coming down this morning because the
sun was shining and he saw a lot [of] new cars for the first
time in eighteen years.

—Notation in a death house log for condemned inmate
David Brewer at 1:39 PM on April 28, 2003, the day
before his scheduled execution

IT IS late November of 2005, and John Hicks is trying to reach his mother.
A recording says her phone isn't taking calls at the moment. It's early, six
o'clock in the morning, but Hicks has already been up almost an hour. He's
shaved, made the bed in his small room, gotten dressed, and then settled in
to read the Bible for a while. He tries his mother again at 6:40 AM, but still
no luck. He decides to take a shower, hoping she'll be available once he is
through. Hicks knows he doesn't have long to reach her. After almost twenty
years in prison, he's scheduled to be executed in just over three hours.[1]

Condemned inmates in Ohio have been waiting behind bars to die since
Edward Stolcupp spent just over two months in a Chillicothe jail in the
summer of 1804, the second year of Ohio statehood, anticipating his
hanging for the murder of Asa Mounts in a fit of jealous anger. Stolcupp
had gone to trial May 14, 1804, for the shooting death of Mounts the previous December and was executed on August 3, 1804.[2]

There is a world of difference between the last day of a condemned inmate then and today—begin with TV and phones—and yet in some ways hardly anything has changed. A stream of visitors still marches in and out of the prison hoping to see the inmate and pay their last wishes. The prisoner waiting to die receives hand-and-foot service that would have been scoffed at during any of his previous days behind bars. Oftentimes a hint of hope remains, the possibility of a last-minute court delay, serving both to mask the purpose of the day and to emphasize its finality even further. An aura of quasi-honor attaches to the condemned killer, who becomes a type of momentary celebrity, a schizophrenic cross between an elder statesman whose every wish is granted and a circus sideshow whose every action is pitied. They are terminal patients without the disease.

Yet some things aren't at all the same, beginning perhaps with the rules surrounding visits and visitors on that last day. Around 1 AM on December 7, 1877, a reporter for the *Columbus Evening Dispatch* went to the Knox County Jail in Mount Vernon to talk with William Bergin, scheduled to die about twelve hours later for the shooting death of Thomas McBride earlier in the year. Bergin waved him off, telling him he didn't want to talk to reporters. The intrepid journalist then gave the somewhat implausible explanation that he wasn't looking for an interview but merely wanted to bid him good-bye, at which point Bergin began to talk about his case and the waiting he'd endured, including the comfort he'd received from various letters, all of which comments conveniently ended up in the paper's next-day account of his execution.[3]

For some lucky inmates, the authorities helped with the press of visitors—up to a point. In Cleveland in 1869, condemned inmate Lewis Davis at first received regular and pleasant visits from his wife, his spiritual adviser—the Reverend A. H. Washburn—friends, reporters, and others while waiting to die for the shooting death of farmer David Skinner during a robbery the previous fall. "Not few have been the expressions of surprise from those who for the first time looked into his face," the *Cleveland Leader* noted. "His deportment to visitors was uniformly courteous and gentlemanly, while his language and manner evinced a degree of refinement which few who entertain the popular idea of such a person would expect." As the week of Davis's hanging arrived, however, the sheriff was besieged with requests from people wanting to visit the unlucky man. "See here,

Mister, I wouldn't mind givin' you four shillins if you'll let me go in there!" one man begged after his request was denied. The sheriff, who received other bribe offers of up to ten dollars, solved the problem by creating a lottery—dropping the names of all who had applied by the Monday before the execution into a hat and then drawing a list of lucky winners. Lucky for them, if not for Davis. "Dire were the lamentations of those who failed to draw prizes," the *Cleveland Leader* noted.[4]

Today's condemned inmate chooses whether to see a spiritual adviser; his counterpart in the nineteenth century may not have had the choice. On Saturday, December 10, 1808, two ministers went to the Adams County jail cell of David Beckett to browbeat him about his continuing allegation that another man was also implicated in the murder for which he was about to hang. After the first minister, Lorenzo Dow, was unsuccessful in his questioning, a second minister, Rev. Robert Dobbins, gave it a try, reminding Beckett how terrible it would be to go before his maker with a falsehood upon his soul. At last Beckett relented and acknowledged that he alone was guilty of the crime. He was then bound and taken to the gallows, where he spoke for forty-five minutes, urging young people to avoid vice, including intemperance, gambling, and poor company, before he was hanged in midafternoon.[5]

Henry Ducolon, sentenced to hang in Toledo for shooting and robbing Frederick Boorman, met with his minister just before his 1865 execution and announced, "I die happy; I could die a dozen deaths for the love of God."[6] But not all inmates were pleased with these ministerial visits. In 1858, a few minutes before Albert Myers was hanged for killing a fellow inmate at the Ohio Penitentiary, the prison chaplain went to visit Myers in his cell "but was repulsed with oaths and abuse" and had to withdraw without achieving whatever goal he had in mind.[7]

The history of inmates' last days is filled with attempts to make their final hours as comfortable as possible. In Cincinnati, as Patrick McHugh awaited his January 25, 1861, execution for killing his wife, Sheriff John Armstrong used his own money to buy anything "which would add to the doomed man's comfort or pleasure during the short time he had to remain on earth."[8] When Ohio was preparing to execute William Wiley and William Haas in the state's first use of the electric chair in 1897, jailers gave them as much to eat as they wanted and allowed them to smoke some fine cigars sent over by the former county treasurer, Samuel Kinnear, who included a note expressing his deepest sympathy.[9] Henry LeCount, who killed a witness whose testimony had sent him to prison for seven years, was so highly regarded by his guards, and his jailhouse behavior was so good, that the guards wept on the day of his execution in late November 1852.[10]

Not all prisoners were content to accept such largesse and wait for their walk to the scaffold. While some attempted suicide—and at least two succeeded—others tried a different type of escape. On July 21, 1869, John Griffin, having lost all legal attempts to avoid his upcoming execution, used as a pretext the departure of a minister who had come to visit him and, seizing the moment when a guard was distracted, made a rush for the door with three other inmates. The attempt was ill-fated. Crowds hearing of the possible escape rushed the prison, and Griffin was back in his cell within fifteen minutes. He was executed eight days later, professing his innocence to the end.[11]

Once Ohio moved executions to the state penitentiary in Columbus in 1885, it performed them on a scaffold in a wing known as the Annex on the far east end of the penitentiary's East Hall. Inmates awaiting execution were housed in a ground floor cell called "No. 1, first A." The night of the execution, they were moved to the cell immediately above it and adjoining the scaffold, "No. 1, second A," known also as the death cell. After 1897, the state moved the electric chair to the space directly under the trap of the gallows. Nearby, but out of sight of the chair, was a large cage where the condemned prisoner would spend his final days. These inmates could request outdoor exercise but to do so had to walk past the electric chair, which was covered in cloth when not in use. As nineteenth-century Columbus historian Marvin Fornshell noted, "What effect this may have upon them is difficult to imagine but it is only reasonable to believe that it is very depressing."[12]

Throughout the twentieth century, the Annex was the scene of prisoners praying, reading the Bible, receiving visitors, and waiting. In early May of 1922, two condemned men, twenty-six-year-old John Valden, of Columbus, and forty-one-year-old George Bush, of Youngstown, both black, each sentenced to die for separate murders, spent several hours each day before their execution reading scripture. On their last day, May 2, they prayed and sang as Bush led them in camp-meeting songs.[13] In 1933, Athay Brown, convicted of killing a Cleveland woman during an argument, spent his last hours meeting with his son and then his wife, Rosie, who was serving time at the state women's prison on a robbery charge. Athay and Rosie chatted for a few minutes, then kissed each other good-bye. Athay eschewed a final meal of his own choosing and instead ate a little of the chicken dinner prepared by the prison for the general population. In his last act, he signed a statement in the presence of a chaplain that his wife was innocent of her crime because he had driven her to his mother's house on the night in question. Strapped into the chair, he lifted his head long enough to stare at the crowd of forty witnesses in the room, including reporters, deputy sheriffs, and prison guards.[14]

On June 7, 1954, the last woman executed in Ohio, Betty Butler, received her final visitors, including her husband, her mother, and her five-year-old daughter and six-year-old son. On Friday, June 11, the day of her execution, she attended a special religious service before the drive from the women's prison to the state penitentiary. She requested only milk, apricots, toast, and scrambled eggs with cheese for her last meal. She walked to the electric chair holding a rosary and wearing a black-and-pink print dress, white oxford shoes, and bobby socks. She was pronounced dead at 8:10 PM after three bursts of electricity over a minute. Robert Griffin, the second-to-last person executed in Ohio under the state's old law, ate a final meal of fried chicken, French fries, and peach pie with vanilla ice cream, smoked cigarettes, and was baptized a Roman Catholic.[15]

In 1972, after the state closed the penitentiary in Columbus, prison officials moved the electric chair and death row to the newly opened Southern Ohio Correctional Facility in Lucasville at the far southern end of the state. The state housed condemned inmates in a separate wing at Lucasville for the next twenty-three years, including in 1978, when the U.S. Supreme Court's decision in Lockett v. Ohio emptied death row. After the 1981 law was enacted, inmates were kept in their cells on Lucasville's J Block almost twenty-four hours a day, allowed out briefly three days a week to shower and shave. Lights went on at 6 AM each morning and stayed on until 11 PM at night. Cells were empty but for a cot, toilet, sink, and mirror, a polished metal plate bolted to the wall. There was little to do but sleep. Relations with guards could be rocky, and it was not uncommon for some inmates to fill paper bags with feces and urine, then launch them at a passing guard. "Bombing them out," they called it.

Over time, the prisoners slowly gained access to radios, TVs, and daily newspapers from their hometowns. By swapping these papers, some prisoners could read five or six papers from around the state each day. Eventually, inmates were allowed out of their cells for longer and longer periods of time. They gained recreation rights, shooting hoops outside or just jogging around the enclosed basketball court. They got access to a regular library and law library. Dale Johnston, a convicted double-murderer who spent five and a half years on death row in Lucasville before appeals courts reversed his conviction and death sentence, said the worst aspect was the total loss of control. "You ate when they told you to, what they told you to, where they told you to," he would recall. "If somebody really wants vengeance, they don't want the death penalty. They want somebody locked in a cage for the next twenty-five or thirty years of their life. That is true vengeance."[16]

After the 1993 Lucasville riot, the state decided to move death row to Mansfield Correctional Institution while keeping the death chamber in Lucasville. In 2005, the state, its vaunted supermax prison in Youngstown nowhere near capacity and facing continuing tight budgets, decided to move death row again, transferring inmates to the Ohio State Penitentiary in Youngstown, where they remain housed today. (The state's two women on death row in 2007 were imprisoned at the Ohio Reformatory for Women in Marysville, northwest of Columbus.) Today, death row consists of two blocks of 126 cells apiece. Each block is divided into eight pods, fifteen or sixteen cells per pod, one inmate to a cell, with a common area in the middle. Prisoners can be out of their cells several hours a day, either in the common area or in outdoor recreation sessions scheduled three times a day. (In 2004, two inmates used this opportunity to climb up drifts of accumulated snow in an unsuccessful escape attempt using ropes they had constructed of sheets and black electrical tape.) Visitors come Wednesday through Sunday from 8 AM to 2:30 PM. There is a phone in each pod for collect calls. Seventy-two hours before a scheduled execution, the prison puts an inmate on twenty-four-hour watch.[17] After resuming executions in 1999, Ohio carried out the sentences in the evening, consistent with the practice from decades ago. But concerned about the effect of the long days on staff and the cost of overtime, the state ended that practice after the second execution, that of Jay D. Scott, and now schedules the executions for 10 AM.

In 1879, Cleveland inmate Charles McGill spent his months in jail reading, receiving visitors, writing letters, and penning his autobiography, including an account of living with the woman he left his wife and children for, Mary Kelley, who became a prostitute after McGill abandoned her; later he would hunt her down and shoot her as they lay together in "Laura Lane's temple of lust." Despite the passage of time, note how similar McGill's days awaiting execution were to those of Joseph Clark, sentenced to die more than a century later for killing gas station attendant David Manning during a 1984 robbery. "I spend my days talking to friends. Playing chess, playing cards. That's during the day. At night I do a little reading. I read the Bible. I write letters."[18]

Christopher Newton, another volunteer, who was sentenced to die for killing a prison cellmate over a chess game (he became enraged when Jason Brewer, his fellow prisoner, kept giving up whenever Newton placed him in check), spent his time before his 2007 execution relaxing as much as possible, listening to music, and reading the Bible. James Filiaggi, convicted of chasing down his ex-wife and shooting her as she cowered in a neighbor's house, watched the Cleveland Browns and the Ohio State football team on TV, suffering along with the rest of Ohio at the university's 41–14 drubbing at the hands of the University of Florida in the 2006 national championship game. Stephen Vrabel, the killer who stuffed his girlfriend and daughter in the freezer, read court decisions, including the Supreme Court rulings on his own case, and watched a lot of television. To his surprise, he enjoyed it. "My life is watching TV," he would observe. "There's a lot of good shows on TV."[19]

Reading, watching TV, playing cards, and listening to music are common throughout Ohio prisons, but no one pretends that death row is the same as other cellblocks. In normal prisons, an inmate's departure has a much different meaning than the exit of a prisoner from death row. And the wait is always on death row inmates' minds, far different than the dragged-out discipline of doing one's time for a noncapital offense, a wait accelerated and painfully enhanced by the imposition of an execution date. As Jerome Campbell put it after his sentence was commuted in 2003,

"When you're given a date at Mansfield, every day, no matter how much you try not to think about it, you're thinking, 'I've only got twenty days left, ten days left.'"[20]

One of the things inmates must do during those last days is formulate the statement they will make, if they choose, in their last minutes. As we have seen, these proclamations could take up much of an afternoon in the nineteenth century as inmates took the opportunity to plead their case one last time, proclaim their innocence, or use their circumstances to warn others away from a similar fate. "My heart it was blacker than the blackest hat you ever saw," Return Ward, hanged in Toledo in 1857 for the murder of his wife, said during a long, rambling speech to about fifty witnesses gathered inside the jail yard. "But now I am going to heaven, where I hope to see you all."[21]

Statements in the modern death penalty era are far less theatrical and tend, for the most part, to reflect the quiet, aseptic events that executions have become. The process is simple: once the inmate is strapped down, the warden leans forward, positions a microphone above the prisoner's face, and asks if the prisoner has anything to say. The prisoner's response at that moment has varied wildly over the years.

Wilford Berry chose to say nothing at all. The next man to die, Jay D. Scott, said simply, "Tell my family and friends I send my love. Don't worry. Tell them I'm all right." Ernest Martin, executed in 2003 for killing a store owner during a robbery, spoke for about three minutes, calmly likening himself to Jesus Christ, and said he was being put to death on the basis of false testimony. John Byrd, who acknowledged his participation in the death of Monte Tewksbury but denied actually killing him, was angry and defiant. "The corruption of the state will fall," he said. "Governor Taft, you will not be re-elected. The rest of you, you know where you can go." (Taft, reelected in 2002, authorized twenty-two additional executions after Byrd's.) In 2004, asked if he had any last words, William Zuern, being put to death for stabbing a prison guard, said, "Nope." In 2005, William Smith said during a four-minute final statement, "I accept this responsibility and I ask you to forgive me and my sins against others." He continued, "I don't consider this to be the right thing but the Lord has put his burden on me and I accept this responsibility." It remains one of the longest speeches since Ohio resumed executions. Newton, his execution delayed by more than an hour while guards tried to find a vein, was less solemn. "Yes, boy, I could sure go for some beef stew and a chicken bone. That's it."[22]

Although the Department of Rehabilitation and Correction has always been careful in what it says about an inmate's final twenty-four hours, an archive of material exists that offers a detailed look at what happens to prisoners from the time they arrive at Lucasville until their deaths. After Ohio resumed executions in 1999, the state began documenting prisoners' last days down to the minute and second through a computer log kept by a rotating team of guards who sit just outside the holding cell down the hall from the death chamber. The state has compiled logs for all twenty-six executions, as well as a twenty-seventh log for Richard Cooey, who came within hours of execution in 2003 before winning a delay. These logs document everything that happens right up until a funeral director leaves with the body following the execution.

Some of the logs show inmates accepting responsibility for what they did. Scott Mink was sentenced to death in 2001 for beating his sleeping parents to death the year before for money to feed a drug habit. He dropped his appeals and was executed in 2004, the fastest time between sentencing and execution under the new law. At 7:16 AM on July 20, 2004, three hours and eleven minutes before Mink is executed, the log notes, "Family members tell I/M [for inmate] Mink how much they love him and he returns the feelings of love for them." When Mink's family members asked him to remember to forgive himself, he said he had. "And he is sorry," the log adds at 7:24 AM.

Other logs indicate little remorse. On October 12, 2004, a guard asked Adremy Dennis if he needed anything. "A chopper out of here," Dennis replied with a laugh. Convicted of shooting an Akron man in his driveway in a 1994 robbery, Dennis blamed the victim for disobeying an order not to move. Dennis's log also records a substantial last meal (or "special meal," as the prison calls it, since it's eaten the day before an execution): fried catfish, garlic bread, and three pieces of pie—pumpkin, pecan, and sweet potato. He stuffed himself, then talked about being sick to his stomach. At 7:07 AM on October 13, three hours and three minutes before he was declared dead, he took Pepto-Bismol to relieve his stomachache.

The logs show that some inmates sleep fitfully or hardly at all. Herman Ashworth, who beat a man to death in Newark during a robbery, stayed awake from the moment he arrived at the prison at 9:22 AM on September 26, 2005, until he was declared dead at 10:19 AM the next day. He spent his night writing letters, listening to music, watching TV, including *Monday Night Football,* smoking, and drinking Mountain Dew. He showed little emotion until the end when, at 9:09 AM, the log notes that he was "on his knees softly sobbing."

The prison logs also cast daily habits and decisions in a new light. At 4:21 PM on February 18, 2002, a guard put an uneaten salad ordered by John Byrd "in refrigerator for later if he requests it." But in Byrd's case, later never came. One of the first things Joseph Clark did upon waking up on May 2, 2006, his last morning, was to put on deodorant. William Smith, executed March 9, 2005, for stabbing a woman then raping her as she lay dying, cleaned his cell, washed his windows, walls, and doors, then selected a fantasy novel, *Child of Flame,* from the prison library. Laughter is also common, even as execution time nears. "I think I'll have one more cigarette," Mink quipped, "and then quit." His joke came at 9:29 AM, an hour before his death.

While the day of reporters barging into the cells of condemned inmates to bid them farewell is long past, many inmates are in constant communication with friends and family to the end, either through phone calls or by receiving visitors during their last day, many times on the morning of the execution. Willie Williams, of Youngstown, sentenced to die for killing four men execution-style in a dispute over drug territory in a public housing unit, talked on the phone much of the night before he died. He also had twelve visitors during his day in Lucasville, including his mother, his sister, and a niece, the morning he was put to death. "Inmate Williams and mother talking about children that look alike enough to be twins," the log for Williams notes at 7:56 AM on October 25, 2005, less than two and a half hours before he died. In 2007, Filiaggi, who had been a popular student at Ohio University in the early 1990s, received a record twenty-four visitors, many of them former teammates on the university's rugby team.

In the nineteenth century, sheriffs sometimes administered whiskey to nervous prisoners on their way to the gallows. In 1812, the American Indian John Omic grabbed the wooden posts supporting the crossbeam of the gallows in Cleveland and refused to let go until he was given two pints of whiskey. As recently as 1979 in Florida, a warden gave death row inmate John Spenkelink two belts of whiskey before he was executed for killing a traveling companion. In recent years across the country, sedatives and tranquilizers have replaced the belt of liquor to help calm prisoners. At least nineteen of the country's thirty-eight death penalty states now offer sedatives and antianxiety drugs to condemned inmates. Prisoners in eleven of those states took the state up on its offer over the past dozen years. Another four death penalty states prohibit the drugs, including Texas, which has the country's busiest execution chamber.

Florida allows members of the execution team to offer inmates Valium or a related drug two hours before a prisoner is scheduled to die. At least one inmate in Arkansas was prescribed a sedative in recent years. In Montana, condemned killer Duncan McKenzie received the sedative Versed before his 1995 execution. In Mississippi, inmate Bobby Glenn Wilcher took Valium an hour before he was executed on October 18, 2007. He also took the drug the previous July 11, before the U.S. Supreme Court temporarily stopped his execution with thirty minutes to go. In Utah, Joseph Mitchell Parsons received a mild sedative through his IV before the lethal chemicals began flowing prior to his 1999 execution. The remaining states that allow sedation are Arizona, California, Connecticut, Georgia, Indiana, Kansas, Kentucky, Maryland, Nevada, Pennsylvania, South Dakota, and Washington. States willing to talk about the process are transparent in their reasoning. As Brian Hauswirth, spokesman for the Missouri Department of Corrections, put it, "It helps keep the inmate calm and we think that's good, not just for the inmate but for the staff as well."[23]

In Ohio, nine of twenty-six inmates put to death since Ohio resumed executions in 1999 took the medication before they died by injection. Five inmates declined the drugs, and records don't indicate if drugs were offered in the remaining cases. On April 28, 2003, Ohio prison officials gave David Brewer the antianxiety drug Ativan three times the day before his execution and at 6:03 AM the next day, four hours and seventeen minutes before he was declared dead. The other drug most commonly given to condemned inmates in Ohio is Vistaril, an antihistamine sometimes prescribed as a sedative. Such drugs are used frequently because they are on the state's list of medicines that medical staff are allowed to prescribe.

Ohio does not provide details about the drugs and prescriptions, saying they are confidential under state open records law because they are part of inmates' files.

The American Medical Association prohibits doctors from participating in executions but allows them to relieve an inmate's suffering ahead of time, which could include giving someone a tranquilizer. Jonathan Groner, an Ohio State University surgeon who opposes the death penalty and writes frequently about lethal injection, says physicians who prescribe drugs before an execution are in a gray area ethically. "Bringing the physician into arm's reach of the execution chamber lends a veneer of medical respectability to the proceedings," he said. "I'm personally wary of this illusion of medical healing for the purpose of killing." But assistant U.S. attorney William Schenck, a death penalty supporter who as a county prosecutor oversaw David Brewer's execution for choking and stabbing a woman to death, said it's humane to give inmates sedatives if they want them. "There's no reason to torture anyone or make them go through any kind of terrible anxiety before they're executed," he says.

In Ohio, nurses generally deliver the drugs to inmates. The American Nurses Association has some concerns about this process. Laurie Badzek, director of the association's Center for Ethics and Human Rights, says prison nurses should ensure that inmates are evaluated individually and that inmates are not given Vistaril or any drugs on the basis of standing orders. Edwin Voorhies, warden at the Southern Ohio Correctional Facility, said a staff doctor or psychiatrist prescribes drugs to inmates on an individual basis only after closely assessing them to see what their mood is and whether the drugs should be offered. As he described it, "a great deal of effort goes into preparing the condemned felon mentally for what he's about to face. . . . Our goal is to get them to walk peacefully into that chamber."[24] That is usually what happens, whether as a result of medication or for other reasons. As we have seen, only one inmate, Lewis Williams, struggled before dying; coincidentally or not, there is no record of Williams taking any sedatives.

Documents unsealed in 2007 offered additional insights into how the state carries out its executions. The Department of Rehabilitation and Correction had long declined to release its exact protocols, saying they were protected under an exception to the open records law. But two defendants in Lorain County, Ruben Rivera and Ronald McCloud, fought for the documents as part of an unusual motion in their death penalty case (unusual for a county-level trial): they argued that the state's execution process was unconstitutional because it didn't guarantee a quick and painless death. Judge James Burge ordered the state to produce the protocols so he could determine for himself. After the state turned over a 632-page binder of execution procedures to Burge, the *Elyria Chronicle-Telegram* successfully pressed him to release the documents. Among other details, the state's material showed that execution team members undergo training at least four times a year, that at least one member must be a nationally certified pathologist, and that team members practice using an artificial arm they inject with water. The documents also included several booklets on how to administer the drugs and handle the equipment used in the process. One manual written by and for nurses included this advice for someone who can't fix a blocked IV line: "call your surgeon and beg forgiveness." The documents also revealed the signal the warden gives to start the lethal chemicals: he buttons his jacket as he stands by the condemned inmate.[25]

In addition to Lewis Williams and his struggles, two other executions did not go as the state wished. Clark, the Toledo gas station attendant killer, had faced execution longer than all but 11 of the 193 men on Ohio's death row at the time he entered the death chamber in 2006. Before he went to prison, Clark was a drug addict, and the abuse was apparent in his ravaged veins. After Voorhies read the fifty-seven-year-old Clark his death warrant on May 2, 2003, at 9:56 AM, the medical team entered Clark's cell and started working on his arms. It was clear right away that it was not going to be easy. "As an observer for the insertion of the IV catheters, I noted that Mr. Clark's veins were not going to be easy to find," one member of the team would observe later.

It took the team four minutes to place the shunt in Clark's left arm, much longer than the process normally took—in some inmates it was finished inside a minute—but not entirely out of line with the time for other prisoners over the years. At 10:02 AM, the team began working on Clark's right arm and continued without success for twenty minutes to insert the shunt. "Going with one arm," the log for Clark's execution notes at 10:22 AM. The team escorted Clark into the death chamber, strapped him down, and allowed him his last statement, in which he said he had asked God for forgiveness for his crime and also to forgive those participating in the execution. The warden gave the signal for the chemicals to begin flowing at 10:33 AM. At 10:37 AM., Clark pushed himself up on the table, straining against the straps, and announced, "It don't work."

Over the next forty-five minutes the medical team tried to reinsert the shunts as Clark lay on the gurney in a gruesome parody of the patient enduring discomfort from the medical personnel trying to help him. Guards did their best to comfort Clark. "I assisted by holding the inmate's feet, patting them in an attempt to calm him down," one team member wrote in a report about the incident. At one point, a team member rolled up Clark's right pants leg to search for a vein. How much Clark suffered is unclear. Witnesses could hear him moan and groan as team members tried to find a usable vein. Team members noted afterward that he did not appear to be in pain. But he was also ready for the whole thing to end. "Can you just give me something by mouth to end this?" he asked the medical team. They couldn't; state law allowed only one path to death. As the search for a working vein continued, prisons system director Terry Collins ordered the curtain to the adjoining witness room drawn. "I could feel the tension rising inside the viewing chamber, and upon that time closed the curtain," the team member who drew the curtain noted. "I personally felt this was a very wise decision to alleviate extra stress upon all witnesses until the team could determine what happened."

At 11:17 AM, forty minutes after Clark sat up to announce the process wasn't working, the team managed to insert a shunt in his right arm. Collins ordered the curtain reopened and gave the signal to try again. This attempt failed too. A team member noticed Clark move his left foot and realized he'd tried to administer the drugs through the original IV line by mistake. He noted, "Once I switched to proper IV line execution was completed successfully." Nine minutes later, Voorhies announced the time of death as 11:27 AM.[26]

One year and four executions later, on May 24, 2007, execution team members worked almost ninety minutes past their deadline of 10 AM to find a usable vein in the fleshy arms of Christopher Newton, obese at six feet and 265 pounds. But this time, prison workers weren't panicking. Chastened by their experience with Clark, the workers, to avoid problems on the gurney, took their time and did not rush the process in the holding cell. This was according to new execution protocols established after the Clark debacle that allowed the team leeway if problems arose with the veins. The more significant delay came when Newton was finally strapped to the table and Voorhies gave the signal to begin at 11:37 AM. Sixteen minutes passed before the time of death, during which time Newton's stomach heaved, his chin quivered and twitched, and his body twice mildly convulsed within its restraints. It took Newton more than twice as long to die as any other inmate since 1999, far surpassing the average time of seven and a half minutes. Groner, the Ohio State surgeon and student of lethal injection, suggested that the chemicals weren't flowing properly or in the right dosage, since the pancuronium bromide, the second of the three drugs, should have paralyzed Newton. For their part, prison officials did not acknowledge a problem. They produced no incident reports because, as they put it, there hadn't been an incident. The new protocols worked, and although Newton had taken longer to die, there hadn't been a problem on the table as there had been with Clark, they said. As prisons spokeswoman Andrea Dean put it the next day, "The team took as much time as needed to find good veins. There was no artificial time line to hurry up and find veins."[27]

The following month, the family of Joseph Clark sued the state in federal court, charging that his execution had violated his constitutional rights protecting him from cruel and unusual punishment.

———

John Hicks, still trying to reach his mother on the morning of November 29, 2005, has now been on death row for almost twenty years. Twenty years earlier, Hicks, a cocaine addict in Cincinnati, had traded his VCR to drug dealers for about fifty dollars worth of cocaine. After taking the drugs, he realized that he needed to get the VCR back before his wife wondered where it was, so he decided to steal money from his mother-in-law, Maxine Armstrong. Entering her apartment on August 2, 1985, he found his five-year-old stepdaughter, Brandy Green, asleep on the couch. He woke her and took her to bed and then strangled Armstrong, first with his hands and then with a clothesline. He left her apartment with about three hundred dollars and some credit cards and used some of the money to buy back his VCR and buy more cocaine. Hicks then realized that his stepdaughter could identify him as the last person in the apartment. He returned and tried to suffocate the girl, first with a pillow, then finally strangling her with his hands. She struggled, and Hicks covered her mouth and nose with duct tape while she was still breathing. He received the death penalty for the girl's murder.

At 8:08 AM, a guard finally gets Hicks's mother on the phone for him. She and her son talk for four minutes. The conversation over, Hicks asks to speak to Rev. Gary Sims, the prison system's spiritual advisor, who often stays with inmates during their final day at Lucasville. At 8:15 AM, he asks for another dose of Vistaril to calm his nerves and receives fifty more milligrams. He spends the next ninety minutes visiting with Sims and reading the Bible. He goes to the bathroom twice. He sips from a cup of water. At 9:57 AM, Voorhies reads the death warrant to Hicks, and one minute later team members begin inserting the shunts into his arms. They finish the job at 10:08 AM and escort Hicks into the death chamber. He makes a final statement at 10:14 AM. "It begun with a syringe in my arm, and it ends with a needle in my arm," the forty-nine-year-old Hicks says. "It's come full circle. I realize that."[28]

The time of death is 10:20 AM. Relatives of Armstrong who witness the execution say they are satisfied with his death; his actions, they say, were the result of a disregard for life, not the influence of drugs. Hicks is the 999th person to die nationally under the country's modern death penalty laws.

NINE

Freakish or Fair

Some people say they don't believe in capital punishment.
They haven't had murder knock at their door.

—*Nana Young, whose daughter, Laura, was one of two victims
killed in a 1991 robbery at a Columbus restaurant*

JUDGE DANNY Boggs had had enough. The Reagan appointee to the
U.S. Sixth Circuit Court of Appeals in Cincinnati had always been aghast
at the treatment his liberal colleagues on the court had given death
penalty appeals over the years. The court had the reputation as friendly
to such appeals, so much so that proponents like Attorney General Betty
Montgomery publicly criticized the panel as a hindrance to carrying out
capital punishment in the state. Boggs had long been at odds with Judge
Boyce Martin, a Carter appointee and for several years chief judge of the
appeals court. Boggs's frustration came to a head in 2001 as death row
inmate John Byrd waged a series of legal battles to prevent his execution
for the 1983 murder of convenience store clerk Monte Tewksbury. Byrd
had raised a claim of innocence late in the game after an affidavit emerged
from one of the participants in the crime who said it was he, not Byrd,
who killed Tewksbury. (Prosecutors said the codefendant, John Brewer,
was lying to save his friend, and a statement from another codefendant
seemed to back this up.) A three-judge panel initially denied Byrd's

appeal. But on September 11, 2001—a day when other events would overshadow developments in the case—the full court reversed the panel and allowed the appeal to continue. This prompted a blistering dissent from Boggs. "This act was taken in response to no apparent motion, it had no jurisdictional basis, and it was done without providing any notice to some members of the court," he wrote. "What we hold, apparently, is that death-sentenced prisoners need not resort to creative legal tactics to come within this court's jurisdiction. So prisoners may file anything, regardless of statute or prior law, and the en banc court may stay their execution for any length of time it chooses." And then the kicker: "The truth may be that for this prisoner, a majority of the active members of this court would grant a stay based on a hot dog menu."[1]

If Boggs was frustrated at how often the court delayed executions, Martin was fed up with the nature of the cases coming before him and was convinced death penalty laws just weren't working. His response to Martin's hot dog menu was his own dissent in 2005 in the case of Brian Moore, a Kentucky prisoner sentenced to death for killing a seventy-year-old man during a robbery. Two judges, including Boggs, voted to deny Moore's federal habeas corpus appeal. Martin dissented, arguing that Moore deserved a new sentencing hearing to allow details of a horrible childhood to be presented. "I have been a judge on this Court for more than twenty-five years," Martin concluded. "After all these years, however, only one conclusion is possible: the death penalty in this country is arbitrary, biased and so fundamentally flawed at its very core that it is beyond repair." His kicker: "But lest there be any doubt, the idea that the death penalty is fairly and rationally imposed in this country is a farce."[2]

The court's yin and yang approach to capital punishment was exasperating to both supporters and opponents of the death penalty. But they weren't the only ones scratching their heads at the divisions. In 2006, a three-judge Sixth Circuit panel denied a request by cult killer Jeffrey Lundgren to join a federal lawsuit challenging the constitutionality of lethal injection, and Lundgren was executed on October 24 of that year. Yet on December 1, 2006, another three-judge panel delayed the execution of condemned killer Jerome Henderson to allow him to join the same lawsuit. U.S. District Court judge Gregory Frost, overseeing the lawsuit in Columbus, noted this discrepancy with dismay. As a judge, he explained, he was confronted with two different decisions by two different appeals court panels, both concerned with the same legal issues and both reaching completely opposite, unexplained conclusions. Frost went on to say, "This Court's inability to discern the appellate rationale for denying or granting a stay does not promote confidence in the system, does not promote consistency in court decisions, and does not promote the fundamental value of fairness that underlies any conception of justice."[3]

Confidence, consistency, fairness. After more than two hundred years of laws governing the death penalty in Ohio, after more than a quarter century under the state's newest capital punishment law, and after almost thirty executions under that law and with dozens of inmates still facing a death sentence, which is it? Has Ohio's system for providing a just punishment for the worst of the worst killers been fairly implemented? Or is it, in the words of the *Furman* majority more than thirty years ago, still applied in a manner so arbitrary as to be freakish?

In his concurring opinion in *Furman,* Justice William Brennan pointed out the obvious: the United States was executing but a tiny fraction of the people who committed heinous murders or rapes each year. Thousands of such crimes were carried out annually (rape was still a death-eligible crime in 1972), yet states were executing only about fifty individuals a year. "When a country of over 200 million people inflicts an unusually severe punishment no more than 50 times a year, the inference is strong that the punishment is not being regularly and fairly applied," Brennan charged. "When the punishment of death is inflicted in a trivial number of the cases in which it is legally available, the conclusion is virtually inescapable that it is being inflicted arbitrarily. Indeed, it smacks of little more than a lottery system."

Brennan's argument helped sway the court to ban capital punishment as unconstitutional in part because the country's death penalty laws appeared to be applied with no pattern or uniformity. A certain number of murders were committed each year, a certain number of people were sentenced to die for those murders, but there was no logical connection between the two categories. It was a persuasive argument—for four years at least, until *Gregg v. Georgia*—but hardly new. Governors in Ohio had been saying the same thing for more than a century.

In the year 1859, Ohio prosecutors indicted about thirty-six hundred individuals for a variety of crimes committed throughout the state, including about eighty murders. Of that figure, about thirteen hundred were convicted at the end of the judicial process, or just over one of every three criminals initially charged. As Governor Salmon Chase pointed out, the low number of convictions compared to indictments amounted to a defect in the administration of justice. Fixing this problem was not a matter of passing a new law, but rather requiring increased vigilance and firmness by those who carried out the law. However, Chase added, there might be one area where a change in the law was necessary, and that was the way courts dealt with first-degree murder, which carried the possibility of a death sentence. It might be worth authorizing judges at their discretion to sentence defendants either to death or to life in prison. How else to deal with a situation in which juries were apparently acquitting offenders rather than sentencing them to die? In his annual address to lawmakers, Chase said, "I am persuaded that, in many instances, murder escapes all punishment, or all adequate punishment, through the reluctance of juries to find verdicts which must necessarily be followed by sentence of death."[4]

More than fifty years passed in Ohio, and yet this concern persisted. From the years 1900 to 1922, the state saw 1,652 murder convictions. During the same time there were 64 executions, or fewer than 4 electrocutions for every 100 people convicted of murder. In the case of first-degree murder, the ratio was even higher—only 1 of every 5 convictions resulted in an execution. Not infrequently, some of the worst offenders ended up receiving sentences meant for second-degree murders, crimes where the offense was not deliberate or premeditated. And none of these figures, Governor Harry Davis observed in 1922, included the numbers of people who committed murders and either weren't caught or were arrested but, for a variety of reasons, weren't prosecuted. "Under such circumstances," Davis said, "it is not a far-fetched conclusion that the man who plans a murder in cold blood, if he considers at all the possibility of capital punishment, looks upon it as too remote to let it influence him."[5]

This issue of fairness, voiced in the nineteenth century, continues to echo through the twentieth century and into our own time and cuts to the heart of the debate over capital punishment. Is a system that hands down the ultimate penalty to a small—very small—percentage of those eligible for that penalty being implemented fairly? Is the fact that those who receive a death sentence deserve the punishment an adequate process—

regardless of whether others equally deserving do not? Opponents of capital punishment will argue that the low ratio of death sentences to capital crimes is evidence on the face of an arbitrary system. Supporters will argue that just because not everyone who speeds is caught is no reason for police to stop enforcing the traffic laws.

What appears not subject to debate is that capital punishment is carried out unevenly in Ohio and plagued by numerous flaws inherent in a system subject to human error and subjectivity. No one is exempt from this conclusion, whether juror, prosecutor, defense attorney, or judge. Of course, the same could be said of almost all elements of the state's criminal justice system, not just the death penalty system, yet there is no outcry to drastically reform the way we punish criminals not facing execution. The reason for the difference, the reason we need a transparent death penalty system, has been reiterated many times by the U.S. Supreme Court. "Death, in its finality, differs more from life imprisonment than a 100-year prison term differs from one of only a year or two," Justice William Brennan wrote in his dissent in the 1987 case *McClesky v. Kemp.* Death, the court reminds us again and again, is different.

Start with prosecutors, those elected lawyers responsible for bringing accused murderers to justice once police have made an arrest. As we have already seen, state and federal courts have long expressed reservations about their behavior. Twice since 1981, the Ohio Supreme Court chastised prosecutors for going too far in their arguments. The first ruling dealt with a particularly savage murder committed by Rhett DePew in Oxford in southwest Ohio. Late in the evening of November 23, 1984, DePew and his girlfriend, Deborah Sowers, drove to the home of Tony and Theresa Jones looking for money; DePew had once rented space in the basement of the house. Armed with a large knife, DePew entered through the rear door of the house, believing it to be empty, and started his search. As he approached a bedroom, he was unexpectedly confronted by Theresa Jones and other members of her family. He "freaked out" and "just started swinging" with his knife, stabbing Theresa at least fourteen times, her seven-year-old daughter, Aubrey, twenty-one times, and Theresa's twelve-year-old sister five times. DePew then set fire to clothing in Theresa's closet. On his way out he found a baby crying in a back bedroom. In his only act of mercy, he wrapped the child in a blanket and left her on the porch of the house next door. Tony Jones returned from work late that night to find the house in flames; firefighters arriving on the scene discovered the three bodies inside. After his arrest, DePew went to trial in the summer of 1985. As the case proceeded, John Holcomb, the Butler County prosecutor, declared at a pretrial hearing that he did not care whether DePew received fair treatment. He later told the jury of an alleged knife fight that had not been introduced in evidence as a sign that DePew was guilty of wrongdoing. He also showed a photograph of DePew next to a marijuana plant, a picture irrelevant to the charges before the jury, and in his closing arguments suggested that any sentence less than death could result in parole.

On appeal to the Ohio Supreme Court, DePew argued that these comments and activities constituted such grave misconduct that it called his entire conviction and sentence into question. Justice Andy Douglas, a Democrat from Toledo, found them to be harmless and outweighed by the overwhelming evidence against DePew. But he went on to say that the issue of lawyers' behavior could not be ignored. "While the prosecutorial misconduct in this case does not require a reversal of appellant's sentence," Douglas wrote in the court's August 31, 1988, opinion, "we express our mounting alarm over the increasing incidence of misconduct by both prosecutors and defense counsel in capital cases." For two justices, however, Douglas did not go far enough. Herbert Brown and Craig Wright both dissented, saying the prosecutors' misconduct was so egregious that DePew's death sentence should be reversed. Wright called it "prosecutorial conduct of the worst sort," and concluded, "Once again, the majority denounces the prosecutorial misconduct obvious in this case, but allows it to continue unheeded, permitting the state to further chip away at the right to fundamental due process and a fair trial."[6] Ultimately, the federal courts agreed with DePew's arguments and threw out his death sentence; he was resentenced in March 2005 to three consecutive life terms.

In his opinion, Douglas pointed out that prosecutors, defense attorneys, and judges all needed to do a better job making sure capital trials were conducted fairly. Eleven years later, in the Angelo Fears case, the court revisited the issue again and expressed, if anything, deeper concerns with the way prosecutors were handling cases. "While we realize the importance of an attorney's zealously advocating his or her position, we cannot emphasize enough that prosecutors of this state must take their roles as officers of the court seriously," Justice Francis Sweeney wrote in the court's September 8, 1999, decision upholding Fears's conviction and death sentence. "As such, prosecutors must be diligent in their efforts to stay within the boundaries of acceptable argument and must refrain from the desire to make outlandish remarks, misstate evidence, or confuse legal concepts."

The evidence of misconduct in Fears's case included making fun of Fears's defense attorney, introducing past evidence of other misdeeds by Fears in violation of trial procedure, and giving the jury false information—such as wrongly alleging that Fears pistol-whipped a robbery victim. All this was too much for Chief Justice Thomas Moyer, who voted to overturn Fears's death sentence. Time and time again, Moyer complained, the court had raised the issue of prosecutorial misconduct. Time and time again, he said, the court had given prosecutors the benefit of the doubt and said their bad behavior wasn't enough to change the outcome of a trial. But despite all the court's efforts to set limits and warnings against inappropriate conduct, Moyer said, some prosecutors continued to unabashedly cross the line of vigorous but proper advocacy. The result had the most dire of implications, he said: "In doing so, they taint the fairness of our criminal justice system."[7]

As Douglas pointed out in the *DePew* case, prosecutors weren't the only ones to blame. From the earliest days of the new law, poorly paid defense attorneys with no training in capital punishment cases had been doing their best—or worst—representing defendants. Their efforts were often minimal and based in large part on the number of cases they needed to carry to make a living. David Doughten, the veteran Cleveland defense attorney, says many good lawyers simply won't take the cases because of the amount of work and meager remuneration. He puts it bluntly: "The majority of people on death row who shouldn't be on death row is the fault of the defense bar and that vestige still exists today."[8]

In fact, a review of Sixth Circuit decisions overturning death sentences finds that since 1981, the court has overturned thirteen of those sentences because of poor legal counsel, or 61 percent of all such sentences it reversed during that time period. By contrast, only two of the reversals cited prosecutors' mistakes. In July 2007, for example, the court overturned the 1985 death sentence of Dewaine Poindexter out of Hamilton County, condemned to die for fatally shooting his ex-girlfriend's boyfriend, saying attorneys hadn't done enough to turn up evidence that could have persuaded a jury not to sentence Poindexter to death. This pattern led Boggs to suggest in 2006 that defense attorneys were better off doing a purposely shoddy job of representing a death row client in the hope of getting a reversal than actually trying to put on an adequate defense. His comments won a sharp rebuke from his Sixth Circuit colleague Judge Martha Craig Daughtrey, who said that defense attorneys "representing the absolute pariahs of society are frequently hamstrung by a critical lack of relevant experience, an obvious lack of time and resources, or both."[9] Ohio is not alone in this situation. The Ninth U.S. Circuit Court of Appeals, whose jurisdiction includes California, blamed inadequate representation in twelve of the twenty-five death sentences it has overturned under that state's new law.[10]

By the mid-1980s, the state supreme court had become so concerned about the quality of representation available to death row inmates that it created a committee to study the problem and come up with solutions. The committee's response, adopted in 1987, was Rule 20, a set of basic criteria for defense attorneys who wanted to be certified as capital lawyers in the state. Chief among these criteria are a series of seminars on capital cases that lawyers must take before becoming certified. The creation of Rule 20 addressed a fundamental problem with the law in the early days, which boiled down to a lack of experience on all sides of the death penalty system, from judges to prosecutors to defense attorneys. But by its very nature this rule couldn't deal with other serious issues, such as pay and the stress of handling such cases. In 2003, a survey by the state supreme court committee overseeing Rule 20 found that attorneys still felt pay was inadequate for representing inmates in capital cases both at trial and on appeal to the supreme court. Attorneys also felt judges weren't appointing lawyers to such cases in "a fair and equitable manner." Worse, the survey found a sharp decline in the number of attorneys handling death penalty appeals after a conviction. In 1995, 207 lawyers were certified as appeals attorneys, a figure that dropped to 143 by 1999 and 117 by 2003, the year of the last report on Rule 20. (The number was down to 110 by 2007.) The report blamed pay and the requirement that lawyers file their arguments with the supreme court just three months after the official notice of a conviction reaches the court. Now that Ohio had entered the age of executions, the report concluded, keeping Rule 20 strong was as important as ever. The question raised by this conclusion, of course, is whether the state's capital defendants are getting the very best representation if pay is still a top concern of those being asked to defend them.[11]

This brings us to judges, who must oversee the unwieldy and complicated arena that is a modern death penalty trial, a combustible mix of crusading prosecutors, overworked defense attorneys, struggling jurors, perpetrators of horrific crime, and courtrooms full of grieving people, sometimes on both sides of the case. The record on judicial misconduct is thin, in part because they are mere referees watching over the actions of players whose mistakes are the ones that count, and perhaps in part because those who rule on misconduct—state and federal appeals court judges—may be reluctant to criticize their fellow jurists.

But beyond any error a judge may or may not commit, or allow, he or she is granted one option under Ohio law that can greatly influence the outcome of a capital punishment trial. The law says that a judge cannot sentence "up," that is, change a life sentence to death, but the judge can sentence "down," that is, overrule the jury's death sentence. This is an exceedingly rare occurrence in Ohio, but it has happened, and more than once or twice. Eight times since 1981, county judges, who are elected and must face the consequences of their actions in the courtroom, have nonetheless weighed the evidence before them and rejected a jury's death sentence for a lesser punishment, usually life in prison with no chance of parole.

The first time it happened, in 1983, the state's law was just two years old when Judge Nicholas Holmes of Ross County Common Pleas Court rejected the death sentence for Drewey Kiser, who had been convicted of fatally shooting Don Writsel during a robbery. Holmes cited Kiser's age—he was twenty-three at the time of the murder—lack of a significant criminal history, and a mental-illness diagnosis of alcoholism. Holmes also pointed out that a death sentence would not have been proportional to the three other death sentences in Ohio at the time. "It is not the act of murder in its various forms which must be weighed by the Court," Holmes concluded. "Rather, it is the circumstances surrounding the act which must be weighed against the circumstances of the actor at the time of the murder."[12]

The last time this happened to date in Ohio was in 2002, when an Ashland County judge overturned the death sentence of a man convicted of shooting his estranged wife. But we must look at one earlier reversal to see this judicial option in the full context of whether Ohio's system is fair. Christopher Fuller, of Hamilton, had committed a crime shocking to even the most hardened of sensibilities, killing his two-year-old daughter after trying to rape her. He was tried and sentenced to death in 2000. But Judge Matthew Crehan of Butler County Common Pleas Court took another look at the case. He examined Fuller's job supporting his family, his military service, his lack of a prior criminal record, and the remorse he showed over the girl's death. He concluded, referring to his decision, "By not following the jury's recommendation of death, you will be sentenced to spend the rest of your life in prison with little to think about but what you did to that little girl."[13]

To opponents of the death penalty, Crehan's decision was a wise and brave exercise in judgment that looked at the totality of facts in the case and rose above a knee-jerk desire for vengeance for such a young victim. But where are supporters of the death penalty left by such a ruling? How to accept a system that allows a killer like Christopher Fuller to go free? Aren't such crimes, which tear a jagged hole in the basic fabric of society, the type of behavior the death penalty was created to deal with?

Crehan's ruling also reminds us of the role of juries in capital cases, a role so enormous as sometimes to be overlooked while we focus on how good a job the prosecutors, defense attorneys, and judges do. The judgments of juries underscore the disparities in the capital system, especially when jurors convening in the same county around the same time reach different conclusions about death-eligible crimes. In 2003 in Franklin County, that geographic stronghold of moderate juror behavior in the face of immoderate crime, two separate juries sentenced James Conway to death not once but twice. It was a rare instance of someone facing execution for two unrelated capital murders. (In the first crime, Conway stabbed a man to death with a pickax in 2001 for fear he'd snitch about Conway's involvement in a shooting. In the second crime, Conway shot and killed an innocent bystander in 2002 when a fight erupted outside a strip joint between Conway's gang and another group.) Both Conway and his victims were white. Two years later, another Franklin County jury spared Vernon Spence for killing three young people execution-style at an apartment near Ohio State University, a botched drug robbery that had sent shock waves through the community. Spence was black, his victims, including a twenty-one-year-old woman, were white. Leading up to the trial, prosecutors offered plea bargains to Spence's codefendants to build their case against Spence. But in the end the jury, while convicting Spence of the crime, couldn't reach a consensus about death in this most brutal of killings. As county prosecutor Ron O'Brien would say, reflecting on the outcome, the system as it is constructed allows one member of a jury to have a pocket veto, "for good, bad or illegitimate reasons."[14] All that must happen in a capital case is for a juror who felt one way while being quizzed by attorneys before selection to have a change of heart once the time for making the ultimate decision arrives.

In the case of Conway and the pickax murder, jurors both black and white were able to sentence him to death even though the killing was largely a dispute between fellow criminals. In the case of Spence, a single vote, that of an African American juror, was enough to spare Spence even though the killings involved three largely innocent victims (Spence and his codefendants had robbed them of five pounds of marijuana and seventy dollars in cash). Former Franklin County Judge Dale Crawford, who presided over both cases, has long watched the effects of race, gender, emotion, and other factors play out in jurors' decisions in capital cases. Ohio law requires jurors to sentence someone to death if they find that the aggravated factors in a crime outweigh any evidence in favor of the perpetrator of the crime. But jurors don't always follow that law, Crawford reflects. As a result, the jury system does produce different outcomes. To erase those differences is to eradicate the system. "When we put the people through this horrible, horrible process to decide whether someone lives or dies, we're asking them to do something they're not trained for and could never have anticipated what they're going to go through," Crawford says. "We have to be prepared to accept the results of that process. If we don't like the results, we need to change the process."[15]

The more closely we examine the capital punishment system in the state, the more results we find we might not like, whether it's a crime that deserved a death penalty where the offender escapes death, or a crime whose conduct was less heinous but where the result was a sentence of death nonetheless. Sitting on Ohio's death row in 2007, for example, were two men convicted and sentenced in murder-for-hire schemes. In Trumbull

County in 1995, Jason Getsy was hired by John Santine to kill a business rival; as the crime unfolded, Getsy shot and wounded the rival, Charles Serafino, and killed his mother, Ann Serafino. Getsy, just nineteen at the time, was the only one of four people implicated in Ann Serafino's death to receive the death penalty.

Two years later, in Hamilton County, Ahmad Fawzi Issa was allegedly hired by Linda Khriss to kill her husband, Maher Khriss, owner of Save-Way Supermarket. Issa provided weapons to a man named Andre Miles, who robbed and then shot and killed both Maher Khriss and his brother, Ziad, on the evening of November 22, 1997. In the subsequent legal proceedings, Linda Khriss was acquitted, Miles was sentenced to life in prison, and Issa—who, unlike Jason Getsy, didn't actually kill anyone—was sentenced to death.

In Getsy's case, a three-judge panel of the Sixth Circuit found the disparity in sentencing too great and, on August 2, 2006, rejected the death sentence. Wrote Judge Gilbert Merritt, "This is a contract murder case with irreconcilable jury verdicts leading one defendant to be sentenced to death and another—the defendant who initiated, contracted for, and paid for the murder—to be sentenced to life imprisonment." The court also upheld a rare instance of alleged misconduct by a judge. The trial judge had socialized with the assistant prosecutor leading the case against Getsy by attending a party during the trial. That was enough to warrant a hearing on the alleged misconduct. A year later, reflecting the deep divide on the court, the full Sixth Circuit voted 8 to 6 to overturn the panel's decision and reinstate Getsy's death sentence.[16]

In Issa's case, the state supreme court upheld his death sentence despite the disparity in sentencing. As Justice Andy Douglas observed, the court had ruled previously that such a disparity is not enough to overturn a sentence if the sentence is not illegal or an abuse of discretion. He wrote in the court's 2001 decision, "We find that the penalty imposed in this case is neither excessive nor disproportionate when compared with other capital cases in which an aggravated murder was committed for hire."

Not unexpectedly, Justice Paul Pfeifer found this reasoning specious, as he pointed out in his dissent. The facts were clear, he noted: "Issa did not kill; Issa was not present during the killing; the actual killer did not receive the death penalty. If ever a sentence of death deserved to be vacated because of proportionality, this is it."[17]

Once again, two sentences of death that seem fair to neither side of the capital punishment debate. For those who support capital punishment, what comfort is there in the fact that John Santine—who planned the Serafino killings in detail—escaped death row, while the teenager who pulled the trigger did not? For those who oppose the death penalty, how fair is it to express outrage that Ahmad Fawzi Issa received a death sentence when the alleged mastermind of the plot and the man who carried out the killings did not?

As we have learned, more people in Ohio end up on death row for killing a white person than for killing a black person. This suggests an uneven outcome for black victims of violent death, who deserve justice no matter the color of their skin. It also suggests, contrary to popular belief, a system that may be lenient on black defendants, since the majority of black homicide victims are killed by fellow blacks. As we have also seen, half of all the state's capital cases, charges meant for the worst of the worst, end in plea bargains, including deals for those accused of extremely heinous crimes. This suggests an uneven outcome for perpetrators dependent on factors that may have little to do with the nature of the crime and everything to do with how an individual prosecutor decides to proceed. And as we have also seen, one's likelihood of receiving a death sentence in Ohio varies dramatically based on where the crime is committed. This suggests an uneven outcome based purely on the politics of terrain.

Many prosecutors, the courts tell us, are guilty of misconduct in how they have handled trials whose outcome is literally a matter of life or death. Many defense attorneys, the courts also tell us, perform so badly on behalf of their clients that the defendants they represent are denied a fair trial. Judges, as we have seen, are occasionally guilty of injecting human bias into a system of laws and rendering decisions that reject the consensus of a community as embodied in a jury of ones peers. Jurors, with no training and a complex system of legal requirements to follow, sometimes choose to follow their hearts instead of the law.

The evidence is overwhelming: the death penalty law in Ohio, crafted more than twenty-five years ago with the best of intentions, after a thorough debate by representative government, in the hope of its being an equitable tool for punishing the worst of the worst, has been implemented in an uneven fashion from its earliest days. One need look no farther than Hamilton County in the southwest and Cuyahoga County in the northeast to see the truth of the matter for oneself.

The morality of that unevenness is an entirely different question, and one that is not the subject of this book. Suffice it to say that the proper outcome when one person kills another in a manner the state deems worthy of a possible death sentence has been left up to local communities for the duration of human history, not to mention the blip of Ohio's two-hundred-plus years on the scale of time, and that outcome will always be different from place to place and murder to murder. What is clear, however, is that this unevenness should be as much a concern for those who favor a system that sentences certain killers to death as those who oppose such an approach. If the system is so imbalanced, both sides must ask, what is the purpose of the law to begin with?

As former Ohio governor Thomas Herbert wrote, when he decided to commute the capital sentence of a convicted murderer whose accomplice had not received the death penalty, "'I am impelled to commute the sentence of Ames [to the same sentence received by his cohort] not for any sympathy for Ames, but in order that it may not be said that Ohio failed in comparative justice.'"[18]

The Future

Life without parole means it's over. The only way they'll get out is in a pine box or if the governor lets them out.

—*Don White, Clermont County prosecutor*

ON NOVEMBER 13, 2002, Representative Jean Schmidt, a Republican lawmaker from southwest Ohio, held a news conference at the Ohio Statehouse to promote a bill making a change in sentencing guidelines for cases of aggravated murder. With her were Clermont County Prosecutor Don White and Angela Wilson, whose fifteen-year-old son, Christopher Alford, had been murdered two years ago that day. Schmidt was promoting a bill, dubbed the "Chris Alford law," that would give judges a new sentencing option in cases involving a charge of aggravated murder without an accompanying death penalty factor such as rape or robbery. The idea was to provide the second-harshest penalty under Ohio law after a death sentence without the added burden of proving a capital case. The concept seemed a fair enough alternative for prosecutors seeking to resolve a heinous murder case without having to accept a lesser sentence carrying the possibility of parole. The proposal may also bring the state another step closer to the end of the death penalty.

As history makes clear, predicting the demise of capital punishment is hardly new. In 1836, the Ohio House judiciary committee concluded that many of the state's most intelligent and patriotic citizens were opposed to the death penalty. The "time may indeed be rapidly approaching," the committee reported, "when its repeal may be accomplished, with the approbation of a majority of the people."[1] Governor Harry Davis uttered similar sentiments almost a century later. "I believe the public is gradually awaking to this fact," he said in 1922, "That the death penalty is serving no purpose, (except dispensing with the necessity of feeding, housing and providing work for the prisoner) which cannot be accomplished with much better effect in the interest of society, by imprisonment, and the public's will to abolish executions will be expressed in many states before many more years."[2] Forty-two years later—during which time Ohio put 229 men and three women to death—Governor Michael DiSalle wrote that it "is gratifying to know that the last barbaric relics of the Middle Ages are beginning to recede into their own darkness; that in our own time we may expect to see the twilight of hopelessness transformed into the dawn of hope; that the time may not be far off when we can say to those who have stumbled in the shadows, 'Night need not fall.'"[3]

Since DiSalle wrote those words, Ohio has seen its death row emptied twice—in 1972 after *Furman* and in 1978 after *Lockett*—only to be quickly filled up again. There is no clamor to end capital punishment. Lawmaker Shirley Smith's death penalty study bill died three times, had a brief moment of success in 2004 when anti–death penalty liberals and pro-life religious conservatives teamed up to approve the measure in the House, then skidded to a halt in the Senate the next day where the Senate president said the bill wouldn't advance. Republican governors George Voinovich and Bob Taft supported the death penalty, as does Democratic Governor Ted Strickland, who says, simply, "This is the law of the state of Ohio."

For those who wish to end capital punishment, therefore, the front door still appears closed. The back door of the death penalty system is another matter. If the news of the early 2000s was the speedy resumption of executions in Ohio, the story by the end of the decade may be the shrinking of the pool of applicants. Executions in Ohio have proceeded at a fairly steady rate, between four and six a year for the past few years.

But death row, meanwhile, is getting smaller. The population was above 200 in the years when Ohio resumed executions after the thirty-six-year gap. Today it hovers near 180. Executions are partly to blame for this drop: twenty-six deaths in eight years is not an insignificant number. Court decisions taking inmates off death row also play a role, as do natural causes; when multiple killer Jerry Hessler, of Columbus, died of a heart attack in 2003, he was not the first death row inmate to expire for health reasons. But most significantly, in a correctional version of birth- and death-rate demographics, the row is not filling up as quickly as it is emptying out.

Beginning in 1996, Ohio lawmakers for the first time allowed juries and judges to consider life without parole (LWOP) as an option in capital cases. The impact was clear and immediate. In 1996, counties sentenced eighteen offenders to death. In both 2006 and 2007, that figure had fallen to four. The popularity of this alternative sentence was no surprise. Public opinion polls, which consistently show high support for the death penalty, also find that that support drops considerably when respondents are presented with LWOP as an option. (It drops even farther with the option of life without parole plus a requirement that inmates provide restitution for the relatives of their victims, an option not currently available in Ohio.)

This brings us back to the Chris Alford law. Having a new avenue for dealing with murder cases, prosecutors appear to be decreasing their use of the death penalty right from the start, especially with those cases that might have been on the edge of qualifying for a death penalty indictment in the past. From 2000 through 2004, capital indictments across the state ranged from a low of eighty-two in 2001 to a high of ninety-seven in 2004, according to data collected by the state supreme court. In 2005, the figure dropped to seventy-three, then fell further to fifty-five in 2006 before leveling off to sixty-six in 2007. Meanwhile, the number of life without parole sentences rose by more than two-thirds in the three years since the law took effect compared with the three years before, when forty-five inmates entered prison with the permanent life sentence.[4]

One of the most dramatic decreases was in Franklin County, where indictments dropped from an annual rate well above twenty to just five each in 2005 and 2006 and to only three in 2007. County prosecutor Ron O'Brien says the law is now one of several factors that he considers in a new approach to capital punishment. Previously, O'Brien's office focused only on the elements that make a case eligible for a death penalty. Called aggravating factors, those include other crimes committed during homicides, such as rape, robbery, or burglary, as well as whether the victim was a child or a police officer. Today, O'Brien also looks at factors that could cause a jury to have mercy on a defendant—such as the perpetrator's age, mental health, criminal background, and upbringing, as well as the strength of the evidence—before deciding whether to bring a possible death penalty charge. "We want to try to focus on those cases that are the worst of the worst homicide defendants that are death penalty eligible, and cases where we believe a jury will return a death verdict," O'Brien says.[5]

These significant sentencing changes are of little comfort to those already on death row. But the alternative offered by the Chris Alford law, along with the option of LWOP, are a sign that the future of the death penalty may be less an abrupt end than a slow withering. As the late State Public Defender David Bodiker reflected, "I think it's becoming less attractive. I think the public has grown tired of the constant argument about whether it works or doesn't."[6]

Corresponding with these reductions were dramatic legal developments on the state and national level. In September 2007, the U.S. Supreme Court agreed to hear the first challenge to a method of execution since 1879, when it upheld Utah's use of the firing squad. The appeal came from two inmates on death row in Kentucky, Ralph Baze and Thomas Clyde Bowling Jr., who claimed that lethal injection as practiced by the state amounted to cruel and unusual punishment, in violation of the Eighth Amendment.[7] The decision to hear the case created a de facto moratorium on executions across the country that lasted almost seven months. On the same day that the court accepted the case, the last inmate put to death in 2007 died when Texas executed Michael Richard, 49, for a 1986 shooting. Over the next several weeks, the high court put some executions on hold while lower courts around the country did the same in anticipation of the arguments in early January for and against lethal injection. As a result of this unofficial moratorium, the number of executions nationally in 2007 dropped to forty-two, the lowest in thirteen years. Meanwhile, the approximately 110 death sentences imposed across the country were the lowest number in thirty years.[8] This pause in executions, unprecedented in the modern history of capital punishment, lasted until April 16, 2008, when a divided U.S. Supreme Court upheld the Kentucky process of putting people to death. Writing for the majority in the 7-to-2 decision, Chief Justice John Roberts said that the protocols followed by Kentucky were sufficient to safeguard against a mishandling of the drugs that could constitute a violation of the Eighth Amendment. Petitioners had "not carried their burden of showing that the risk of pain from maladministration of a concededly humane lethal injection protocol, and the failure to adopt untried and untested alternatives, constitute cruel and unusual punishment," Roberts wrote.[9] Although Justice John Paul Stevens concurred with the majority, he also said for the first time he believed the death penalty was unconstitutional. He based his position on a similar finding by Justice Byron White in the court's 1972 *Furman* ruling, which he quoted: "I have relied on my own experience in reaching the conclusion that the imposition of the death penalty represents 'the pointless and needless extinction of life with only marginal contributions to any discernible social or public purposes.'"[10] Within days of the ruling several states indicated they were lifting their moratoria, and on May 6, 2008, Georgia executed the first inmate of the post-Baze era. But the nation's high court was not finished with the death penalty. If the Baze decision was a victory for death penalty supporters, the court's second major ruling on capital punishment in 2008 bolstered opponents. On June 25, a strongly divided court struck down a Louisiana law permitting the death penalty for the rape of a child who did not die. The 5-to-4 decision effectively concluded the work the court began in 1977 when it rejected the death penalty for the rape of adult women. In his opinion for the majority, Stevens said he couldn't discount the years of anguish that would follow the rape of a child. But he went on: "Evolving standards of decency that mark the progress of a maturing society counsel us to be most hesitant before interpreting the Eighth Amendment to allow the extension of the death penalty, a hesitation that has special force where no life was taken in the commission of the crime."[11]

Adding to the national drama were major developments in New Jersey and Nebraska. When New Jersey voted to abolish its death penalty in the closing days of 2007, it became the first state in decades to take such action. Although New Jersey hadn't executed anyone in years, the move was startling given that capital punishment still receives widespread, though narrowing, support across the country. In Nebraska, the state supreme court in February 2008 ruled that electrocution—the state's only method of execution—constituted cruel and unusual punishment. That left the fate of ten death row inmates up in the air as the state and defense attorneys argued over whether the men could ever be put to death under the state's current law.

In Ohio, an injection lawsuit similar to the Kentucky challenge contends that one of the three drugs used in the injection process, pancuronium bromide, known by the trade name Pavulon, could leave inmates conscious before they die. By the end of 2007, federal judge Gregory Frost had allowed twenty inmates to join the lawsuit, first brought by inmate Richard Cooey in 2004, which challenges the constitutionality of lethal injection based on the Eighth Amendment prohibition against cruel and unusual punishment. Similar challenges across the country had temporarily halted executions in California, Missouri, and Maryland, among other states, before the Supreme Court's Baze decision froze capital punishment altogether. The Cooey injection lawsuit was still pending in the summer of 2008.

As we have already seen, Lorain County Common Pleas Judge James Burge ordered the state to produce its protocols for executing inmates after two offenders facing death penalty trials argued that death by injection constituted cruel and unusual punishment. Then, on June 10, 2008, Burge ruled the state's injection process was unconstitutional because two of the drugs used—pancuronium bromide, which causes paralysis, and potassium chloride, which stops the heart—can cause pain. It was an unusual decision for a trial court, and even Burge conceded he did not believe the ruling would affect executions in Ohio unless it persuaded the legislature to change the wording of the injection statute.[12] Yet the Burge decision, along with the high court's Baze ruling and the Cooey lawsuit, presented one more complication to the state's continuing pace of executions.

As 2007 came to a close, two high-profile death penalty cases in Ohio neared conclusions that would raise new doubts about the implementation of capital punishment in the earliest years of the law. After years of appeals, death row inmate Ken Richey, sentenced to die for a 1986 fire that killed a two-year-old girl in Putnam County, finally won release after federal courts said his lawyers mishandled his case; expert defense testimony, the courts said, could have contended that the fire wasn't intentionally set. In the Van Wert County case of John Spirko, years of DNA testing by the state ended with the attorney general's announcement that investigators had failed to find anything that matched Spirko to the crime scene. This bolstered what his attorneys had long argued, that he was innocent of the crime.

Even as we predict the future of capital punishment, those whose lives were wrapped up in the death penalty system over the past four decades must carry on regardless of what happens. In Akron, the children of slain pawnbroker Sydney Cohen still contend with their loss more than thirty years after Sandra Lockett, her brother, and their New Jersey acquaintances tried to figure out a way to raise some quick cash. Cohen's daughter, Arlene Schwartz, says the events surrounding her father's death are still too painful to recount. Lockett herself was left permanently debilitated by her experience. After she was freed from death row in 1978, she still had several years to serve on the charge of murdering Cohen. Finally released in 1993, she reentered the world with few friends, no money, and no skills. She worked briefly for Cleveland defense attorney David Doughten but found it hard to adjust to a regular schedule. In 1995, she was sentenced to thirty-two days in jail for stealing cosmetics at a drugstore. She struggled with a drug addiction and missed parole meetings and counseling sessions. Eventually she was sent back to prison in 1997 on parole violations, getting out in 2003 with few prospects. Today she lives in Akron on disability and is trying to write a book about her experience. "I just take life one day at a time," she says.[13]

Leonard Jenkins, the first man condemned under the new law and one of eight whose sentences were commuted by Governor Richard Celeste, remains in prison. Celeste became ambassador to India, then took a job as president of Colorado College, where he still serves today. The relatives of Wilford Berry Jr. live quietly in Ashland, Ohio; the relatives of his victim, Charles Mitroff Jr., including his children, have scattered around the country, and now only his sister and widow are left in the Cleveland area. The parents of Emily Murray, who live in Cold Spring, New York, are still involved in their efforts to spare Gregory McKnight from execution. Paul Pfeifer remains a justice on the supreme court, along with Chief Justice Thomas Moyer. Richard Finan, forced out of the legislature by term limits, is a consultant and lobbyist in Columbus. Bob Taft teaches education policy at the University of Dayton. Betty Montgomery, after a stinging defeat in November 2006 in her effort to regain her old job as attorney general, is a lawyer running her own consulting firm, also in Columbus. State prisons director Reggie Wilkinson, at the time the longest-serving prisons chief in the country, retired in 2007 and shortly afterward announced his opposition to the death penalty, saying it was no longer needed given the option of sentences such as life without the possibility of parole.

Favoring capital punishment or opposing it, the architects and engineers of the state's death penalty law have a variety of views on the future of executions. Wilkinson says it could be decades, if ever, before the system is abolished, a move that will depend on several factors. "It depends on positions that prosecutors take. It depends on positions that judges will impose. It depends on how the media portrays it. It depends on how well educated people are on justice in general," he says. Pfeifer is convinced the law has been applied too broadly, to the types of cases, such as domestic disputes, it wasn't intended to cover. Where the future is concerned, he says, it may be time for a change. "I think it well to ask ourselves if we are well served as a nation and well served as a society by continuing to have the death penalty," he says.[14]

Where Pfeifer questions the need for capital punishment, a surprising prediction of its demise comes from no less than Moyer. "The fact that death penalty cases are decreasing in Ohio does not trouble me," the chief justice says in an interview for this book. "I was never one who thought it was just wonderful to put someone to death." He goes on to say that he will not be surprised if in the future the death penalty was reserved for a far more limited number of crimes than it is today. In fact, he says, "I would not be extremely surprised if the death penalty were abolished in Ohio so long as life without parole was maintained." The key, he says, is what appears to be a changing sentiment in the community, as more and more people come to feel that spending the rest of your life behind bars is suitable punishment for taking a life.[15]

As we have seen, predictions of the collapse of capital punishment are neither new nor reliable. A majority of Ohioans still support the death penalty today, as have three of the last four governors and both chambers of the legislature along bipartisan lines. As Taft reflected, "In the immediate foreseeable future I don't think it should change." Juries still impose death sentences in the state, albeit more rarely, and those sentences are mostly upheld by the state's highest court, including by Pfeifer and Moyer. There are also societal factors, some deeply engrained in the American character, that weigh heavily against abolition. As Montgomery says, "There's always going to be a case out there that screams out for what appears to be an obvious death penalty application and it's going to be very hard for the policy makers to just ignore that." Those cases could include multiple killings, the death of a child or a pregnant woman, or the death of a police officer. A murder in a small town or less populated county may bring a far louder cry for the ultimate justice than in a big city. And there is no surer predictor for changes in attitudes toward capital punishment than fluctuations in the crime rate. As defense attorney David Stebbins notes, there are events on the streets of every community that could reverse the current trend toward seeking and imposing fewer death sentences. The decline in such sentences will continue, he says. "But it will be a long time before you see states like Ohio and Texas back away completely from the death penalty."[16]

The comments of Moyer and Pfeifer, along with developments in the law and in the courts, suggest it's worth paying close attention to this latest round of forecasting. For proponents of capital punishment, the possibility exists of a greatly restricted law reserved, as lawmakers originally envisioned, for the very worst of the worst and no one else. For opponents of the death penalty, DiSalle's dawn of hope may be a ways off, but for the first time since the de facto moratorium of the 1960s, the sky may be again growing lighter.

Executions in Ohio, 1803–85

The information in this appendix comes from the Espy File.

Adams County

David Beckett, white, hanged December 10, 1808, for killing his traveling trader companion, John Lightfoot, by beating him to death with an axe

Allen County

Andrew Brentlinger, white, hanged April 7, 1872, for stabbing his wife to death

Ashland County

Charles Steingraver, white, hanged January 30, 1852, for killing ten-year-old Clarinda Vantilburg

William H. Gribben and George A. Horn, white, hanged May 16, 1884, for killing Henry Williams

Belmont County

Thomas D. Carr, hanged March 24, 1870, for the murder of fourteen-year-old Louisa Fox

Butler County

George Schneider, white, hanged June 19, 1885, for killing his mother, Margaret Schneider, in a rage over a remark she made about his wife
John Griffin, hanged July 29, 1869, for the murder of Uzile Prickett

Coshocton County

Frank Ept, white, hanged September 29, 1876, for the murder of Abraham Wertheimer, son of the store owner Ept worked for

Cuyahoga County

John Omic, American Indian, hanged June 26, 1812, for killing two white fur trappers
John Hughes, white, hanged February 10, 1866, for shooting his seventeen-year-old ex-mistress, Tamzen Parsons, after she refused to return to him
Alexander McConnell, white, hanged August 10, 1866, for killing Rose Colvin with an axe after she caught him stealing clothes in her boardinghouse
Lewis Davis, white, hanged February 13, 1869, for shooting David Skinner during a robbery
John Cooper, black, hanged April 25, 1872, for killing James Swing after Swing refused to lend him six dollars
Stephen Hood, black, hanged April 29, 1874, for murdering his fourteen-year-old stepson, Greenbury Hood
William Adin, white, hanged June 22, 1876, for the murder of his wife, his stepdaughter, and a woman who had given them shelter
Charles McGill, white, hanged February 13, 1879, for the murder of his ex-mistress, Mary Kelley

Darke County

Monroe Robertson, white, hanged July 16, 1880, for the murder of Wiley Coulter

Erie County

Edward Evans, white, hanged September 30, 1840, for killing merchant John Ritter in front of his store after he refused to sell him whiskey

Fairfield County

David Work, white, hanged October 14, 1836, for the murder of Christopher Hocker (trial moved to Perry County because of "public excitement")

Fayette County

William Smith, white, hanged December 21, 1867, for the murder during a robbery of John Gray for a few hundred dollars in gold and cash

Franklin County

Leatherlips (American Indian, Wyandot), executed by tomahawk in June 1810 for befriending whites
James Clark, white, hanged February 9, 1844, for killing prison guard Cyrus Sells at the Ohio State Penitentiary
Esther Foster, black, hanged February 9, 1844, for killing Louisa White at the Ohio State Penitentiary
Albert Myers, white, hanged December 17, 1858, for the murder of Richard Neville, fellow inmate at the Ohio State Penitentiary
James Greiner, white, hanged October 17, 1885, for the murder of Margaret Seeling

Gallia County

James Lane, executed September 9, 1817 for the murder of William Dowell

Geauga County

Benjamin Wright, hanged May 15, 1823, for the murder of a man named Warner

Greene County

Jesse Ransbottom, white, hanged January 25, 1850, for cutting the throat of his wife, Fannie, in a drunken rage

Hamilton County

Phillip Lewis, black, hanged November 27, 1826, for the murder of Thomas Isdell over an old dispute

John W. Cowan, white, hanged November 27, 1835, for killing his wife, Mary, and their two children with an axe

Byron Cooley, white, hanged November 25, 1837, for fatally shooting John Rambo

John Washburn, white, hanged January 6, 1837, for killing William Beaver

Mathias Hoover, white, hanged June 30, 1837, for killing William Beaver

David Davis, white, hanged June 30, 1837, for killing William Beaver

Henry LeCount, white, hanged November 26, 1852, for the murder of William Clink

Patrick McHugh, white, hanged January 25, 1861, for the murder of his wife

Samuel Case, George Goetz, and Alexander Olgus, white, hanged April 30, 1867 for the murder of James Hughes

George A. Price, black, hanged July 9, 1880, for the murder of his former employer, Villie Black

William McHugh, white, hanged May 2, 1884, for fatally stabbing his wife, Sophie McHugh

Benjamin Johnson, black, hanged September 12, 1884, for beating to death a couple and their adopted daughter, then selling their bodies to a medical college

John Hoffman, white, hanged December 16, 1884, for shooting his son, Edward

Joseph Palmer, black, hanged July 15, 1885, for killing his employer, stables owner William Kirk, for $245

Henry County

Job Cowell, white, hanged August 11, 1865, for the murder of William Treadway, a fellow prison escapee

Wesley Johnson, white, hanged May 29, 1884, for the axe murders of George and Isabella Williams for $26 and a silver watch to support a girlfriend

Hocking County

Elias Primmer, hanged November 26, 1856, for the murder of John Fox

Huron County

Ne-go-sheck and Ne-gon-a-ba, American Indians, hanged July 1, 1819 for the murder of muskrat trappers John Wood and George Bishop

Jackson County

John W. Jackson, white, hanged May 11, 1883, for the murder of farmer Samuel Hull

William Jones and Luke Jones, brothers, white, hanged February 29, 1884, for shooting farmer Anderson Lackey during a robbery

Laban Stevens, white, hanged May 23, 1884, for shooting Anderson Lackey

Knox County

William Bergin, white, hanged December 7, 1877, for shooting Thomas J. McBride

Lawrence County

Andrew Price, white, hanged April 2, 1869, for killing Louis Halgenberg

Logan County

Andrew Hellman, hanged January 12, 1843, for killing his wife and poisoning all but one of his children

Lucas County

Return Ward, white, hanged June 12, 1857, for the murder of his wife, Olive, when she tried to leave him

Michael Beaudien, white, hanged June 24, 1859, for the murder of fellow French settler Antoine Upal

Henry Ducolon, hanged March 24, 1865, for shooting and robbing Frederick Boorman

Mahoning County

Charles Sterling, white, hanged April 21, 1877, for the murder of fourteen-year-old Elizabeth Grombacher

Medina County

Fred Streeter, white, hanged February 26, 1864, for the murder of Shubal Coy, his wife, and their son

Miami County

George Mitchell, black, hanged September 17, 1880, for the murder of his wife, Anna (Stickney) Mitchell

Monroe County

Peter King, white, hanged May 28, 1880, for the murder of David Trembly during an apparent robbery

Montgomery County

John McAfee, hanged March 28, 1825, for the murder of his wife

Francis Dick, white, hanged September 8, 1854, for killing his mother-in-law, Elizabeth Young, and her sixteen-year-old son, Jim

John W. Dobbins, white, hanged April 15, 1864, for killing John Lindenmood

James Murphy, white, hanged August 25, 1876, for the murder of Colonel William Dawson

Harry Adams, white, hanged June 15, 1877, for the murder of Henry Mullharren, a soldier at the national military home

Muskingum County

Solomon Shoemaker, hanged January 12, 1844, for the murder of his brother

Portage County

Henry Aunghst, white, hanged November 30, 1816, for the murder of Epaphras Matthews

David McKisson, white, hanged February 9, 1838, for killing his sister-in-law, Catherine McKisson

Jack Cooper (alias Samuel Wittum), white, hanged April 27, 1866, for fatally beating auctioneer John Rhodenbaugh in a robbery

Putnam County

John Goodman, white, hanged December 30, 1874, for the murder of John and Susan Haywood

Richland County

J. M. Ward, white, hanged June 12, 1857

Edward Webb, hanged May 31, 1878, for the murder of farmer William Finney during a robbery

Ross County

Edmund Stolcupp, white, hanged August 3, 1804, for shooting Asa Mounts

Thomas Dean (alias Henry Thomas), white, hanged March 6, 1846, for killing merchant Frederick Edwards

Perry Bowsher, white, hanged June 21, 1878, for shooting Columbus turnpike toll-gate keepers Ann and Edmund McVey

Sandusky County

George Thompson, white, hanged July 12, 1844, for shooting eighteen-year-old Catherine Hamler for repeatedly refusing his proposals of marriage

John Radford, white, hanged October 12, 1883, for the murder of his wife, Anna

Shelby County

Alfred Artis, black, hanged February 23, 1855, for starving to death his twelve-year-old daughter, Emma, by keeping her chained in a room

Stark County

Christian Bechtel, white, hanged November 2, 1833, for killing his wife with an axe while she slept

G. A. Ohr and George Mann, hanged June 25, 1880, for the murder of John Wattmough during a robbery

John Sammitt, also hanged June 25, 1880, during the same execution, for the murder of Chris Spuhler, an upcoming witness in Sammitt's burglary trial

George McMillan, hanged July 20, 1883, for shooting his wife, Augustine, with whom he frequently argued

Summit County

James Parks, white, hanged June 1, 1855, for killing William Beatson

Henry Hunter, white, hanged November 21, 1871, for the murder of Robert and Elizabeth Gargett, parents of his ex-fiancee, Chloe Gargett

Trumbull County

Ira Gardner, white, hanged November 1, 1833, for stabbing to death sixteen-year-old Frances Maria Bell

Tuscarawas County

John Funston, hanged in New Philadelphia on December 30, 1825, for the murder of William Cartnell, a postboy shot while delivering the mail

Van Wert County

Daniel McGraw, white, hanged in the period 1839 to 1841 for killing a man in a fight at a grocery

Warren County

Samuel Coovert, white, hanged August 24, 1866, for hatcheting to death a farm hand, Jesse Couzens, and three daughters of the Roosa family, Alice Belle, Francis, and an infant girl

Washington County

Hanson Bumgardner, hanged February 15, 1867, for killing John T. Enbanke

Wayne County

John Callihan, white, hanged December 3, 1880, for the murder of John Tormie during a fight at the county fairgrounds

Williams County

Andrew Tyler, white, hanged January 26, 1849, for killing a five-year-old boy whose disappearance he initially helped investigate, claiming to have clairvoyant powers

Wood County

George Porter, white, hanged November 5, 1830, for shooting Isaac Richardson for not paying Porter for work he had done

Carl Bach, white, hanged October 12, 1883, for fatally stabbing his wife, Mary Bach

Wyandot County

Soo-de-nooks, American Indian (Wyandot), executed October 8, 1830, by tribesmen by firing squad for killing Too-ra-hah-tah, another Indian, in a fit of drunkenness

Wyandot Indian, executed by the tribe for killing an elderly Indian man, October 1840

The Eight Ohio Death Row Volunteers since 1999

Wilford Berry, thirty-six, of Cleveland, convicted of the shooting death of his boss, Charles Mitroff Jr., in 1989. Executed February 19, 1999.

Stephen Vrabel, forty-seven, of Struthers, convicted of the 1989 gun slayings of his girlfriend, Susan Clemente, and their three-year-old daughter, Lisa. Executed July 14, 2004.

Scott Mink, forty, of Union, convicted of bludgeoning to death his parents, William and Sheila Mink, in 2000. Executed July 20, 2004.

Herman Dale Ashworth, thirty-two, of Newark, convicted of beating Daniel Baker to death in 1996 in an alley in Newark. Executed September 27, 2005.

Rocky Barton, forty-nine, convicted of the 2003 shooting death of his wife, Kimbirli Jo Barton, forty-four, with a shotgun in 2003 outside their farmhouse in Waynesville, about thirty-five miles northeast of Cincinnati. Executed July 12, 2006.

Darrell Ferguson, twenty-eight, of Dayton, convicted of the Christmas Day, 2001, killing of Thomas King, sixty-one, and the slayings the next day of Arlie Fugate, sixty-eight, and his wife, Mae, sixty-nine. Executed August 8, 2006.

James Filiaggi, forty-one, of Lorain, convicted of killing his ex-wife, Lisa Huff Filiaggi, in 1994. Executed April 24, 2007.

Christopher Newton, thirty-seven, convicted of killing his cellmate, Jason Brewer, while incarcerated at Mansfield Correctional Institution in 2001. Executed May 24, 2007.

Eight Ohio Cases in Which Judges Have Thrown Out a Death Sentence since 1981

1983

Jury's death sentence for Drewey Kiser, of Williamsport, convicted of fatally shooting Don Writsel during a robbery, overridden by Judge Nicholas Holmes Jr. of Ross County Common Pleas Court. Holmes cited Kiser's age (twenty-three), lack of previous significant criminal history, and mental-illness diagnosis of alcoholism. Holmes also pointed out that a death sentence would not have been proportional to the three other death sentences in Ohio at the time.

> It is not the act of murder in its various forms which must be weighed by the Court. Rather, it is the circumstances surrounding the act which must be weighed against the circumstances of the actor at the time of the murder.[1]

1987

Jury's death sentence for defendant Alonzo Wright, of Cleveland, convicted of fatally shooting Grover Lang during a robbery, overridden by Judge Frank J. Gorman of Cuyahoga County Common Pleas Court. Gorman cited the shooting victim's decision to rush Wright instead of obeying a request to look for money.

> It is the Court's considered opinion that, had not the victim charged the defendant, (which he had every right to do,) the victim would still be alive. Under these circumstances, it is the opinion of the Court that the death sentence is not appropriate.[2]

1988

Jury's death sentence for defendant John Parsons, of Worthington, convicted of shooting a man as he fled from his burning home, overridden by Judge Dale Crawford of Franklin County Common Pleas Court. Crawford cited Parsons's background and lack of a prior criminal record and said a death sentence would not be equivalent to five other death sentences imposed in Franklin County up to that time.

> The strength to impose the death penalty is the same strength to deny its imposition in a case where the penalty is not appropriate.[3]

1989

Jury's death sentence for defendant Eddie Robertson, of Dayton, convicted of fatally shooting Stephanie Hiatt in a 1988 robbery, overridden by Judge William MacMillan Jr. of Montgomery County Common Pleas Court. MacMillan cited Robertson's lack of a significant criminal history, his relative youth (thirty), his pursuit of education beyond high school, and the lack of an advance plan to kill anyone. MacMillan said it appeared Robertson shot Hiatt on the spur of the moment, fearing that she recognized him.

> It is this Court's conclusion that the death penalty must be cautiously and sparingly imposed on any fellow human-being. . . .

The present case does not fall within the perceived objective of mandatory destruction of life.[4]

1999

Jury's death sentence for defendant Gregory Crawford, of Valley City, convicted of beating Gene Palmer to death during a robbery, overridden by Judge Mark Wiest of Wayne County Common Pleas Court. Wiest cited Crawford's age (thirty-seven), his good behavior in jail, his strong relationship with his family, his work completing his high school degree, and his conversion.

> The question then becomes, can the court say beyond a reasonable doubt that the commission of a brutal murder in order to avoid being caught for a robbery and burglary outweighs the facts that the defendant has the potential to be a productive inmate and is a loving son, grandson and brother who believes in God.[5]

2000

Jury's death sentence for defendant Christopher Fuller, of Hamilton, convicted of killing his two-year-old daughter after trying to rape her, overridden by Judge Matthew Crehan of Butler County Common Pleas Court. Crehan cited Fuller's job supporting his family, his military service, his lack of a prior criminal record, and the remorse he showed over the girl's death.

> By not following the jury's recommendation of death, you will be sentenced to spend the rest of your life in prison with little to think about but what you did to that little girl.[6]

2001

Jury's death sentence for defendant Timothy Hancock, convicted of killing his prison cellmate, Jason Wagner, at Warren Correctional Institution, overridden by Judge Neal Bronson on technical grounds. Bronson said the jury had improperly received a number of items of evidence, including photos of the victim's body, statements made to police, and the rolled-up bedsheet that Hancock used to strangle Wagner. Bronson resentenced Hancock to death in 2003 after the Twelfth Ohio District Court of Appeals overturned his decision to substitute a life sentence for the jury's recommendation of death.

> Consequently, the court has determined that the sentencing
> phase was a prejudiced proceeding and declares a mistrial in
> that phase.[7]

2002

Jury's death sentence for defendant Brian Siler, of Nankin in Ashland County, convicted of shooting his estranged wife, Barbara Siler, overridden by Judge Jeffrey Runyan of Ashland County Common Pleas Court. Runyan cited a number of factors in Siler's defense, including the absence of a criminal background and active participation in church and the community. Runyan also questioned the burglary charge against Brian Siler—an added count that made the crime a capital case—pointing out that he had broken into his own home. Runyan then questioned whether the death sentence was an attempt by the community to avoid responsibility for failing to do more to prevent Barbara Siler's death.

> The court notes that this case demonstrates a horrible failure by
> this community to deal with the issue of domestic violence. Some
> of this community's finest citizens—clergy, counselors, and
> others were all involved. But none the less, we as a community
> failed Barb Siler. This court asserts that our desire for the death
> penalty is indeed in part an attempt to shift the blame to one
> person, the defendant.[8]

Significant Events in the History of the Death Penalty in Ohio

1788: Marietta Code, first criminal statutes of the Northwest Territory, sets out five crimes punishable by death: treason, murder, arson, burglary, and robbery resulting in death.

1805: Ohio limits death penalty to treason, murder, rape, fatal arson, and maiming.

1815: Capital punishment limited to first-degree murder and treason.

1824: Death penalty limited to first-degree murder.

1836: A House select committee presents a bill proposing to abolish the death penalty, but the motion fails to win approval.

1844: Legislature restricts executions to enclosures near a jail out of public view and limits the number of witnesses.

1850: Delegates to the Constitutional Convention of 1850–51 vote 50 to 34 to reject a proposal that would have abolished capital punishment.

April 29, 1885: Lawmakers vote to move executions to the Ohio State Penitentiary in Columbus.

July 31, 1885: Valentine Wagoner hanged in the prison annex at the Ohio State Penitentiary, the first man hanged at the state pen after lawmakers moved executions to the central location in Columbus.

1896: The General Assembly passes a law requiring all people sentenced to death for crimes committed after July 1, 1896, to die by electric chair.

April 21,1897: William Haas and William Wiley executed for separate crimes, the first to die in the Ohio electric chair.

September 3, 1912: Ohio voters defeat a proposed constitutional amendment to abolish the death penalty 303,246 to 258,706, a margin of 44,540.

December 12, 1938: Anna Marie Hahn, of Hamilton County, is the first woman executed in Ohio in the twentieth century and one of only four to be put to death between 1844 and the present.

1949: Ohio executes fifteen men, the highest number in any year.

1957: Three days before convicted killer Henry Bundy is scheduled to die, new evidence arises that will ultimately exonerate him.

March 15, 1963: Donald Reinbolt, twenty-nine, dies in the electric chair in the Ohio State Penitentiary, the last offender executed by electrocution and the last put to death for thirty-six years.

May 3, 1971: In *Ohio v. Crampton,* the U.S. Supreme Court upholds the right of a jury to sentence someone to death even without concrete instructions from a judge.

June 29, 1972: In *Furman v. Georgia,* the U.S. Supreme Court, by a 5-to-4 vote, declares Georgia's death penalty law unconstitutional, effectively wiping out forty state capital punishment statutes.

July 12, 1972: In *State v. Leigh,* the Ohio Supreme Court, reacting to *Furman,* overturns the death sentence of John Leigh, convicted of fatally shooting a female teller and three woman customers during a bank robbery in Delhi Township in Hamilton County.

January 2, 1974: After a seven-year rewrite of the state's criminal code, Ohio's new death penalty law goes into effect, creating a list of aggravating and mitigating factors that must be weighed before sentencing a defendant to death.

July 2, 1976: In *Gregg v. Georgia,* the U.S. Supreme Court upholds the constitutionality of new death penalty laws in Florida, Georgia, and Texas.

Nov. 24, 1976: In *State v. Bayless,* the Ohio Supreme Court upholds the constitutionality of Ohio's 1974 capital punishment law.

July 3, 1978: In *Lockett v. Ohio,* the U.S. Supreme Court rejects Ohio's first attempt to rewrite its capital punishment law, ruling in favor of Sandra Lockett, sentenced to death for killing an Akron pawnbroker in a robbery. The decision commutes the death sentences of 120 inmates, including four women, to life in prison.

October 19, 1981: Following the court's mandates in *Lockett,* Ohio successfully enacts its modern death penalty statute.

December 17, 1984: The Ohio Supreme Court upholds the new law's constitutionality when it affirms the conviction and death sentence of Leonard Jenkins for killing a Cleveland police officer.

January 10, 1991: In his final days as governor, Richard Celeste commutes the death sentences of four men and four women to life in prison, including Jenkins.

July 7, 1993: New law allows condemned inmates to choose injection or the electric chair.

November 9, 1994: Voters approve a constitutional amendment, dubbed "rocket docket," eliminating state appellate courts from the death penalty process and requiring offenders sentenced to death to appeal directly to the Ohio Supreme Court.

1995: Death row moved to Mansfield Correctional Institution to ease conditions at the Southern Ohio Correctional Facility, site of a prison riot in 1993 that killed a guard and ten inmates.

November 7, 1995: By a vote of 1,791,341 to 732,674, Ohio voters approve a constitutional amendment making it more difficult for a governor to issue blanket commutations to death row inmates.

July 17, 1996: Two years later, lawmakers closed what they considered a formidable loophole in the 1981 law, a measure that required the original jury in a capital case to hear a resentencing. Proponents said ten condemned killers had used a 1987 state supreme court ruling to escape their death sentence on a technicality.

February 19, 1999: Wilford Berry, a volunteer who waived his rights of appeal, is executed by injection, the first man put to death in Ohio since Reinbolt.

November 21, 2001: Governor Bob Taft signs a bill into law removing electrocution as a means of capital punishment.

June 26, 2003: Taft commutes the death sentence of Jerome Campbell to life in prison after questions are raised about evidence introduced at his trial.

2004: Ohio executes seven inmates, second in the nation behind Texas and the most in one year since 1949.

2005: Ohio moves death row to the super maximum-security facility in Youngstown to save money.

June 9, 2006: The execution of Joseph Clark takes more than an hour after an IV fails to deliver the lethal drugs properly because of circulation problems with his veins, damaged by years of preprison drug abuse. The case is cited in lawsuits nationally seeking to declare injection unconstitutional.

NOTES

INTRODUCTION

1. Associated Press, "Civil Rights Group Sues to Make Entire Execution Public," September 26, 2003, AP Electronic News Archive; AP, "Lewis Williams Executed for 1983 Fatal Robbery after Struggle with Guards," January 14, 2004, AP Archive.

2. Ohio Department of Rehabilitation and Correction, execution timeline, Lewis Williams, January 14, 2004, ODRC, Columbus, Ohio.

3. Damian Guevara, "After 21 Years on Death Row, Woman's Killer Is Executed," *Cleveland Plain Dealer*, January 15, 2004.

4. Raymond Paternoster, interview by author, April 14, 2005.

5. AP, "Hundreds of Killers Escape Death Sentences through Plea Bargains," June 6, 2005, AP Archive.

6. AP, "Capital Cases Hard for Smaller Counties," May 6, 2005, AP Archive; David Landefeld, interview by author, June 10, 2004.

7. AP, "Race, Geography Can Decide Death Penalty Cases," May 6, 2005, AP Archive.

8. AP, "Federal Appeals Judge Calls Vote on Execution Illegal," January 15, 2004.

CHAPTER I: EARLY JUSTICE

1. "Executions," *Old School Republican and Ohio State Gazette*, February 9, 1844; "Execution of William Clark and Hester Foster," *Ohio State Journal*, February 9, 1844; "The Hanging," *Ohio State Tribune*, February 10, 1844; Charles C. Cole Jr., "The Last Public Hanging," *Columbus Monthly*, December 1993; Alfred E. Lee, *The History of the City of Columbus* (Columbus: Franklin County Genealogical and Historical Society, 2000), 78, 581; Ed Lentz, *Columbus: The Story of a City*, The Making of America (Charleston, S.C.: Arcadia, 2003), 66; William Martin, *History of Franklin County* (Columbus: Follett, Foster, 1858), 422–23; Dan Morgan, *Historical Lights and Shadows of the Ohio State Penitentiary* (Columbus: Ohio Penitentiary Printing, 1893), 115–17.

2. Robert Francis Harper, *The Code of Hammurabi, King of Babylon, about 2250 B.C.* (1904; repr., Honolulu: University Press of the Pacific, 2002), 118–19; William Seagle, *Men of Law* (New York: Macmillan, 1947).

3. Hayley R. Mitchell, ed., *The Complete History of the Death Penalty* (San Diego, Calif.: Greenhaven, 2001); Michael Kronenwetter, *Capital Punishment: A Reference Book* (Santa Barbara, Calif.: ABC-CLIO, 1993); Stuart Banner, *The Death Penalty: An American History* (Cambridge, Mass.: Harvard University Press, 2002), 6–8.

4. Ohio Legislative Service Commission, *Capital Punishment,* staff research report no. 46, LSC, Columbus, Ohio, 27.

5. Banner, *Death Penalty,* 141.

6. Albert Post, "The Anti-Gallows Movement in Ohio," *Ohio History* 54, no. 2 (1945): 105.

7. Henry Howe, *Historical Collections of Ohio,* 2 vols. (Columbus: H. Howe and Son, 1896), 1:343; L. Edward Purcell, *Who Was Who in the American Revolution* (New York: Facts on File, 1993).

8. Henry A. Ford and Kate B. Ford, *History of Hamilton County, Ohio* (Cleveland, Ohio: L. A. Williams, 1881), 334.

9. A. A. Graham, *A History of Fairfield and Perry County* (Chicago: W. H. Beers, 1883), 45–46.

10. "Execution of Jesse Ransbottom," *Xenia Torch Light,* January 31, 1850; Espy File, data collected by researchers M. Watt Espy and John Ortiz Smylka and made available through the Inter-University Consortium for Political and Social Research, as collected and archived by the Ohio State Public Defender's Office, Columbus, Ohio; "Execution of James Parks," *Cleveland Facts,* June 1, 1855, Espy File.

11. Joseph Antrim, *History of Champaign and Logan Counties* (Bellefontaine, Ohio: Press Printing , 1872), 120–27.

12. Howe, *Historical Collections of Ohio,* 1:497; Crisfield Johnson, *History of Cuyahoga County, Ohio* (Philadelphia, Pa.: D. W. Ensign, 1879), 57, copy in Espy File; Soo-de-nooks file, Espy File.

13. William DeBeck, *Murder Will Out: The Murders and Executions of Cincinnati* (Cincinnati, 1867), 13–15; A. J. Baughman, *History of Ashland County* (Chicago: S. J. Clark, 1909), 119–21.

14. "The Law Violated, The Law Vindicated," *Ohio Liberal,* June 5, 1878, copy in Espy File.

15. "Crime and Casualty," *Ohio State Journal,* May 29, 1880.

16. "The Execution of Albert Myers, the Murderer of Richard Neville," *Ohio State Journal,* December 18, 1858.

17. "Dropped into Eternity," *Ohio State Journal,* October 17, 1885, copy in Espy File.

18. "A Life For a Life," *Coshocton Democrat,* October 3, 1876, copy in Espy File; "Ept's Exit," *Daily Evening Dispatch,* September 29, 1876.

19. "Execution of W. S. Bergin, *Columbus Evening Dispatch,* December 7, 1877; "Mt. Vernon Miscellany," *Columbus Evening Dispatch,* December 8, 1877; "The Execution at Mt. Vernon Yesterday," *Ohio State Journal,* December 8,

1877; H. M. Fogle, *The Palace of Death, or, The Ohio Penitentiary Annex* (Columbus, 1908), 21; "Almost Decapitated," *Columbus Evening Dispatch,* September 30, 1885.

20. "Ben. Johnson, Burker," *Columbus Evening Dispatch,* September 12, 1884.

21. "The Hughes Murderers," *Ohio State Morning Journal,* May 2, 1867.

22. "A Triple Tragedy," *Columbus Evening Dispatch,* June 25, 1880.

23. Fogle, *Palace of Death,* 16–17; "Wagner's Doom," *Columbus Dispatch,* July 31, 1885.

24. "Message of the Governor of Ohio, to the Thirty-sixth General Assembly, Begun and Held in the City of Colu [*sic*] Monday, December 4, 1837," executive documents, annual reports, Ohio Historical Society Archives Library, Columbus, Ohio, call no. FLM 293, reel 1; Post, "Anti-Gallows Movement," 106.

25. *Acts of a General Nature Passed by the Forty-second General Assembly of the State of Ohio* (Columbus: State Printer, 1844), 71; "List of Acts," *Ohio State Journal,* March 9, 1844; Research staff, Ohio Legislative Service Commission, *Capital Punishment,* 9.

26. J. V. Smith, *Report of the Debates and Proceedings of the Convention for the Revision of the Constitution of the State of Ohio,* 1850–51 (Columbus: S. Medary, 1851), 2:22–35.

27. Durbin Ward, *Legislative Report on the Subject of Capital Punishment,* House of Representatives Select Committee on Capital Punishment, March 9, 1853, Ohio Historical Society archives, call no. 343.2 Oh3, 12–13.

28. Cesare Beccaria, *On Crimes and Punishments,* trans. Henry Paolucci (Indianapolis, Ind.: Bobbs-Merrill, 1963), 45, 50.

29. Isaac Wright, *Minority Report, Senate Select Committee on Capital Punishment,* March 6, 1854, Ohio Historical Society archives, call no. Ohio Docs OGA 1:20-4: M666/854, 8–9.

30. "Message of the Governor of Ohio to the Fifty-third General Assembly," executive documents, annual reports, January 3, 1859, 88–89, Ohio Historical Society archives, call no. FLM 293, reel 18.

31. Isaiah Pillars, *Report in Favor of the Abolition of Capital Punishment to the House of Representatives,* 1873, Ohio Historical Society archives, Ohio Docs. OGA, 98.4-1:Ab 154/873, 4.

32. Harry Davis, *Death by Law,* (Columbus: Federal Printing, 1922), 23 (reprinted from *Outlook* magazine).

33. "The Question of Capital Punishment," *Congressional Digest,* August–September 1927, Columbus Metropolitan Library microfilm collection, 235.

34. Legislative Service Commission, *Capital Punishment,* 11.

35. Banner, *Death Penalty,* 184–87; Mark Grossman, *Encyclopedia of Capital Punishment* (Santa Barbara, Calif.: ABC-CLIO, 1998), 140–41; "Death at Last Comes to Wm. Kemmler," *Columbus Evening Dispatch,* August 6, 1890.

36. "William Haas' Last Day," *Columbus Dispatch,* April 7, 1897; "Haas' Unexpected Respite," *Columbus Dispatch,* April 8, 1897; "Quick and Certain Were the Deaths of Haas and Wiley," *Columbus Dispatch,* April 21, 1897.

37. Ohio Department of Rehabilitation and Correction, "Ohio Executions," *Ohio Department of Rehabilitation and Correction,* http://www.drc.state.oh.us/Web/Executed/executed01.htm; Hugo Bedau, ed., *The Death Penalty in America: Current Controversies* (Oxford: Oxford University Press, 1997), 8–11; Legislative Service Commission, *Capital Punishment,* 22.

38. "Grocer Is Found Shot to Death," *Columbus Citizen-Journal,* August 29, 1961; "Grocer's Wallet Found," *Columbus Citizen-Journal,* August 30, 1961; "Grocer's Funeral Thursday," *Columbus Citizen-Journal,* August 31, 1961; "Ex-Con Shows Cops How He Brutally Killed Grocer," *Columbus Citizen-Journal,* September 9, 1961; "State Asks Death in Reinbolt Trial," *Columbus Citizen-Journal,* February 16, 1962; "Jury Deliberates Fate of Reinbolt; Ask Death," *Columbus Dispatch,* February 16, 1962; "Reinbolt Is Found Guilty; Execution Date to Be Set," *Columbus Dispatch,* February 17, 1962; "Reinbolt to Die in Chair Friday," *Columbus Dispatch,* March 15, 1963; "Reinbolt Dies in Chair for '61 Murder," *Columbus Dispatch,* March 16, 1963; "Reinbolt Executed," *Columbus Citizen-Journal,* March 16, 1963; AP, "14 Minutes Reporter Will Never Forget," March 1, 1998, AP Archive.

CHAPTER 2: A NEW LAW

1. "Death Row Erupts in Cheers at Ohio Pen," *Columbus Evening Dispatch,* June 29, 1972; "Lucas County Has 5 on Death Row," *Toledo Blade,* June 29, 1972; "14 from County Escape Death Penalty," *Cincinnati Enquirer,* June 30, 1972; Wink Hess and Tony Mangine, "Local Response to Ruling Mixed," *Columbus Citizen-Journal,* June 30, 1972; Susan Q. Stranahan, "15 from County Escape Spectre of Electric Chair," *Cleveland Plain Dealer,* June 30, 1972.

2. Rudolph v. Alabama, 375 U.S. 889 (1963); Stuart Banner, *The Death Penalty: An American History* (Cambridge, Mass.: Harvard University Press, 2002), 248; Barry Latzer, *Death Penalty Cases: Leading U.S. Supreme Court Cases on Capital Punishment* (Boston: Butterworth-Heinemann, 1998).

3. State v. Crampton, 18 Ohio St. 2d 182, 248 N.E.2d 614 (1969); McGautha v. California, 402 U.S. 183, 207 (1971); AP, "Few Death-Row Inmates to Face Early Execution," *Toledo Blade,* May 4, 1971.

4. AP, "Governor Clarifies Statement on Law," *Columbus Dispatch,* July 27, 1981; Roger Blair, interview by author, December 18, 2006.

5. "Lawmaker to Press Two-Trial Proposal," *Columbus Dispatch,* May 4, 1971.

6. *Bulletin,* 109th General Assembly of the State of Ohio, Regular Session, January 4, 1971, Ohio Historical Society archives, call no. Ohio Docs. 328.771 Oh3l 109th; David Lore, "House Dumps Effort to End Death Law," *Columbus Dispatch,* March 22, 1972.

7. Furman v. Georgia, 408 U.S. 238 (1972).

8. State v. Leigh, 31 Ohio St. 2d 97, 285 N.E.2d 333 (1972); "Bandits Killed His Wife, He Wanted Them to Die," *Cincinnati Enquirer,* June 30, 1972.

9. "Norris Optimistic about Passage of Criminal Code Revision on Bill This Year," Ohio Report, Gongwer News Service, October 31, 1972, vol. 50, report no. 211, 1, archives of Gongwer News Service, Columbus, Ohio.

10. Harry J. Lehman and Alan E. Norris, "Some Legislative History and Comments on Ohio's New Criminal Code," *Cleveland State Law Review* 23 (Winter 1974): 9; David Lore, "Ohio Legislature Approves Revision of Criminal Code," *Columbus Dispatch,* December 15, 1972; David Lore, interview by author, December 3, 2006.

11. State v. Bayless, 48 Ohio St. 2d 73, 357 N.E.2d 1035 (1976); William Canterbury, Charles Montague, and Michael Cull, "Suspect Seized in Slayings of Funeral Director, Wife," *Akron Beacon Journal,* February 27, 1974; "Bayless Will Be Tried as Adult in Slayings," *Akron Beacon Journal,* February 28, 1974.

12. Woodson v. North Carolina, 428 U.S. 280 (1976).

13. David Lore, "Capital Punishment Ruling Hushes Lucasville Death Row," *Columbus Dispatch,* July 3, 1976.

14. State v. Lockett, 49 Ohio St. 2d 48, 358 N.E.2d 1062 (1976); Max Kravitz, Brief for Petitioner, Lockett v. Ohio, 438 U.S. 586 (1978); Sandra Lockett, interview by author, June 21, 2007.

15. Lockett v. Ohio, 438 U.S. 586 (1978); Answer Brief of Plaintiff-Appellee, State v. Lockett, 49 Ohio St. 2d 48, 358 N.E.2d 1062 (1976).

16. Lockett, interview; Brief of Defendant-Appellant, State v. Lockett, 49 Ohio St. 2d 48, 358 N.E.2d 1062 (1976); Bob Von Sternberg and Jan Clark, "Slain Pawnbroker 'Dealt in Humanity,'" *Akron Beacon Journal,* January 16, 1975.

17. Stephan Gabalac, interview by author, November 17, 2006; James Rudgers, interview by author, November 22, 2006; Fred Zuch, interview by author, January 12, 2007; Answer Brief of Plaintiff-Appellee.

18. Max Kravitz, interview by author, November 9, 2006.

19. Ibid.; David Hess, "Supreme Court Airs Lockett Case Appeal," *Akron Beacon Journal,* January 18, 1976.

20. Glenn Waggoner, "Non-triggerman Law Challenged," *Columbus Dispatch,* January 18, 1976.

21. Lockett, 438 U.S. at 633.

22. Richard McBane, "Death Penalty Ruling Sifted for Guidance," *Akron Beacon Journal,* July 4, 1978; Jim Strang, "Ruling Bitter for Widow," *Cleveland Plain Dealer,* July 4, 1978; Graydon Hambrick, "Death Row Inmates, ACLU Jubilant over Ban on Executions," *Columbus Dispatch,* July 4, 1978.

23. Robert Ruth, "House OKs Capital Punishment Bill," *Columbus Dispatch,* February 22, 1979.

24. "Senate Defeats Attempt to Force Vote on Death Penalty Bill," Ohio Report, Gongwer News Service, November 29, 1979, report no. 232, 3, Gongwer archives;

"Second Attempt to Force Senate Vote on Death Penalty Bill Fails," Ohio Report, Gongwer News Service, February 20, 1980, report no. 288, 2, Gongwer archives.

25. Richard Finan, interview by author, November 14, 2006.

26. United Press International, "Senate Rushes into Hearings on Death Penalty Bill," *Columbus Citizen-Journal,* January 7, 1981.

27. Ohio Legislative Service Commission, *Capital Punishment,* staff research report no. 46, LSC, Columbus, Ohio, 40–41.

28. Lawrence Herman, interview by author, December 1, 2006; Robert Ruth, "Death Penalty Actually 'Murder,' Senate Panel Told," *Columbus Dispatch,* January 15, 1981; UPI, "Proposed Death Penalty Bill Is Attacked as Morally Wrong," *Columbus Citizen-Journal,* January 15, 1981.

29. UPI, "Strict Death Penalty Law Urged for Ohio," *Columbus Citizen-Journal,* January 8, 1971; Robert Ruth, "Miller Favors Death Penalty Bill," *Columbus Dispatch,* January 8, 1971; UPI, "Legislators Put Strength in Death Penalty Bill, Drop Plan to Eliminate Juries from Sentencing," *Columbus Citizen-Journal,* January 23, 1981.

30. Robert Ruth, "Testimony Assails Death Penalty," *Columbus Dispatch,* January 29, 1981; AP, "Panel Rejects Life Term as Alternative to Death Penalty," *Cleveland Plain Dealer,* January 29, 1981.

31. Terry Tranter, interview by author, December 3, 2006.

32. UPI, "Death Penalty Bill Modified to Eliminate Jury Sentencing," *Columbus Citizen-Journal,* May 7, 1981.

33. UPI, "Ploy to Cancel Death Penalty Short-Circuited," *Columbus Citizen-Journal,* January 29, 1981; AP, "Panel Urged to Reject Death Penalty Plan," *Cleveland Plain Dealer,* February 19, 1981; "Death Penalty Bill Hearings Conclude," *Columbus Dispatch,* May 22, 1981; David Hartley, interview by author, December 15, 2006.

34. AP, "Bill Reviving Death Penalty Cleared by House Committee," *Cleveland Plain Dealer,* June 4, 1981; William Carlson, "Ohio House Votes 67–31 to Revive Death Penalty," *Cleveland Plain Dealer,* June 11, 1981; Bill Mallory, interview by author, December 3, 2006.

35. Alan Norris, interview by author, January 23, 2007; Harry Lehman, interview by author, February 9, 2007; Tranter, interview.

36. State v. Jenkins, 15 Ohio St. 3d 164, 473 N.E.2d 264 (1984); John Coyne and John Hagan, "Policeman Slain by Bank Robber," *Cleveland Plain Dealer,* October 22, 1981; John Hagan, "Death Row for Jenkins," *Cleveland Plain Dealer,* April 17, 1982.

37. State v. Jenkins, 15 Ohio St. 3d at 204, 473 N.E.2d 300.

38. Ibid., 168; 473 N.E.2d at 273.

39. Ibid., 206; 473 N.E.2d at 301.

40. Ibid., 238; 473 N.E.2d at 325.

41. Ibid., 177; 473 N.E.2d at 279.

CHAPTER 3: THE VOLUNTEER

1. AP, "Ohio Resumes Capital Punishment with Volunteer," February 20, 1999, AP Archive; AP, "Protesters Carry Signs, Hold Candles at Prison," February 20, 1999, AP Archive; Bill Sloat and Mary Beth Lane, "Berry Executed; First in Ohio in 36 Years," *Cleveland Plain Dealer,* February 20, 1999; Ohio Department of Rehabilitation and Correction, Operation Execution, memo, March 10, 1999, ODRC, Columbus, Ohio; Andrea Dean, e-mails to author, January, February, March 2007.

2. Sloat and Lane, "Berry Executed"; JoEllen Lyons, Ohio Department of Rehabilitation and Correction, e-mail to author, August 31, 2007.

3. AP, "Death Row Full Up, but Expansion Planned," March 25, 1988, files of AP Ohio wire, Columbus, Ohio; Dick Kimmins, "Ohio's Chair Upgraded," *Cincinnati Enquirer,* October 7, 1992.

4. Robert Goldberg, Report of Psychological Assessment, court-ordered pretrial assessment of Berry, July 14, 1990, State v. Berry, case no. 93-2592, Ohio Supreme Court, box P108; Sharon Pearson, Psychological Evaluation, competency evaluation commissioned by Ohio Public Defender's Office, State v. Berry, case no. 93-2592, Ohio Supreme Court, box P106.

5. Pearson, Psychological Evaluation, 3, 8; Goldberg, Report of Psychological Assessment, 9.

6. Goldberg, Report of Psychological Assessment, 4; Pearson, Psychological Evaluation, 3, 10; Defendant-Appellant's Response to State of Ohio's 8-20-98 Status Report, State v. Berry, case no. 93-2592, Ohio Supreme Court, box P106, 11.

7. Goldberg, Report of Psychological Assessment, 8; Application for Executive Clemency for Wilford Berry, 5, Department of Rehabilitation and Correction, Ohio Parole Board, January 23, 1998.

8. Pearson, Psychological Evaluation, 6, 8.

9. Berry clemency application, iii; Goldberg, Report of Psychological Assessment, 5.

10. Goldberg, Report of Psychological Assessment, 11, 13; Berry clemency application, 6; Mary Beth Lane, "The Man Who Wants to Die," *Cleveland Plain Dealer,* February 14, 1999.

11. AP, "Ohio Carries Out First Execution since 1963," February 19, 1999, AP Archive; Elaine Quigley, interview by author, March 15, 2007.

12. Richard Bowler, interview by author, February 22, 2007.

13. Ibid.

14. Berry clemency application, 1; Don Bean, "2 Indicted in Killing of Fleet Ave. Baker," *Cleveland Plain Dealer,* December 15, 1989.

15. Don Bean, "Defendant in Baker's Death Decides on Trial by 3 Judges," *Cleveland Plain Dealer,* July 27, 1990; Goldberg, Report of Psychological Assessment, 2; State v. Berry, 72 Ohio St. 3d 354, 356, 650 N.E.2d 433, 435, 437

(1995); State v. Berry, 1993 Ohio App. Lexis 5101, at *5 (judgment affirmed); State v. Lozar, 1992 Ohio App. Lexis 2627 (judgment affirmed).

16. Berry, 72 Ohio St. 3d at 357, 650 N.E.2d 433, 437; Lozar, 1992 Ohio App. Lexis 2627, at *1; William Florio, interview by author, January 24, December 13, 2007.

17. Stan Voorhees, interview by author, February 22, 2007; Berry, 72 Ohio St. 3d at 355, 650 N.E.2d 433, 435–36; Lozar, 1992 Ohio App. Lexis 2627, at *3–4.

18. Berry, 1993 Ohio App. Lexis 5101, at *23–24; Bean, "2 Indicted in Killing."

19. Quigley, interview; Berry, 72 Ohio St. 3d at 359, 361, 650 N.E.2d 433, 439–40.

20. Defendant-Appellant's Response, 11; Berry, 1993 Ohio App. Lexis 5101, at *42; Don Bean, "Jury Recommends Death for Baker's Killer," *Cleveland Plain Dealer,* August 2, 1990.

21. John Hagan, "Teen-Age Killer Sentenced to 53-Year Term," *Cleveland Plain Dealer,* August 16, 1990.

22. Reggie Wilkinson, interview by author, August 2, 2007.

23. Richard Celeste, "Executive Clemency: One Executive's Real Life Decisions," *Capital University Law Review* 31, no. 2 (2003): 139–42; Richard Celeste, interview by author, April 10, 2007.

24. Mary Beth Lane, "Celeste Commutes Eight Death Sentences," *Cleveland Plain Dealer,* January 11, 1991.

25. McCleskey v. Zant, 499 U.S. 467 (1991).

26. AP, "Supreme Court Ruling Gives Go-Ahead for More Executions," June 28, 1996, AP Archive.

27. Betty Montgomery, interview by author, January 29, 2007.

28. Alan Johnson, "Shortening Death Appeals, Linking Schools Proposed," *Columbus Dispatch,* January 6, 1994.

29. AP, "Defense Lawyer, Victims' Mother Differ on Death Penalty Appeals," April 12, 1994, files of AP Ohio wire, Columbus, Ohio; Catherine Candisky, "Victim's Family Begs for Speedy Death Appeals," *Columbus Dispatch,* April 8, 1994.

30. Michael L. Radelet, Hugo Adam Bedau and Constance E. Putnam, *In Spite of Innocence* (Boston: Northeastern University Press, 1992); Thomas Suddes, "Death-Penalty Amendment Advances," *Cleveland Plain Dealer,* May 13, 1994.

31. Callins v. Collins, 510 U.S. 1141 (1994); Mark Costanzo, *Just Revenge* (New York: St. Martin's, 1997), 1.

32. State ex rel. Maurer v. Sheward, 71 Ohio St. 3d 513, 644 N.E.2d 369 (1994).

33. AP, "Convict Wants to Be Executed; Supreme Court Orders Psychiatric Tests," November 29, 1995; Wilford Berry, letters to Chief Justice Thomas Moyer, April 21, 1995, and June 1, 1995, Berry file, Ohio Supreme Court, box P106.

34. Berry, handwritten motions of July 11, 1995, and October 23, 1995, Berry file, Ohio Supreme Court, box P106.

35. Pearson, Psychological Evaluation, 13–14; Mary Beth Lane, "The Life He Wants to Leave," *Cleveland Plain Dealer,* March 1, 1998.

36. Anderson v. Buell, 516 U.S. 1100 (1996); Benjamin Marrison, "Court Says No to Execution," *Cleveland Plain Dealer,* January 25, 1996; Ohio Parole Board, In re: Wilford Berry, report, September 15, 1995, Berry file, Ohio Supreme Court, box P108.

37. Buell, 516 U.S. at 1100 (Scalia, J., dissenting); AP, "Attorney General Looks to End Death Row Stalls," *Cleveland Plain Dealer,* January 26, 1996; Margaret Newkirk, "Execution Watch Likely to Be First of Many Trips to Brink," *Akron Beacon Journal,* January 26, 1996; Mark Weaver, interview by author, April 18, 2007.

38. Pearson, Psychological Evaluation, 20; Robert Alcorn, report to Judge Carolyn Friedland on Berry mental competency, April 9, 1997, 6, Berry file, Ohio Supreme Court, box P106; Phillip Resnick, report to Chief Justice Thomas Moyer on Berry psychiatric examination, April 24, 1996, 7, Berry file, Ohio Supreme Court, box P106.

39. "7 Death-Row Inmates Hurt in Riot," *Cleveland Plain Dealer,* September 7, 1997; Lane, "Man Who Wants to Die"; Ohio State Public Defender staff, interview by author, January 26, 2007; Ohio State Highway Patrol, report of investigation, case no. 97-08170-0200, Ohio Supreme Court, box P108.

40. Alan Johnson, "Death Row Case Is Debated—Again," *Columbus Dispatch,* September 25, 1997.

41. Alan Johnson, "Berry's Family Files Appeal to Halt Execution," *Columbus Dispatch,* February 20, 1998; Jon Craig, "'Volunteer' Threatens Mother," *Akron Beacon Journal,* January 28, 1999.

42. Joe Andrews, interview by author, August 19, 2007; Dean, e-mail, August 20, 1997; Ohio State Public Defender staff, interview.

43. Southern Ohio Correctional Facility, Operation Volunteer, log of Wilford Berry's last twenty-four hours, ODRC, Columbus, Ohio, 7; ODRC, Operation Execution memo; Andrews, interview; Mary Anne Sharkey, e-mail to author, March 9, 2007.

44. Southern Ohio Correctional Facility, Operation Volunteer log, 2; Pearson, Psychological Evaluation, 13; Ohio Department of Rehabilitation and Correction, Reimbursement of Execution for Inmate Wilford Berry, memo, February 25, 1999, ODRC, Columbus, Ohio; AP, "Parole Board Permits Wilford Berry's Execution," February 13, 1998, AP Archive.

45. Southern Ohio Correctional Facility, Operation Volunteer log, 6; AP, "Ohio Resumes Capital Punishment with Volunteer"; Bill Sloat and Mary Beth Lane, "Berry Executed."

46. Quigley, interview; AP, "Berry Was Changed Man before His Execution, Minister Says," February 25, 1999, AP Archive.

CHAPTER 4: THE ROLE OF RACE

1. State v. McKnight, 107 Ohio St. 3d 101, 837 N.E.2d 315 (2005); video archive of oral arguments before the Ohio Supreme Court, March 19, http://www.sconet .state.oh.us/videostream/archives/2005/default.asp#march.

2. Philip J. Schwarz, *Twice Condemned: Slaves and the Criminal Laws of Virginia, 1705–1865* (Baton Rouge: Louisiana State University Press, 1988), 26, 81–82.

3. William J. Bowers and Glenn L. Pierce, "Arbitrariness and Discrimination under Post-*Furman* Capital Statutes," *Crime and Delinquency* 26, no. 4 (1980): 575–76.

4. Ohio Legislative Service Commission, *Capital Punishment,* report, 1971, LSC, Columbus, Ohio, 14; Death Penalty Information Center, http://www .deathpenaltyinfo.org/executions.php.

5. Legislative Service Commission, *Capital Punishment,* 62, 74–75.

6. Espy File, data collected by researchers M. Watt Espy and John Ortiz Smylka and made available through the Inter-University Consortium for Political and Social Research, as collected and archived by the Ohio State Public Defender's Office, Columbus, Ohio; "Death Row Current Residents," "Former Death Row Residents under 1981 Law," data compiled by Ohio State Public Defender's Office, "More Information on Death Row," *Ohio State Public Defender's Office,* http://opd.ohio.gov/dp/dp_Moreinfo.htm.

7. Walter Berns, *For Capital Punishment: Crime and the Morality of the Death Penalty* (Lanham, Md.: University Press of America, 1979).

8. Maxwell v. Bishop, 398 F.2d 138 (8th Cir. 1968).

9. McClesky v. Kemp, 481 U.S. 279 (1987); Stuart Taylor, "Death Case Bias Argued in Court," *New York Times,* October 16, 1986.

10. Hugo Adam Bedau, ed., *The Death Penalty in America: Current Controversies* (New York: Oxford University Press, 1997); Death Penalty Information Center, "The Federal Death Penalty System: A Statistical Survey (1988–2000)," *Death Penalty Information Center,* http://www.deathpenaltyinfo .org/article.php?scid=29&did=196; University of Maryland, "UM Study: Race, Geography Factors in Md. Death Penalty Decisions," news release, January 7, 2003, *University of Maryland Newsdesk,* http://www.urhome.umd.edu/news-desk/SocIss/release.cfm?articleID=265; AP, "Racial Disparities Found in Death Penalty," *Atlanta Journal-Constitution,* January 8, 2003.

11. Rosina Maynard, *Ohio's Other Lottery System: The Death Penalty* (Columbus: Rosina Maynard, 1980), Columbus Metropolitan Library.

12. Bowers and Pierce, "Arbitrariness and Discrimination"; Jefferson Holcomb, Marian Williams, and Stephen Demuth, "White Female Victims and Death Penalty Disparity Research," *Justice Quarterly* 21, no. 4 (2004): 877–902.

13. David Doughten, interview by author, February 4, 2005.

14. John Murphy, interview by author, March 7, 2008.

15. U.S. Department of Justice, Federal Bureau of Investigation, *Crime in the United States,* 2005, Table 3.129.2005, *Sourcebook of Criminal Justice Statistics Online,* http://www.albany.edu/sourcebook/pdf/t31292005.pdf.

16. Ernest van den Haag, "Why Capital Punishment?" in *The Leviathan's Choice: Capital Punishment in the Twenty-first Century,* ed. J. Michael Martinez, William Richardson, and D. Brandon Hornsby (Lanham, Md.: Rowman and Littlefield, 2002), 37; John C. McAdams, "Race and the Death Penalty," in Martinez, Richardson, and Hornsby, *Leviathan's Choice,* 176.

17. Grand jury indictments against Gregory Stamper and James White, case nos. 95CR 11-6280, November 3, 1995, and 96CR 11-6471, November 27, 1996, Franklin County Common Pleas Court records; Stamper and White plea bargains, November 20, 1996, and September 16, 1997, Franklin County Common Pleas Court records; "1 Sentenced, 1 Nabbed in Deaths of 2 Others," *Columbus Dispatch,* November 21, 1996; "Murder Suspect Pleads Guilty after Key Testimony," *Columbus Dispatch,* September 17, 1997; Sandra Craig, interview by author, May 14, 2004.

18. State v. Jackson, 92 Ohio St. 3d 436, 751 N.E.2d 946 (2001); "Jury Recommends Death for Killer," *Columbus Dispatch,* January 30, 1998; "Judge Sentences Killer to Death," *Columbus Dispatch,* February 20, 1998; Doug Stead, interview by author, February 3, 2005; Don Schumacher, interviews by author, May 8, May 18, 2007; Franklin County prosecutor's office, e-mail to author, June 14, 2007.

19. Bostic testimony, State v. McKnight, trial transcript, case no. 01-CR-7230 (2001), 995–1087, Ohio Public Defender's Office, Columbus, Ohio; Kevin Mayhood, "Woman Recalls Watching Slaying in '92," *Columbus Dispatch,* December 23, 2000; Frank Hinchey, "Though Miles Apart, Families United by Grief over Lost Kin," *Columbus Dispatch,* April 1, 2001; McKnight, 107 Ohio St. 3d 101, 837 N.E.2d 315.

20. Appellant's Merit Brief, November 3, 2003, State v. McKnight, Ohio Supreme Court, Columbus, Ohio, 3.

21. State's Memorandum Opposing Appellant's Motion for Reconsideration, December 10, 2005, State v. McKnight, Ohio Supreme Court, Columbus, Ohio, 19.

22. McKnight, 107 Ohio St. 3d 101, 116–17, 837 N.E.2d 315, 338–39; State v. McKnight, trial transcript, case no. 01-CR-7230 (2001), 67–68, 354–72.

23. "State's Memorandum," 9; State v. McKnight, 107 Ohio St. 3d 101, 114, 837 N.E.2d 315, 336.

24. "State's Memorandum," 19; State v. McKnight, trial transcript, case no. 01-CR-7230 (2001), 360.

25. "State's Memorandum," 5; State v. McKnight, 107 Ohio St. 3d 101, 118–19, 837 N.E.2d 315, 339.

26. State v. McKnight, 107 Ohio St. 3d 101, 102–4, 837 N.E.2d 315, 326–27.

27. Timothy Gleeson, interviews by author, May 8, 2007, and May 14, 2007.

28. Kathleen Murray Sworn Statement, October 22, 2002, State v. McKnight, Ohio Supreme Court, Columbus, Ohio; Gleeson, interview by author, August 22, 2007.

29. State v. McKnight, trial transcript, case no. 01-CR-7230 (2001), 369, 1020, 1077; Tom and Cynthia Murray, interview by author, August 20, 2007.

30. Gleeson, interview, May 8, 2007; "State's Memorandum," 7, 21.

31. Murray, interview.

CHAPTER 5: THE BARGAINING OF DEATH

1. AP, "Hensley: 'I Turned into Something I Couldn't Control,'" April 4, 2000, AP Archive.

2. Ibid; AP, "Man Pleads Guilty to Killing Girls, Bible Studies Teacher," March 7, 2000, AP Archive; Steve Wearly, interview by author, June 18, 2007.

3. Wearly, interview; James Stevenson, interviews by author, October 8, 2003, and June 5, 2007; Mark Kimbler, interview by author, January 5, 2004; Christine Henderson and Glenn Daniel, "No Hensley Trial Means Cost Savings for County," *Sidney Daily News,* March 9, 2000.

4. U.S. Department of Justice, Federal Bureau of Investigation, *Crime in the United States,* 2002, Table 5.46.2002, http://www.albany.edu/sourcebook/pdf/t5462002.pdf.

5. Doug Stead, interview by author, February 3, 2005.

6. AP, "Hundreds of Killers Escape Death Sentences through Plea Bargains," June 6, 2005, AP Archive.

7. AP, "Death Penalty Frequently Sought, Rarely Imposed in Franklin County," April 4, 2004, AP Archive.

8. Nebraska Crime Commission, *The Disposition of Nebraska Capital and Non-capital Homicide Cases (1973–1999): A Legal and Empirical Analysis,* October 10, 2001, 21–22,66–67, http://www.ncc.state.ne.us/documents/other/homicide.htm; Russell Stetler, "Commentary on Counsel's Duty to Seek and Negotiate a Disposition during Capital Cases," *Hofstra Law Review* 31, no. 4 (2003): 1157; Capital Defender Office, "Capital Punishment in New York State: Statistics from Eight Years of Representation, 1995–2003," August 2003, http://www.nycdo.org/8yr.html; Alan Finder, "Death Penalty Is Challenged in State Court," *New York Times,* October 15, 1998; "New York's Capital Mistake," *New York Times,* November 27, 1998.

9. AP, "Hundreds of Killers"; AP, "Man Who Gave Plea Bargain to Green River Killer Dies," May 26, 2007, AP Archive.

10. Stevenson, interviews.

11. AP, "Man Pleads Guilty to Killing 4 People," February 4, 2001, AP Archive; AP, "Hundreds of Killers."

12. Joe Deters, interviews by author, October 7, 2003, and June 3, 2005.

13. AP, "Hundreds of Killers"; David Doughten, e-mails to author, June 5, 2007, and June 6, 2007; David Stebbins, e-mail to author, June 6, 2007.

14. Wearly, interview; Steve Wearly, e-mail to author, August 23, 2007.

15. Kort Gatterdam, interview by author, June 5, 2007; Stevenson, interview, June 5, 2007.

CHAPTER 6: GEOGRAPHY AS JUDGE

1. Hayley R. Mitchell, ed., *The Complete History of the Death Penalty* (San Diego, Calif.: Greenhaven, 2001), 24.

2. University of Maryland, "UM Study: Race, Geography Factors in Md. Death Penalty Decisions," news release, January 7, 2003, *University of Maryland Newsdesk,* http://www.urhome.umd.edu/newsdesk/SocIss/release.cfm?articleID=265"; AP, "Racial Disparities Found in Death Penalty," *Atlanta Journal-Constitution,* January 8, 2003; Rick Halperin, Texas Coalition to Abolish the Death Penalty, e-mail to author, November 28, 2007.

3. AP, "Analysis Shows Varied Application of Death Sentence in 1983 Cases," August 22, 2005, AP Archive.

4. AP, "Groups Demand Stop to Executions in Ohio," May 19, 2005, AP Archive.

5. Don Schumacher, interview by author, May 8, 2007; Ron O'Brien, interview by author, June 18, 2007.

6. AP, "Death an Unlikely Sentence for Cutts," September 2, 2007, AP Archive.

7. Jack Palmer, "Felony Sentencing Philosophy Reflects Community Values," *Defiance Crescent-News,* April 30, 2007; David Webb, interview by author, June 19, 2007.

8. "Maximum Fee Schedule by County—Trial Level," Ohio Public Defender's Office document; AP, "Capital Cases Hard for Smaller Counties," May 6, 2005, AP Archive Perry Ancona, interview by author, June 19, 2007.

9. County Commissioners' Association of Ohio, State Reimbursement to the Counties for the Defense of Indigent Persons, 2005 memo to the House Transportation and Justice Subcommittee, CCAO, Columbus, Ohio.

10. Carmen Marino, interview by author, April 12, 2007.

11. Memorandum and order, March 24, 2006, D'Ambrosio v. Bagley, case no. 1:00 CV 2521, U.S. District Court, Northern District of Ohio, Cleveland.

12. Arthur Ney, interview by author, June 19, 2007.

13. Ohio Parole Board, In re: John William Byrd, Jr., #175145, clemency report, August 23, 2001, ODRC, Columbus, Ohio; Greg Meyers, e-mail to author, August 23, 2007.

14. Steve Eckstein, interview by author, June 8, 2004.

CHAPTER 7: DIMINISHING MERCY

1. Ohio Parole Board, In re: Jerome Campbell, #A211-228, clemency report, May 2, 2003, ODRC, Columbus, Ohio; State v. Campbell, 2003-Ohio-3201, 3–4; State v. Campbell, trial transcript, case no. B-8900095 (1989), 1143.

2. State v. Campbell, Defendant's Exhibit I, Exhibit J, Application for Executive Clemency for Jerome Campbell, April 18, 2003, Ohio Public Defender's Office.

3. AP, "Governor Grants Clemency for First Time," June 26, 2003, AP Archive; Campbell clemency report, 7.

4. Herrera v. Collins, 506 U.S. 390 (1993); Dan Kobil, "The Quality of Mercy Strained: Wresting the Pardoning Power from the King," *Texas Law Review* 69, no. 3 (1991): 569–641.

5. State v. Woodard, 68 Ohio St. 3d 70, 623 N.E.2d 75 (1993).

6. Ohio Adult Parole Authority v. Woodard, 523 U.S. 272 (1998).

7. *A Pen Picture of Newark and Vicinity as It Appeared in* 1818 (Columbus: Columbus Printing Company, 1887), 29–31; *Allen County Directory* (Lima, Ohio: Stanley and Keator, 1878), 140, copy in Espy File, data collected by researchers M. Watt Espy and John Ortiz Smylka and made available through the Inter-University Consortium for Political and Social Research, as collected and archived by the Ohio State Public Defender's Office, Columbus, Ohio; "A Fiend's Fate," *Columbus Evening Dispatch,* July 9, 1880; "A Triple Tragedy," *Columbus Evening Dispatch,* June 25, 1880.

8. "Smith's Neck Saved," *Ohio State Journal,* April 29, 1891; "The Governor's Reasons," *Ohio State Journal,* April 30, 1891.

9. Michael DiSalle, *The Power of Life or Death* (New York: Random House, 1965), 57–58.

10. Ibid., 5, 204.

11. Ibid., 47–58; "Slayer Saved from Chair; Is Given Life," *Columbus Dispatch,* April 22, 1960.

12. DiSalle, *Power of Life or Death,* 27–28, 58.

13. Ohio Governor Pardon Record, 1963–75, 103, Ohio Historical Society Archives, call no. series 669, copy BV2936.

14. Lee Leonard, "Death Penalty's Revival Generated Heated Debate," *Columbus Dispatch,* February 20 1999.

15. Richard Celeste, "Executive Clemency: One Executive's Real Life Decisions," *Capital University Law Review* 31, no. 2 (2003): 139–42.

16. Richard Celeste, interview by author, April 10, 2007.

17. Cathleen Burnett, *Justice Denied: Clemency Appeals in Death Penalty Cases* (Boston: Northeastern University Press, 2002); Austin Sarat, *Mercy on Trial: What It Means to Stop an Execution* (Princeton, N.J.: Princeton University Press, 2005).

18. Ohio Legislative Service Commission, *Capital Punishment,* staff research report no. 46, LSC, Columbus, Ohio, 64; Edmund Brown, *Public Justice, Private Mercy: A Governor's Education on Death Row* (New York: Weidenfeld and Nicolson, 1989).

19. Death Penalty Information Center, "Clemency," *Death Penalty Information Center,* http://www.deathpenaltyinfo.org/article.php?did=126&scid=13; Sarat, *Mercy on Trial,* 37–66; Burnett, *Justice Denied,* 162.

20. Ohio Governor Pardon Record, 226.

21. Bob Taft, clemency statements 1999 to 2006, obtained from the governor's office, Columbus, Ohio, copies on file with the author.

22. AP, "Family of 1988 Murder Victim Wants Ohio to Execute Killer," June 19, 2003, AP Archive.

23. Joe Wilhelm, e-mail to author, August 23, 2007; AP, "Governor Grants Clemency for First Time," June 26, 2003, AP Archive; AP, "State to Move Spared Death Row Killer from Prison," July 1, 2003, AP Archive.

24. AP, "State to Move Spared Death Row Killer"; AP, "Former Prosecutor Defends Handling of Campbell Trial," July 3, 2003, AP Archive; Patrick Dinkelacker, interview by author, June 21, 2007.

25. Bob Taft, interviews by author, October 30, 2006, and August 28, 2007.

26. AP, "Death Penalty Supporters, Opponents Write Ohio Governor's Office," February 17, 2007, AP Archive.

27. Ted Strickland, "Governor's Statement Regarding Clemency Application of John G. Spirko," statement obtained from governor's office, January 9, 2008, copy on file with author.

CHAPTER 8: LAST DAY

1. Ohio Department of Rehabilitation and Correction, execution timeline, John Hicks, November 29, 2005, ODRC, Columbus, Ohio.

2. Stolcupp file, in Espy File, data collected by researchers M. Watt Espy and John Ortiz Smylka and made available through the Inter-University Consortium for Political and Social Research, as collected and archived by the Ohio State Public Defender's Office, Columbus, Ohio.

3. "The Doomed Man's Last Night," *Columbus Evening Dispatch,* December 7, 1877.

4. Davis file, Espy File.

5. Nelson W. Evans, *A History of Adams County* (West Union, Ohio: E. B. Stivers, 1900), 386–92.

6. Ducolon file, Espy File.

7. "The Execution of Albert Myers," *Ohio State Journal,* December 18, 1858.

8. William DeBeck, *Murder Will Out: The Murders and Executions of Cincinnati* (Cincinnati, 1867), 102.

9. "Quick and Certain Were the Deaths of Haas and Wiley," *Columbus Dispatch,* April 21, 1897.

10. DeBeck, *Murder Will Out,* 50–51.

11. *A History and Biographical Cyclopaedia of Butler County, Ohio* (Cincinnati: Western Biographical, 1882), 264.

12. "Last Day on Earth of Wagner, the Morrow County Murderer," *Columbus Dispatch,* July 30, 1885; Marvin E. Fornshell, *The Historical and Illustrated Ohio Penitentiary* (1903; repr., Columbus: Arthur W. McGraw, 1997), 24–25.

13. "Two Murderers Put to Death at Prison," *Columbus Dispatch,* May 5, 1922.

14. "Slayers Will Die in Chair Tonight," *Columbus Dispatch,* March 10, 1933; "Two Slayers Pay Supreme Penalty," *Columbus Dispatch,* March 11, 1933.

15. "Lausche Refuses to Save Woman's Life," *Columbus Dispatch,* June 11, 1954; "Mother of Two Dies Calmly in Chair," *Columbus Dispatch,* June 12, 1954; "Griffin Will Die in Chair Friday Night," *Columbus Dispatch,* February 15, 1963; "Griffin Calm before Execution," February 16, 1963.

16. Dale Johnston, interview by author, July 18, 2007.

17. W. Keith Fletcher, warden's assistant, Ohio State Penitentiary, to author, July 23, 2007.

18. "Murderer McGill," *Ohio State Journal,* February 13, 1879; Joseph Clark, Ohio Legislative Correspondents' Association (OLCA) pool interview conducted by Paul Kostyu, GateHouse Media, March 21, 2006.

19. Christopher Newton, OLCA pool interview conducted by Laura Bischoff, *Dayton Daily News,* April 30, 2007; James Filiaggi, OLCA pool interview conducted by Marc Kovac, Dix Newspapers/*Youngstown Vindicator,* January 25, 2007; Stephen Vrabel, OLCA pool interview conducted by Michael J. Maurer, ThisWeek Newspapers, July 13, 2004.

20. Jerome Campbell, interview by author, July 1, 2003.

21. Ward file, Espy File.

22. AP, "Scott-Execution," June 14, 2001, AP Archive; AP, "Executed Man's Last Words Accuse State of Using False Testimony," June 18, 2003, AP Archive; AP, "Final Statement of John W. Byrd Jr.," February 19, 2002, AP Archive; AP, "Man Executed for Stabbing Jail Guard to Death with Homemade Knife," June 9, 2004, AP Archive; AP, "Prisoner Asks for Forgiveness in 1987 Stabbing Death," March 9, 2005, AP Archive; AP, "After State's Longest Delay, Man Executed for Cellmate Murder," March 24, 2007, AP Archive.

23. AP, "States Use Drugs to Calm Condemned Inmates before Execution," November 3, 2006, AP Archive.

24. Ibid.

25. AP, "Judge Unseals Documents Detailing Ohio's Lethal Injection Process," December 28, 2007, AP Archive; Brad Dicken, "Inside the Death House: Unsealed Documents Reveal Capital Punishment Protocols," *Elyria Chronicle-Telegram,* December 28, 2007.

26. Ohio Department of Rehabilitation and Correction, incident reports, Joseph Clark execution, May 11, 2006, ODRC, Columbus, Ohio.

27. Ohio Department of Rehabilitation and Correction, execution timeline, Christopher Newton, May 24, 2007, ODRC, Columbus, Ohio; AP, "Time for Inmate to Die Longer Than Other Executions," May 25, 2007, AP Archive.

28. ODRC, execution timeline, Hicks; AP, "Ohio Man Who Killed 2 Relatives Becomes Nation's 999th Execution," November 29, 2005, AP Archive.

CHAPTER 9: FREAKISH OR FAIR

1. In re Byrd, 269 F.3d 578, 581–82 (6th Cir. 2001) (Boggs dissenting).

2. Moore v. Parker, 425 F.3d 250, 270 (6th Cir. 2005) (Martin dissenting).

3. Cooey v. Taft, 2006 U.S. Dist. Lexis 88267, at *10–11.

4. "Message of the Governor of Ohio to the Fifty-third General Assembly," executive documents, annual reports, January 3, 1859, 88–89, Ohio Historical Society archives, call no. FLM 293, reel 18.

5. Harry Davis, *Death by Law* (Columbus: Federal Printing Co., 1922), 11–12 (reprinted from *Outlook* magazine).

6. State v. DePew, 38 Ohio St. 3d 275, 528 N.E.2d 542 (1988).

7. State v. Fears, 86 Ohio St. 3d 329, 715 N.E.2d 136 (1999).

8. David Doughten, interview by author, February 4, 2005.

9. Poindexter v. Mitchell, 454 F.3d 564, 590 (6th Cir. 2006) (Daughtrey concurring).

10. AP, "Incompetent Lawyers Chief Reason for Overturned Death Sentences," July 30, 2006, AP Archive.

11. *Fifth Report of the Committee on the Appointment of Counsel for Indigent Defendants in Capital Cases,* January 2003, Ohio Supreme Court, Columbus, Ohio; Ohio Supreme Court, Office of Public Information, e-mail to author, July 24, 2007.

12. Opinion of the trial judge in capital case, State v. Kiser, January 10, 1983, case no. 82-CR-69, Ross County Common Pleas Court, Chillicothe, Ohio.

13. AP, "Man Gets Life Term, Instead of Death, for Killing His Child," October 9, 2000, AP Archive.

14. Ron O'Brien, interview by author, June 18, 2007.

15. Dale Crawford, interview by author, July 23, 2007.

16. Getsy v. Mitchell, 456 F.3d 575 (6th Cir. 2006).

17. State v. Getsy, 84 Ohio St. 3d 180, 702 N.E.2d 866 (1998); State v. Issa, 93 Ohio St. 3d 49, 752 N.E.2d 904 (2001).

18. Michael DiSalle, *The Power of Life or Death* (New York: Random House, 1965), 58.

CHAPTER 10: THE FUTURE

1. Albert Post, "The Anti-Gallows Movement in Ohio," *Ohio History* 54, no. 2 (1945): 106.

2. Harry Davis, *Death by Law* (Columbus: Federal Printing, 1922), 21 (reprinted from *Outlook* magazine).

3. Michael DiSalle, *The Power of Life or Death* (New York: Random House, 1965), 214.

4. Indictment data compiled by Ohio State Public Defender's Office; life without parole data compiled by the Department of Rehabilitation and Correction; AP, "Ohio Prosecutors Using New Life without Parole Option," June 22, 2008, AP Archive.

5. Ron O'Brien, interview by author, June 9, 2008; AP, "Ohio Prosecutors Using New Life without Parole Option."

6. David Bodiker, interview by author, February 16, 2007.

7. AP, "Justices to Decide Kentucky Death Row Cases Challenging Lethal Injection," September 25, 2007, AP Archive.

8. Death Penalty Information Center, "The Death Penalty in 2007: Year End Report," *Death Penalty Information Center,* http://www.deathpenaltyinfo.org/2007YearEnd.pdf.

9. Baze v. Rees, 2008 U.S. Lexis 3476, at *13.

10. Ibid., at *91.

11. Kennedy v. Louisiana, 2008 U.S. Lexis 5262, at *49.

12. AP, "Ohio Judge Says State Must Change Lethal Injection Law," June 10, 2008, AP Archive.

13. Arlene Schwartz, interview by author, April 2007; Debra Dennis, "Woman Who Broke Ohio Death Penalty Faces Prison Again," *Cleveland Plain Dealer,* March 5, 1997; Sandra Lockett, interview by author, June 21, 2007.

14. Paul Pfeifer, interview by author, December 2, 2006; Reggie Wilkinson, interview by author, August 2, 2007.

15. Thomas Moyer, interview by author, July 5, 2007.

16. Betty Montgomery, interview by author, August 1, 2007; David Stebbins, e-mail to author, July 30, 2007; Bob Taft, interview by author, August 28, 2007.

APPENDIX 3

1. Judge Holmes, opinion of the trial judge in capital case, January 10, 1983, State v. Kiser, case no. 82-CR-69, Ross County Common Pleas Court, Chillicothe, Ohio.

2. Judge Gorman, sentencing opinion, April 24, 1987, State v. Wright, case no. CR-211379, Cuyahoga County Clerk of Courts.

3. Judge Crawford, decision, October 29, 1990, State v. Parsons, case no. 88-CR-279, Franklin County Clerk of Courts.

4. Judge MacMillan, decision, order, and entry of sentence, April 18, 1989, State v. Robertson, case no. 88-CR-3178, Montgomery County Clerk of Courts.

5. Judge Wiest, sentencing, May 24, 1999, State v. Crawford, case no. 98-CR-0185, Wayne County Clerk of Courts.

6. Judge Crehan, quoted in "Man Gets Life Term, Instead of Death, for Killing His Child," October 9, 2000, AP Archive.

7. Judge Bronson, sentencing entry, December 26, 2001, State v. Hancock, case no. 00-CR-19073, Warren County Clerk of Courts.

8. Judge Runyan, trial transcript, sentencing hearing, June 14, 2002, State v. Siler, case no. 01-CRI-08110, Ashland County Clerk of Courts, 12.

SELECTED BIBLIOGRAPHY

Banner, Stuart. *The Death Penalty: An American History.* Cambridge, Mass.: Harvard University Press, 2002.

Bedau, Hugo Adam, ed., *The Death Penalty in America: Current Controversies.* Oxford: Oxford University Press, 1997.

Berns, Walter. *For Capital Punishment: Crime and the Morality of the Death Penalty.* Lanham, Md.: University Press of America, 1979.

Brown, Edmund. *Public Justice, Private Mercy: A Governor's Education on Death Row.* New York: Weidenfeld and Nicolson, 1989.

Costanzo, Mark. *Just Revenge.* New York: St. Martin's Press, 1997.

Davis, Harry. *Death by Law.* Reprinted from *Outlook* magazine. Columbus: Federal Printing, 1922.

DeBeck, William. *Murder Will Out: The Murders and Executions of Cincinnati.* Cincinnati, 1867.

DiSalle, Michael. *The Power of Life or Death.* New York: Random House, 1965.

Fogle, H. M. *The Palace of Death, or, The Ohio Penitentiary Annex.* Columbus, 1908.

Fornshell, Marvin E. *The Historical and Illustrated Ohio Penitentiary.* 1903; reprint, Columbus: Arthur W. McGraw, 1997.

Hixon, Mary, and Frances Hixon, *The Last Hangings, Jackson, Ohio, 1883–1884.* N.p.: Mary Hixon and Frances Hixon, 1989.

Howe, Henry. *Historical Collections of Ohio.* Columbus: H. Howe and Son, 1896.

Lifton, Robert Jay, and Greg Mitchell. *Who Owns Death? Capital Punishment, the American Conscience, and the End of Executions.* New York: William Morrow, 2000.

Martinez, J. Michael, William Richardson, and D. Brandon Hornsby, eds. *The Leviathan's Choice: Capital Punishment in the Twenty-first Century.* Lanham, Md.: Rowman and Littlefield, 2002.

Maynard, Rosina. *Ohio's Other Lottery System: The Death Penalty.* Columbus: Rosina Maynard, 1980.

Morgan, Dan. *Historical Lights and Shadows of the Ohio State Penitentiary.* Columbus: Ohio Penitentiary Printing, 1893.

Ohio Legislative Service Commission. *Capital Punishment.* Staff Research Report no. 46, 1961.

———. *Capital Punishment.* Staff Research Report, 1971.

Post, Albert. "The Anti-Gallows Movement in Ohio." *Ohio History* 54 (1945): 104–12.

Streib, Victor. *The Fairer Death: Executing Women in Ohio.* Athens: Ohio University Press, 2006.

INDEX